THE STANDARD BOOK OF
HOUSEHOLD PETS

The Standard Book of
HOUSEHOLD PETS

by

JACK BAIRD

WITH ILLUSTRATIONS BY
PAUL BROWN

Halcyon House

GARDEN CITY, N. Y.

Foreword

THE STANDARD BOOK OF HOUSEHOLD PETS aims to give you just the information that you want about choosing and caring for dogs, cats, rabbits, birds, fishes, and a number of other favorite pets.

It is the author's hope that the book will prove an indispensable guide for the new pet owner and a source of valuable information for those who have long had and enjoyed pets in their homes.

You will find in this book the most practical sort of advice as to the kind of pet and the particular breed best suited to your home, whether you want a companion for yourself, a friend for your children, or a pet which is especially adapted to training and for exhibiting at shows.

In discussing each kind of pet, the book tells you not only about points to consider and to watch in making a selection, but also exactly how to keep your pet healthy, what food to give and when, how to train for obedience, and what to do in case of sickness.

The section on Dogs, which opens the book, includes a complete, authoritative reference guide giving exact standards for all the recognized breeds, with definitive illustrations. In the other chapters of this section you will find easy-to-follow advice on the care and training of your dog, on mating and pregnancy, on handling young puppies, and on requirements for dog shows and competitions.

The section on Cats also includes a reference guide with the standards for the recognized breeds and colors, as well as dependable recommendations on selection, care, breeding of your cat, and requirements of cat shows.

The third section of the book deals with other small domestic animals: rabbits, squirrels and chipmunks, guinea pigs, white mice, white rats, and hamsters.

The Bird section comes next, with chapters on Canaries, Parrots, Parakeets and Love Birds, Finches, and other caged birds, giving descriptions and illustrations to aid you in making a choice, and all the necessary instructions about feeding and care.

The final section is on Fishes, with chapters of Goldfish, Tropical Fish, and small water animals such as turtles and tadpoles. There is full and detailed information about the requirements for a well-balanced aquarium; and there are descriptions and illustrations of the most popular, interesting, and satisfactory pet fishes, which will aid you in making your choice.

SEVERAL PETS IN THE SAME HOUSEHOLD

As we have already mentioned, this book has separate sections on Dogs, on Cats, on Rabbits and other small domesticated animals, on Birds, and on Fishes. The reader can therefore readily find the information which he or she wants about the choice and care of the kind of pet in which he is especially interested. Many people prefer to have only one pet, and in the five Parts of this book we take up one pet at a time.

In this Foreword, however, we want to take up a few questions which apply to pets of all sorts and include some suggestions for those who are considering having more than one pet.

This book is about Household Pets, and it is certainly true that in the household several different kinds of pets can get along together, just as the various members of the family get along together. And this brings up one of the most important points about the care of pets —they must be an integral part of the home. The family must consider them members of the home group; and the pets must and will learn that they are part of the family.

When a new pet is brought into the home, make the older pet and the newcomer realize that they are equally important to you. If you have a dog, and bring in a cat, by holding the dog under one arm and the cat under the other, you can show them that you care for them both equally. And they will quickly accept this fact; and there will be no jealousy between them if you treat them both equally well. The same, of course, applies to two dogs—of the same or different breeds, or to two cats. The problem is a little different when you have a dog or cat and also birds or fishes. Smaller animals will need some protection, but the dog or cat should be trained by means of warnings (and punishment if it seems necessary) that the birds or fishes must not be disturbed.

There are many good reasons for having several pets in the home. Every member of the family may want to have his or her very own pet, and more than likely each will want a different kind of pet. And actually not very much more time and attention is required in caring for several pets than in caring for one. Here again we have the parallel of the family, where the whole group is enriched by each member; and each member is stronger, more interesting, more companionable, because of the others. In raising pets, apply the same psychology that you apply in raising children: make each pet feel at home, and be sure that it senses that none takes precedence over another. Let the new and old pets have equal favors. Do not incline toward one more than toward another.

SOME FURTHER SUGGESTIONS

The newcomer among the pets may need special protection; this is particularly true of birds and fishes. It is important to place birds in cages which cannot be reached by dogs or cats, and furthermore the cages should be placed so that they cannot be overturned. For this reason a cage hinged on a hanging bracket is very good, since it can be placed high enough to be far out of reach of other pets, and there is no danger of its being knocked over.

Fish should be properly placed where they get what light and heat they need, and also so angled that cats or dogs, either in the spirit of curiosity or depredation, can't get at the tank. A screen put over the top of the fish bowl or aquarium is often a good solution to this problem. The provision of protection is a natural part of the care of defenseless pets.

Rabbits, mice, hamsters, and other small household pets also need proper care and attention, so that they too may live happily and unmolested by possible intruders. Providing the proper cages or runs, placed in the proper spot either in the house or out in the yard, will make you feel confident that the health and security of your pets are being assured.

There is one more thought about the advantages of several pets in the home. Although the whole family may be interested in a single pet, there is no doubt that young, growing children like to feel that they are particularly responsible for the welfare of a special one which they have chosen for themselves. The care, attention, and devotion which young children feel for their pets, and which the pets in turn feel for them is a form of companionship which is one of the great joys of growing up. At one time the writer had a Newfoundland, a Pug, two cats, a canary, a parrot, and some goldfish, and though he was but eight years old, was still able to handle them all.

ACKNOWLEDGMENTS

The author wishes to mention here the great pleasure which he has found in his many years of professional work with pets. As a writer on dogs for many newspapers and magazines in the practical work with his own kennels, and in showing and judging dogs, he has constantly gained new and valuable ideas about the care of pets.

A special word of thanks goes to Paul Brown, outstanding among artists whose favorite subject is animals, for his excellent, clear, and expressive drawings for this book. To the American Kennel Club, the author's hearty appreciation for permission to follow the standards approved by the Club for the various breeds of dogs. And likewise to the Cat Fanciers' Association, Inc., for permission to follow and quote from their standards for colors and for breeds of cats. The author also wishes to express his thanks to Mrs. Eleanor Booth Simmons, well-known for her newspaper columns on cats, for valuable pointers in planning the material on cats; to Mrs. Frederica Lewis Page, for assistance in the preparation of the material on birds; and, more general advice, to Dr. Leonard W. Goss, of the staff of the New York Zoological Society. For assistance throughout the work on the book, the author wishes to make special acknowledgment to his wife, Marge Baird.

J.B.

Contents

FOREWORD   v

Part One

DOGS

I. CHOOSING A DOG   3

   IMPORTANT CONSIDERATIONS WHEN SELECTING A DOG   3

   CLASSIFICATION OF DOG BREEDS INTO GROUPS . . .   9

II. BREEDS OF DOGS 15

   THE SPORTING GROUP 16

     The Sporting Group as a Whole, 16; Irish Setter, 17;
English Setter, 18; Gordon Setter, 18; Cocker Spaniel, 19; English Cocker Spaniel, 21; English Springer
Spaniel, 21; Field Spaniel, 22; Irish Water Spaniel,
23; Sussex Spaniel, 24; Welsh Springer Spaniel, 24;
American Water Spaniel, 25; Brittany Spaniel, 26;
Clumber Spaniel, 26; Pointers, 27; German Short-
haired Pointer, 28; Wire-haired Pointing Griffon,
28; Weimaraner, 29; Chesapeake Bay Retriever, 30;
Labrador Retriever, 30; Golden Retriever, 31; Flat-
coated Retriever, 32; Curly-coated Retriever, 32.

   THE HOUND GROUP 33

     The Hound Group as a Whole, 33; Beagle, 34;
Basset Hound, 35; American Foxhound, 35; English

Foxhound, 36; Black and Tan Coonhound, 37; Harrier, 37; Bloodhound, 38; Basenji, 39; Dachshund, 39; Greyhound, 41; Whippet, 41; Saluki, 42; Borzoi, 43; Afghan Hound, 43; Irish Wolfhound, 44; Scottish Deerhound, 45; Otterhound, 46; Norwegian Elkhound, 46.

THE WORKING GROUP   47

The Working Group as a Whole, 47; Collie (rough), 48; Collie (smooth), 49; Shetland Sheepdog, 49; Old English Sheepdog, 50; Briard, 51; Komondor, 51; Pulik, 52; German Shepherd, 53; Belgian Sheepdog, 54; Doberman Pinscher, 54; Boxer, 55; Rottweiler, 56; Great Dane, 56; Mastiff, 57; Bull Mastiff, 58; Pembroke Welsh Corgi, 59; Cardigan Welsh Corgi, 59; Eskimo, 60; Alaskan Malemute, 61; Siberian Husky, 62; Samoyede, 62; Giant Schnauzer, 63; Standard Schnauzer, 64; Bouvier de Flandres, 64; St. Bernard, 65; Bernese Mountain Dog, 66; Newfoundland, 66; Great Pyrenees, 67; Kuvasz, 68.

THE TERRIER GROUP   69

The Terrier Group as a Whole, 69; Airedale Terrier, 70; Irish Terrier, 71; Welsh Terrier, 72; Lakeland Terrier, 72; Border Terrier, 73; Norwich Terrier, 74; Smooth Fox Terrier, 74; Wire-haired Fox Terrier, 75; Kerry Blue Terrier, 76; Scottish Terrier, 77; Cairn Terrier, 77; Sealyham Terrier, 78; West Highland White Terrier, 79; Lhasa Apsos Terrier, 79; Skye Terrier, 80; Dandie Dinmont Terrier, 81; Bedlington Terrier, 81; White Bull Terrier, 82; Colored Bull Terrier, 83; Staffordshire Terrier, 83; Manchester (Black-and-Tan) Terrier, 84; Miniature Schnauzer, 84.

THE TOY GROUP   85

The Toy Group as a Whole, 85; Pekingese, 86; Pomeranian, 87; Papillon, 87; Japanese Spaniel, 88; English Toy Spaniel, 89; Maltese, 89; Yorkshire Terrier, 90; Toy Poodle, 91; Brussels Griffon, 91; Affenpinscher, 92; Pug, 93; Toy Manchester Terrier, 93; Italian Greyhound, 94; Miniature Pinscher, 94: Chihuahua, 95; Mexican Hairless, 96.

THE NON-SPORTING GROUP 96

The Non-Sporting Group as a Whole, 96; Boston Terrier, 97; French Bulldog, 98; Bulldog, 99; Dalmatian, 100; Poodle (standard and miniature), 100; Chow Chow, 101; Keeshond, 102; Schipperke, 103.

III. CARE OF DOGS 105

KEEPING YOUR DOG HEALTHY 105

FEEDING YOUR DOG 114

GROOMING YOUR DOG 122

TRAINING YOUR DOG 127

CARE OF SICK DOGS 136

IV. BREEDING DOGS 143

MATING 143

PREGNANCY AND DELIVERY 149

CARE OF NEW-BORN PUPPIES 151

V. DOG SHOWS AND OTHER COMPETITIONS . . 155

RACING 155

FIELD TRIALS 157

OBEDIENCE TRIALS 160

DOG SHOWS 165

VI. ORIGIN OF DOGS AND HISTORY OF THEIR DOMESTICATION 177

HOW THE FIRST DOGS SERVED MAN 178

DEVELOPMENT OF PRESENT-DAY BREEDS 181

PREHISTORIC ORIGIN OF DOGS 183

Part Two

CATS

VII. CHOOSING A CAT 187

IMPORTANT CONSIDERATIONS WHEN SELECTING A CAT . 187

CLASSIFICATION OF CAT BREEDS AND THEIR COLOR QUALIFICATIONS 189

VIII. BREEDS OF CATS 195

Domestic Short-haired Cats, 196; Long-haired Cats, 197; Manx Cats, 199; Siamese Cats, 200; Abyssinian Cats, 201; Peke-faced Cats, 202; Japanese Kimono Cats, 202; Other Cat Groups, 202.

IX. CARE OF CATS 203
KEEPING YOUR CAT HEALTHY 203
GROOMING AND BATHING 205
TRAINING 208
CARE WHEN SICK 210

X. BREEDING CATS 213
MATING 213
PREGNANCY 214
DELIVERY AND NURSING 214
CARE OF NEW-BORN KITTENS 214
WEANING KITTENS 215
ALTERING AND SPAYING 215

XI. CAT SHOWS 217

XII. ORIGIN AND HISTORY OF DOMESTICATED CATS 219

Part Three

RABBITS, SQUIRRELS, AND OTHER SMALL DOMESTIC ANIMALS

XIII. RABBITS 223
SELECTING RABBITS AS PETS 223
BREEDS OF RABBITS 224

Angora, 225; Belgian Hare, 225; Broken-colored, 225; Lop-eared, 226; Himalayan, 226; English, 226; Polish, 226; Flemish Giant, 226; Silver, 227; Blue and Tan, Black and Tan, 227; Other Breeds, 227.

FEEDING RABBITS 227
RABBIT HUTCHES 228
BREEDING RABBITS 229

XIV. SQUIRRELS AND CHIPMUNKS 231
    MAKING FRIENDS OF SQUIRRELS AND CHIPMUNKS . . 231
    SQUIRRELS 232
    CHIPMUNKS 233

XV. GUINEA PIGS, WHITE MICE, WHITE RATS, AND HAMSTERS 235
    GUINEA PIGS AS PETS 235
    WHITE MICE AND WHITE RATS 237
    HAMSTERS 239

Part Four

BIRDS

XVI. CANARIES 243
    VARIETIES OR TYPES OF CANARIES 243
    CARE OF CANARIES 244
    BREEDING CANARIES 247
    ORIGIN AND HISTORY OF THE CAGED CANARY . . . 248

XVII. PARROTS, PARAKEETS, AND LOVE BIRDS . . 251
    PARROTS 251
    MACAWS 253
    SHELL PARAKEETS 255
    LOVE BIRDS 257

XVIII. FINCHES AND OTHER CAGED BIRDS 259
    FINCHES 259
    OTHER CAGED BIRDS 262
    SUMMARY OF THE CARE OF SMALL CAGED BIRDS . . . 264

Part Five

FISHES

XIX. PLANNING A WELL-BALANCED AQUARIUM . 269
    CARE OF THE AQUARIUM 269
    PLANTS AND OTHER MATERIALS FOR THE AQUARIUM . 271

XX. GOLDFISH 273
    VARIETIES OF GOLDFISH 273
    CARE OF GOLDFISH 275

XXI. TROPICAL FISH 277
    POPULAR VARIETIES OF TROPICAL FISH AND THEIR CARE 278
        Paradise, 278; Swordtail, 279; Guppy, 279; Chanchito, 279; Jewel, 280; Zebra, 280; Angel Fish, 280; Mollienisia, 280; Platy, 281; Pearl Danio, 281; Tetra, 281; Mouthbreeder Family, 282; Barbus Family, 282; African Killifish, 282.

    POPULAR SMALL DOMESTIC FISHES 283
        Minnow, 283; Other Small Domestic Fishes, 283.

XXII. TURTLES, TADPOLES, AND SALAMANDERS . 285
    TURTLES 285
    TADPOLES 287
    SALAMANDERS 287

    INDEX 289

Part One

DOGS

CHAPTER I

CHOOSING A DOG

A dog is a companion as well as pet. Your dog will be a household friend that you want to have with you for a long time, not a novelty to be discarded with the coming of a new season. For this reason there are many factors that you will want to consider when selecting and buying a dog for your home.

IMPORTANT CONSIDERATIONS WHEN SELECTING A DOG

Deciding What Kind of Dog You Want. Keep in mind first the purpose for which you want the dog. Is it to be a dog which will live with you most of the year, but which you will also want to take out now and then on hunting trips, or is it to be a dog that you want purely for pet-companionship qualities? Or is your dog to be a guardian of your home and family as well as a family pet?

Consider next the surroundings in which the dog will live. The confinement that goes with the modern apartment in a large city is not suited to the well-being of dogs belonging to the larger breeds, especially those of many of the hunting breeds and some of those we know as the working breeds. The confusion and congestion of the city streets and the hard pavements are hardly correct surroundings for a dog that needs much exercise and open-country running for its best health. Although the city-dweller's personal inclination may lean to the hunting dogs or large breeds, he should consider the size of the dog in relation to where it must live most of the year, for a dog in cramped living quarters is in time going to become cramped of disposition or prove a costly drain through illnesses. While changing conditions have robbed many of the dog breeds of their natural work, so that the majority of the country's fifteen million dogs are of the pet-companion type and will be relatively happy any place where their loved humans exist, dog life is shortened through living where exercise in proportion to size cannot be obtained.

If the potential buyer lives in a suburban area where an outdoor kennel may be constructed or a suitable run made for safe exercise, the problem becomes not one of size but of quiet behavior which will not disturb the neighborhood as incessant barking would.

The country-dweller may purchase a dog of any breed which suits his fancy, provided that he, as well as the city- or surburban-dweller, takes into consideration the temperament of the dog to be bought. The disposition of the dog should be suited to that of the purchaser or the relationship between them will not work out to the advantage of either one. A nervous, high-strung person, for example, surely does not want a nervous, flighty dog. In fact, a temperamental dog is not advisable for anyone unless other qualities in the dog are especially desirable and the owner knows how to train a "problem" dog properly.

For the average household the ideal dog, regardless of size, is the quiet but alert dog which barks only when there is need and which is easily taught such good habits as staying off furniture and people. He should be reserved but not unfriendly, sufficiently aggressive to protect his family and possessions without being of the bullying, domineering type that is continually looking for a fight to prove how tough he is.

It is well to consider, in regard to the dog's temperament, whether the dog is being bought for an adult or a child. A puppy of good breeding is generally the best bet for a small child, for the pup will feel that in the youngster he has a pal and will show a happy, contented devotion to him. However, if one must buy a grown dog to go into a home where there are children, care must be taken to get a dog of even disposition and good judgment—one that will not resent the mauling that children are apt to hand out to anything they play with, inanimate or living.

If you have taken into consideration the age and temperament of the person who is to have the dog as a pet, the surroundings the dog will have, and the disposition desired in the proposed pet, and you are disappointed to find you are unable to have that big breed you had your heart set on, take some time out to study breeds, for you can readily find a representative of a smaller breed possessing the same characteristics and abilities, the same nature and expressions as the large breed you had in mind. Inasmuch as there are more than a hundred breeds of dogs now recognized by the American Kennel Club, which is the governing body of purebred dogs in the United States, the potential purchaser, through a little study, can find the exact breed that is suited to the living quarters and temperaments of the family with which the new dog will live.

Later in this chapter we shall mention the six groups into which all the hundred or more breeds are classified; and then in Chapter II we shall take up each of the recognized breeds in turn, giving the reader full information on which to base his choice.

Deciding between a Puppy and a Grown Dog. When you start out to buy a dog, you may wonder whether it is better to get a puppy or a full-grown dog. Each has its advantages. If you get a full-grown dog, you are not running any risk of its developing along physical or temperamental lines other than what you expected. Also, you will avoid the bother of the housebreaking period and probably save yourself some trouble in other phases of training as well. How important this is to you will of course depend on your individual circumstances and inclinations—how much time you have to devote to training and discipline, and how much patience you have in such matters.

With a grown dog, however, particularly one more than a year or so old, you may be taking your chances on the difficulties of winning the love, trust, and devotion which the dog may still feel for his former owner. This is not usually too great a risk, since most dogs of a friendly, happy disposition adapt themselves fairly easily to new owners in spite of their previous attachments.

Points about Puppies. If you acquire a puppy, of course, there will be no problem about loyalty. And if you have the time, facilities, and willingness to raise a dog from puppyhood through the training stages, you are likely to find it extremely rewarding. Most dog-lovers find a deep pleasure in watching the development of their pet from its early phase, when perhaps it is shy and docile, through the time when it learns to play and possibly becomes somewhat mischievous, until it reaches the more settled, wise, and obedient ways of maturity. Whether or not you will enjoy watching this growth process will depend on how

CHOOSING A PUPPY FROM A LARGE LITTER

much patience you have. If the occasional chewing of a slipper or spot on a rug, or the trouble of taking measures to avoid such accidents, will upset you very much, you will be better off with a well-trained adult dog that has outgrown the somewhat scatterbrained playfulness of the untrained puppy. But if you are the sort of person who feels a little damage to property here and there is well worth the joy of a happy, frisky puppy even during his impishly destructive period, then buy a puppy.

If you get a very young puppy, don't be disappointed or think you have a particularly stupid dog when you find he doesn't learn everything perfectly in a few weeks. Sometimes puppies learn quickly and then relapse later into their former ways, and cannot be entirely relied upon for good behavior for many months. Don't let this discourage you. It is necessary to keep on disciplining him, but a young puppy is too easily distracted for you to expect immediate results from your attempts at training. As he grows and develops, he will become less wild in his ways and progressively quicker at learning good habits. Some puppies do, of course, respond very quickly to firm, gentle training. Some scarcely need to be housebroken. But it is best to be prepared for the usual hazards of puppyhood. Thus you will be able to enjoy more thoroughly the feeling that this dog has been your very own from the start and was well worth raising from a pup, as well as the pride that comes from having been responsible for the development of a fine, healthy, and lovable pet.

Willing and eager as you may be not to miss the fun of owning a puppy, you will be wise not to get one that is less than about three months old. For a puppy that is taken away from its mother at too early an age is likely to be troublesome—to cry a great deal, especially at night, and to develop into a nervous, hard-to-train dog.

Deciding between a Male and a Female. Perhaps you have heard dog-owners discussing and disagreeing on the relative merits of males and females as pets. Many who prefer females maintain that females tend to be more affectionate. Other people are unwilling to bother with the precautions necessary during a female's "heat" period and so prefer males. The males in a litter usually cost a little more than the females.

So far as temperament and affection are concerned, probably the most important factors are the owner and the treatment he gives the pet, and the atmosphere of the home in which the pet is raised. Whether male or female, the more affection a dog is given, the more it will give in return. Its upbringing, far more than its sex, will determine its degree of playfulness, devotion, and other desirable qualities.

It is, of course, entirely up to you to decide whether you want to avoid the "heat" and breeding problems of females or whether you feel you might even particularly want to have a dog that will bear pups. Perhaps these matters will make no difference to you, one way or the other. In that case, pick the individual dog that appeals to you the most and fulfills your requirements, regardless of its sex.

Choosing a Healthy Dog. Having finally decided what kind of dog you want, you must next be sure you are getting a healthy puppy or grown dog.

If you want a puppy, it is best always to protect yourself by buying one from a litter, where you have a fairly good chance of getting the right temperament as well as getting a healthy, husky puppy. Of course, there is no guarantee that either you or the breeder can pick what will eventually be the best, for many times successful breeders have ignored puppies of a litter as being inferior, only to have them mature into more healthy, finer-looking, and more successful dogs than their brothers and sisters.

As a rule it is safest to pick the most alert, clear-eyed puppy, centering your attention on neither the largest nor the smallest of a litter. If you pick the largest, there is a good chance that when the dog matures

WHICH ONE WOULD BE YOUR CHOICE?

you will have one that is considerably larger than your mental picture of that breed. If you pick the smallest of the litter you run a risk of getting something that is smaller than you had in mind. Of course, there are many cases where the so-called "runt" of the litter has turned out to be a canine version of the ugly duckling.

Purebreds and Pedigrees. There are many advantages to buying a purebred dog. The "papers" that go with purebreds represent careful breeding to produce a certain type and quality of dog. They enable you to buy the kind of dog you want and to get one of a quality resulting from the time, thought, money, and effort of many breeders over a period of years.

The term "purebred" means that the dog is of purest breeding, produced by generations of matings within that one breed, and one which, bred to a proper mate of that same breed, will reproduce true to type in size, build, coat, temperament, and ability to do a given task. Pure breeding enables you in the United States to make a selection of your breed from among well over 100 recognized breeds at the present time. You can thus be sure of getting the breed that best suits your needs, whether you want a hunting dog, a dog for the work of guardianship of home and family, or a dog bred primarily for companionship.

As a partial further guide, the many pure breeds are classified into what is known as variety groups, which is a heritage from the early Roman days and groups dogs according to the uses or the purposes for which these breeds were developed. These groups constitute the present-day general usage of the breeds. By looking over these variety listings, the potential purchaser can quickly narrow his buying-field down to a few breeds and thus save much time in his final selection.

CLASSIFICATION OF DOG BREEDS INTO GROUPS

The Six Variety Groups. In the next chapter we shall take up each of the individual breeds of dogs. At this point we want to mention that dog breeds are classified into six *variety groups,* as follows:

Group One takes in the more than twenty gun dogs and is known as the SPORTING GROUP; it is made up of the Pointers, Setters, sporting Spaniels, Retrievers and other breeds which do this same type of work.

Group Two is known as the HOUND GROUP and is made up of those sporting dogs accustomed to trailing their game, making good by sense of smell. Some of these dogs work entirely by scent, others by sight, and still others by a combination of the two senses. Here we have nearly all the breeds which have 'hound' as part of their breed name.

Group Three is the WORKING GROUP and includes nearly thirty breeds that were developed for specific working purposes, such as guardianship of livestock, herding, police work, and sundry accomplishments. Here we have mostly large breeds, although a few do not run to too great a size. Although all are noted for quiet courage, some are fast, while others are ponderous. Nearly all these breeds go back hundreds of years.

Group Four is known as the TERRIER GROUP and nearly all of the more than twenty breeds in this group originated in the British Isles, where they were developed for specific hunting purposes and as aides to larger sporting dogs. As the name "terrier" indicates, these dogs, in their working days, "go to earth". Gamesters all, they are fast with body and brain.

Group Five, known as the TOY GROUP, takes in some sixteen breeds developed in many parts of the world primarily as pets; some were developed as house companions of royalty. Despite their small size and the name "Toy", they are all dog.

Group Six in official language is known as the Non-sporting Group, which is rather a misnomer, for while the eight distinct breeds in this group are now classed solely as companions, some have fine working backgrounds, while others in their native lands were valued for their abilities in the hunting field.

There are many other breeds which have been brought in small numbers into the United States, which at present lack classification with any of the above groups and show-wise are rated in the miscellaneous class. Many of the more popular breeds now enjoying a high rating in their own variety classifications have graduated from this group.

Usefulness of Breed Standards. The presentation of the variety group classifications not only narrows the purchaser's search, but also gives an idea of another careful step by which the world of the purebred dog guards and guides the public. Each of the breeds has a standard of perfection by which breeders and judges may guide their efforts and these standards govern type and quality of the individual breeds, which further protects the buyer. Being careful to get what he wants or needs, and finally having been able to classify the dogs that come within his conditions, the wise purchaser will obtain and study a copy of the breed standard, which will give him an excellent idea of just how his dog should look.

Thus informed, the purchaser can be fairly well assured of getting a dog that possesses to a decided degree the type, character, size, and weight called for in the standard of perfection. Thus he can choose the puppy which shows the strongest characteristics of the breed. Of course, one has greater assurance of getting the right dog if one has a chance to see the sire and dam of the puppy and to know of any marked failings in physical or mental characteristics. But simply by using the standards and guides set up in each breed of the purebred dog world, the buyer can fairly well know that the puppy he brings into his house will grow up to have a certain expression, a definite size and way of going, and what the texture and color of his coat will be, as well as what sort of temperament he will have.

Advantages of Purebred Dogs. If the buyer seeks a matured dog, by knowing the standards and something of the history of the breed, he can be most certain that what he is getting is something that is definitely of that breed, and, with no apologies to make, he can have a greater pride of possession, which is often found to count a great deal as time goes on.

The papers that go with a dog, or should, if a person is buying from a kennel with reputation, are the certificate of pedigree and the transfer of ownership to the new master of the dog. The former sets forth the name of the dog, its sire, and its dam, and quite often goes back two, three or more generations, while the latter is the new owner's guarantee that the dog is registered with the American Kennel Club and part of a registered litter.

These papers have great value in protecting the owner, in that they create a re-sale value and also may bring a financial return should it be desired to breed from a female or to use a dog as a sire.

In contrast, the mongrel or crossbred can have no papers and thus is purely a permanent cost, and also with the crossing of two or more breeds, the owner may be certain that there is nothing at all predictable as to size, manner, coat, or other characteristics.

The mongrel litter is always a gamble and a hazard, for there are certain to be physical and temperamental faults emphasized in such a breeding and the owner has no sure guide to follow in handling the situation. After the 'cuteness' of the mongrel puppy (and all puppies are 'cute') has worn off, there is nothing to recommend him. It is well to remember that it costs no more to feed a good dog than a bad one and the good one is easier to look at.

It is foolish to believe the tale that the mongrel is healthier than the purebred, for the average good veterinarian will state that if he had to depend on purebred dogs for a living, he would starve to death. The owner of a purebred, having an investment in cash and pride, will take better care of his dog and not let him become prey to disease or run too many risks along the health line. Those mongrels which do come along and seem to survive everything are merely the survival of the fittest.

Naturally the breeder of good stock is going to take expert care of his dogs because they represent not only a cash outlay, but his reputation hinges on the looks and health of his dogs; he has bred them from the best lines he could obtain, the prime requisite being good health.

The mongrel is the result of a chance or "street" mating of two dogs on the loose and surely they have asked no questions as to each other's health. The result is a litter of puppies no one wants, except perhaps the keeper of an unlicensed pet show who can pick up the dogs for nothing or close to it, and sell the individuals off when still young and cute at a low price. Shoppers who gamble on buying the mongrel pup take a chance of bringing disease into the home and surely risk temperamental outbursts that may result in damage to loved ones.

The fallacy that mongrels are smarter than purebreds may also be disposed of easily and logically. To begin with, the mongrel that does survive street roamings and knows where the best garbage cans are is merely a smart dodger, sly and shrewd, and very unpredictable as to reactions. The best proof that the purebred dog, being a product of careful breeding that had to take into account the ability to do a given job for which that breed was created, is the smarter is evident on every hand.

Many police forces in the United States, and more generally in Europe, use dogs as aides in various parts of their work and all of these dogs are purebreds. The dogs that come through the schooling of the "Seeing Eye" and other training units preparing thousands of dogs to aid the sightless are all purebreds. By far the majority of the dogs that turned in such a remarkable piece of work as war dogs with our Armed Forces during World War II were purebreds, and to them must go credit for saving thousands of American lives and millions of dollars in property.

The purebred succeeds where the mongrel fails in the same way that a kindergarten child isn't given the same tasks that a college graduate would find easy. With humans, the difference is in the amount of education poured in from the outside. With dogs it is that the purebred, developed for years for specific purpose, has his education born within him.

Where to Buy a Dog. It is possible to buy healthy, sound puppies or grown dogs from reputable breeders, and it merely takes a call to a local dog authority or a perusal of the excellent dog magazines, to be set right as to where stock is available in any one of the breeds. It is well to remember always that there are no bad breeds, but that there are bad individuals within any breed, just as there are bad members of human society. The proper selection of dogs for the individual needs and desires has been made simpler of late years through a growing consciousness of public responsibility on the part of reputable breeders. In most cases they will not sell an individual the "wrong" dog, knowing that if they do the dog may bounce back on them and that the bad advertising that comes from wrong placement can be ruinous.

In many cities there are well-kept pet shops, operating under a fine sanitary code, which deal in good dogs and act as clearing-houses for breeding-kennels that are located at distant points. Trained in dogs, the operators of these high-grade shops always try to fit the purchaser with the right dog for his living quarters and temperament, and in many instances will take an order for a puppy or grown dog, if the desired stock is not on hand. Such shops are guarantees of healthy stock because their investments run so high that they cannot risk letting disease creep into their business and ruin more than their hard-won reputation.

Where the prospective purchaser is unable to locate the desired breed within his home territory, a query addressed to the American Kennel Club, 221 Fourth Avenue, New York, N. Y., will bring a prompt reply as to the address of kennels devoted to that breed.

CHAPTER II

BREEDS OF DOGS

Man, in his desire to work with nature, to improve upon it, and to bend a natural creation to his own use, first domesticated dogs many centuries ago and then, to provide a more useful servant, crossed and re-crossed breeds and eventually developed over two hundred distinct breeds which exist in the world today.

In searching for a pet dog, the potential buyer needs to know the physical and temperamental characteristics of the various breeds. Besides all the breeds now recognized by the American Kennel Club, there are probably more than twenty other breeds in the United States that have yet to attain the status of such recognition but which will get there when they have proved true to type in breeding, and when they exist in sufficient numbers and have a general distribution. It is quite likely that dogs from other parts of the world brought to this country by members of the Armed Forces after World War II will add other breeds that may catch the public eye enough to become accepted as purebreds.

It is very helpful for a prospective buyer to go to a nearby dog show where he will find prime specimens of the majority of the breeds. The process is simplified further at shows which are benched, that is, where raised stalls are provided for the entrants, for at the end of each row of benches there are lists of breeds that may be found in that section, and as a rule the majority of the breeds in each group are benched fairly near one another.

THE SPORTING GROUP

The Sporting Group as a **Whole.** Because of their long background of working for and with man in a common livelihood and the generations of practical training that even the softness of civilization has not bred out of them, the dogs classified as belonging to the Sporting Group, or—in the parlance of the competitive purebred sport—Variety Group One, are ideal as household pets. By nature adaptable to all conditions of living and ready to take on any reasonable training, Sporting dogs respond excellently to the simple schooling needed for community living.

The Sporting Group offers a variance in size from the American-type Cocker Spaniel, which averages from 22 to 28 lbs., to the various Retrievers and the Weimaraners, which will weigh as much as 85 lbs. and stand as high as 26 inches. This permits the buyer to select a dog that will fit into the size of the living-quarters of the potential owner, and which also could be, in vacation time, a joy in the field.

The breeds in this group were either naturals or were developed by man for hunting purposes. At the start, these dogs earned their keep, for the majority of breeds were developed from one hundred to several hundred years ago, when man and his family ate better if there were dogs to help locate and bring in the game. We now find more than twenty breeds in the group, bred to some definite standard in physical proportions. Here we find the many breeds of Sporting Spaniels. (The Japanese Spaniel and the English Toy Spaniel belong to Variety Group Five, the Toy group.) Also included in the Sporting group are the several Retriever breeds, most of which owe their development to the North American Continent.

Other members of the group are the pointing breeds, which include the three Setter breeds and the all-purpose breeds such as the Wire-haired Pointing Griffon, the German Short-haired Pointer, and the Weimaraner.

Many of these breeds are of such classic lines and appealing grace as to have won many show honors, while nearly all have proved their intelligence by excellent work in acquiring obedience-test degrees. The combination of physical excellence with intelligence, coming out of many years of being bred to work in the field, has given the public a wide range of healthy, long-lived, easy-to-care-for dogs to make fine pets for the household, regardless of where the owner may reside.

Irish Setter. One of the most colorful of all present-day purebreds is the Irish Setter. With a rich red

IRISH SETTER

coat and an ability to move like flowing gold, he is one of the handsomest dogs of all time. He is endowed also with the real Irish disposition—happy-go-lucky and independent, with a fine sense of companionship and a hardiness that leads to a longer average life-span than is given most breeds. An exceptionally lovable pet, he shows great gentleness and devotion.

Today there may be many of the old red-and-whites across the water, but in the United States all Irish Setters are red. In condition an adult Irish Setter will weigh from 50 to 70 lbs. and stand close to 25 inches high at the shoulder. The body coat is of moderate length, devoid of curl or wave. Ear tips, head, and fronts of legs have fine

short hair, while the backs of legs have straight feathering. The tail-feathering decreases as it gets toward the end of the slightly curving tail that is held almost at back level.

The Irish Setter first came to notice early in the eighteenth century and soon made a name in the British Isles. His ancestry is hard to trace. Very likely it was an English Setter-Pointer and Spaniel mixture with a bit of the Gordon Setter thrown in for good measure.

When first brought to this country, Irish Setters held their own in the top field trials with the best the other breeds had to offer, but breeders became over show-conscious and now there are few that can challenge even in small stakes. But the change brought on great show winnings, and few breeds have so enviable a record in taking best-of-show wins. And in spite of some opinions that Irish Setters are hard-headed, those which have gone into obedience work have been hard to beat.

English Setter. The English Setter is an extremely beautiful breed—one of the best "picture" dogs in the world—and matches its looks not only with fine performance but with a sweetness of disposition that makes it an ideal pet in suburban or country places where it can get enough exercise.

The coat is flat, without curl, of good length, and with no woolly feeling. Colors are black, white, and tan; black and white; blue belton, lemon, and white; lemon belton, orange, and white; orange belton, liver, and white; liver belton; and solid white.

A normally active male English Setter will run from 55 to 75 lbs. and stand from 23 to 25 inches, although

ENGLISH SETTER

the field trial dogs run much smaller than the standard of the breed calls for. Females are slightly smaller than males.

Evidence points to the English Setter as having been a practical working bird-dog as far back as 400 years ago. The most generally accepted theory is that the breed was developed from crosses of the Spanish Pointer, the larger Water Spaniel, and the Springer Spaniel. Out of the combination and the continued development through the years came a dog that won reknown in England and the United States as a finished field dog, equally good as a shooting dog or field trial star, and a beautiful bench show winner.

Ever since the first English Setter came into the United States (before 1875), the rise of the breed has been steady, with none of the falls that have hit other breeds. It would be impossible to enumerate the best in show titles that these dogs have won on the bench in the biggest fixtures in the country.

Gordon Setter. The Gordon Setter is a handsome dog with a shining coal-black coat which has artistically-placed, clearly-defined markings of glossy chestnut or mahogany-red. He stands from 21 to 25 inches high at the shoulder.

Definitely a one-family dog, he is ideal as a companion to young or old. Few more faithful dogs can be found, nor can one sum up more good qualities in one breed than there are in the Gordon Setter.

Although it is an ancient breed equipped with intelligence, a strong, sturdy build, and an extremely loyal disposition, the Gordon Setter is the least-known of the Setter family in the United States. This is simply because no attempt has been made to push the breed into the limelight and therefore few Gordon Setters are bred and few sold.

The breed owes its origin to Scotland, where it played a big part in the sporting history of that country, but it has been from Norway, Sweden, and Denmark that the best specimens have come to the United States, beginning in the years just before World War II.

At one time the Gordon Setter was called the Black and Tan Setter, and it is apparent that while the ancestry was the same as that of other Setter breeds, there was a cross-in of the Black and Tan Setting Spaniel which was so popular in England in the Sixteenth Century.

Although there have been some Gordon Setters that were as racy as other breeds of Setter, they are not fast dogs as a breed, the majority of breeders having preferred to keep the well-built, strong Gordon which, sure and steady and smart as they come, can hunt all day and make sure that no game is missed on his beat. For those who have owned a Gordon and hunted with him in the field, there can be no other shooting dog.

Cocker Spaniel. The name Cocker Spaniel strikes a chord of

COCKER SPANIEL

recognition in more American minds than does the name of any other breed, and the picture conjured up is that of a small, merry dog with soulful eyes. There is hardly a person who, if he has not owned a Cocker Spaniel himself, has not at least known some close friend who has.

The Cocker Spaniel tops all other breeds by far in the official registration of the American Kennel Club; in fact, it is so far ahead of the next breed that one might say there is no second. The same proportion holds true in the records of licensing the millions of dogs in the United States, proving that the Cocker is valued by more people as a pet and companion than is any other breed of dog, as well as rating high for show, field trial, and obedience purposes.

To the city-dweller in his small apartment, or the suburbanite with but a small plot of ground, the Cocker fits into the picture because of small size, adaptability to all conditions, and a general level of temperament that lets the dog get on with adult or child alike, and which makes him truly a family dog.

There is no question but what the eye has a great deal to do with the selection of any pet, and as this is especially true when one considers color, the wide range in the coat colors leaves potential purchasers with much from which to choose. The great numbers of Cockers in the show rings of the country have even led to the establishment of what is known as varieties, from the standpoint of judging.

At the present time there are three varieties in the judging; namely, blacks, any solid color other than black, and the parti-colors, and there is a likelihood that soon there will be a separate division for black and tans. This explanation is given because so many non-technical dog lovers are under the impression that these varieties are not all Cocker Spaniels.

In the solid colors apart from the blacks, there are reds of various depths ranging to that of the Irish Setter color, creams, buffs, liver; while the parti-color division gives us black and white, red and white, a few liver and white, as well as varying combinations of black, tan and white, and the blue roan. Take any of these colors in the flat or slightly waved coat that is at once soft and dense, and with good feathering on the ears, chest, legs and abdomen, and you present a picture to charm any person. It is perhaps the wide range of colors that makes the breed rank as America's Number One dog, both as a pet and a show dog.

The Cocker is the smallest of the sporting spaniels, in fact the smallest of all dogs regularly used as gun dogs, and by standards should run not less than 22 lbs. or more than 28 lbs., although there are many today running into the low 30's. The breed packs a lot of power into its sturdy body, has well-boned legs, and is so muscled as to possess great stamina.

The good Cocker, in addition to being built right, will have a merry wagging tail, whether in your living room, on the street or in his natural habitat of the field. The expression of the Cocker, its eye dark except in the lighter-colored coats which may run to a hazel eye, is one of alertness, with a soft, appealing gaze, backed by real intelligence.

Show-wise, the breed has had few equals in its ability to top the biggest and best shows of the country, and while its field trial work has slumped off in recent years in favor of larger dogs, tens of thousands go into the hunting field every year and acquit themselves well. In the obedience phase of competition, the intelligence and adaptability that makes them so fine a pet shows up and generally the Cocker Spaniels in any given tests can be found "in the money".

The Spaniel family is a very large one and can be traced back to the 14th Century and perhaps further. As time wore on, different districts developed from the general family to fit the needs of the hunting conditions of the territory from which game was to be procured, and eventually the Cocker Spaniel, answering more needs than other breeds, became the most popular of the gun dogs, both in the United States and England. At the present time there is such a type divergence between the English and the American Cocker, that for the past several years they have been judged as separate breeds, although generally called "types".

The Cocker in the hunting field "quarters" the ground ahead of the huntsman's gun at a snappy pace, and after flushing game, stops until the command to retrieve the shot bird is given. The same ease of accepting commands is evidenced in the training of the Cocker as a household pet.

English Cocker Spaniel. The English Cocker Spaniel is a rugged

ENGLISH COCKER SPANIEL

dog with enough size to do a full day's work in the hunting field and yet not so large as to be in the way if his owner lives in a small house or apartment. The same intelligence that makes him a splendid dog for the field makes him readily adjustable to the living conditions of his owner and ready to take on any type of training.

In weight, the English Cocker runs from 26 to 34 lbs., a good size for all conditions. He makes an attractive picture, covered as he is with a glistening wavy or flat coat of medium length and an undercoat

that protects against cold and water. The feathering is never enough to hinder his natural work in the field. In color, the English Cocker runs to roans of blue, liver, red, orange and lemon as well as solids of black, red and liver, and some are black and tan.

He is a merry dog, short of body, standing rather higher on the legs than our more familiar American Cocker, and with a larger head that is packed with common sense. Few breeds are more responsive to training, and this fact, coupled with alertness, courage, and a bright disposition, make him beloved of young and old alike. His stamina makes for ease in raising under any conditions, while his speed of foot and grace in action make him a joy to behold, whether going down the city street, romping in the park, or at his task as a hunting dog.

English Springer Spaniel. While the English Springer Spaniel breed has been kept as a hunting dog, such is its intelligence and merriness of working that the members of this breed have endeared themselves as pets and household companions. Large enough to tackle any type of cover natural to their quarry, they were never bred so large that almost any home could not readily accommodate at least one of the breed. At the shoulder they will average 18 to 18½ inches, and in weight should, in condition, scale

from 42 to 50 lbs., their weight distributed so as to make them able to
go all day in the field in an easy
manner.

The coat is of medium length,
either flat or wavy, and comes in

ENGLISH SPRINGER SPANIEL

liver and white, black and white,
liver and tan, black and tan, liver,
black, roan, as well as black, tan,
and white.

Although not officially recognized
as a separate breed by the Kennel
Club of England until 1902, the
English Springer Spaniel was well
known as a superlative hunting dog
for many years before that, and can
trace its ancestry back for centuries
in the lines of the so-called "spring-
ing spaniel", common parent of all
the present-day land spaniels.

The first of the English Springers
were brought to the United States
solely because American sportsmen
had had such delight in gunning
over them abroad. They bobbed up
here and there and were not exactly
strangers for the many years before
their devotees formed the English
Springer Spaniel Field Trial Asso-

ciation to act as a protective parent
body for them. This was in 1924
and at once field trials for the breed
appealed so much to the competitive
sportsmen and followers of such
events that the English Springer
Spaniel ever since has been a fixture
on the American sporting scene.

Field Spaniel. By nature, Field
Spaniels are very quiet and easy to
get along with, which is one reason
why those who have bred them
have usually raised them with their
own children, finding that they were
lovable pets and of such intelligence
as to remain unspoiled for their
work in the field while being household pets. Their expression is one of
gravity and understanding, accentuated by a long muzzle in which it is
said there has been developed a
"nose" second to none among the
sporting spaniels.

The coat color sought is black,
and unless the dog is supreme in
bodily construction, any other color
would virtually disqualify him in a
show. The Field Spaniel should run
from 35 to 50 lbs. in weight and
stand about 18 inches at the shoulder. He is so built as to possess good
speed and all-day endurance. Extremely intelligent and not of a
"prima donna" nature, the Field
Spaniel has about as much persever-
ance as any hunting breed of which
we know.

The breed is but slightly known
in the United States, even to con-

sistent showgoers, the majority of whom do not realize that the fancies of breeders have threatened from time to time to ruin the breed. At one time their vagaries turned him into a long, low-to-the-ground dog and it took the infusion of Cocker and Springer blood to bring him back to the build that enabled him to do the work for which he was originally created—that of a true land spaniel. Of late years in England, sound heads have persevered and a standard type has been developed, with the result that those who have enjoyed gunning over them and admired their steadfastness may soon bring enough good ones to the United States for American dog-lovers to become acquainted with them.

Irish Water Spaniel. Here is one dog that belies the old tale that a hunting dog is not a top-rank guardian, for the loyalty of the Irish Water Spaniel to his own family is such that he has been quite as highly prized as the protector of the household as for his prowess as a hunting aide.

He stands from 21 to 24 inches at the shoulder and weighs from 45 to 65 lbs. The coat is solid liver in color, covering the neck, back, and sides in tight ringlets, while most of the remainder is longer and either wavy or curly, with the front of the legs covered with shorter hair than the back of the legs.

An outstanding point is the "rat tail", which at the base is covered with tight short curls, tapering off to a fine point at the end. The topknot is another characteristic that stands out.

IRISH WATER SPANIEL

These are eager, fast, enduring, and very intelligent dogs, a fact which has been proved by the smartness of their work in the hunting field and in obedience tests. As the name indicates, they are primarily water dogs and their work as duck retrievers is hard to equal. This is because they not only love the water, winter and summer, but their coats are of such a texture as to shed water readily.

History does not exactly indicate when they first came on the scene, but it is known that the first show classes for them were granted back in 1859, and that for many years before that time, Ireland boasted of a North Country Water Spaniel and a South Country Water Spaniel. Finally leaders of both sections got together and developed this tallest of the spaniel family. Few hunting dogs have had more tales told of them than the Irish Water Spaniel. It is a breed rich in history and accomplishment and a breed that, once seen, can never be forgotten.

Sussex Spaniel. It is not often that Sussex Spaniels come to American shows, but when they are on

SUSSEX SPANIEL

the benches, their appearance calls for much comment from the casual showgoer, who is more often out to pick a pet than for anything else.

The rich golden liver coat is one of their outstanding characteristics and a proof of their pure breeding. These dogs are fairly long and low to the ground, being massive and muscular in build and creating the impression of being rather larger than they actually are, for they run only 35 to 45 lbs. in weight. There is nothing muscle-bound about them, for their action is free and their merry tails advertise their cheerful disposition which leads them to get along well with anyone and to adapt themselves to schooling.

They have not been the subject of heavy importations, mainly because the average American devotee of the sporting breeds wants a faster dog, and often sacrifices the sureness of the Sussex to get a faster dog that is unsure and less easy to "cover". Although lacking the speed of Cockers and Springers, the Sussex has an excellent nose, is a thorough ground coverer and valued for all types of upland game.

Actually this is another case of a dog being bred out of the basic Spaniel family to meet an actual condition, and the Sussex was wanted for types of rough shooting where a lighter, taller or speedier dog would have been at a loss. The breed was accepted for English show classification about 1860 and was developed many years before that time.

One oddity of the breed is that unlike most gun dogs it is inclined to give tongue, as would a hound dog on the scent.

Welsh Springer Spaniel. Stronger and larger than the Cocker Spaniel, but smaller than an English Springer, the Welsh Springer Spaniel can live in city or country with equal ease and is known as a good "keeper", for he seems almost immune to skin troubles and other diseases that afflict the general run of dogs. Years of work with humans has developed to a high degree the desire of the breed to please its people and to help in any way. This has made the dog excellent as a family companion and guardian, and there are numerous instances of members of the breed taking care of children and young animals. It must be said, however, that the Welsh Springer should be started in training at about six months of age, lest he become a lone hunter and thus hard to break.

The coat is flat and thick, of a silken texture, with a woolly protective undercoating. The color is red and white and evidently has been since the earliest days of the breed. Old writings and sketches give proof that in the first days of shooting over dogs, the medium-sized dog used was more like the Welsh Springer than any other type of spaniel known today. Known for centuries in Wales, he has slowly spread through the British Isles and now numbers have gone to America, Australia, and Siam. Extremes of heat or cold do not bother him. He is both a good land and water dog. If developed commercially, the breed could "go to town" because of its many fine qualities.

American Water Spaniel. Another of the few dogs developed in the United States is the American Water Spaniel, known to sportsmen for many decades but little known to the general public and to show-goers because the breeders and users of this likeable breed were afraid of spoiling their pets by show contacts.

Few breeds in any variety group make pets as fine as American Water Spaniels for a family. Small enough to live anywhere, their true Spaniel disposition makes them truly a family dog.

Their coat is of a solid liver or chocolate color and is closely curled; it is dense enough to protect against

AMERICAN WATER SPANIEL

the water and tough cover, yet is never coarse. They stand 15 to 18 inches high at the shoulder, and range in weight from 25 to 45 lbs. Their eyes match the coat, being hazel or brown, and are set wide apart, presenting an attractive, intelligent expression, with boundless enthusiasm.

Although only medium in size, American Water Spaniels are a very powerful breed, highly intelligent, fast, and with a great deal of stamina. They are able to work with authority under any weather, land, or water conditions. Regardless of the type of game sought, they will bring it in. Truly delightful hunting companions from dawn to dusk, they never tire and never cease wagging their short tails merrily.

While the breed is familiar to only a small group of the people who go to shows, the folks back of the breed have, since 1940, taken on American Kennel Club recognition and have begun to put a few specimens in the show rings.

Brittany Spaniel. The Brittany Spaniel is a small dog, closely knit and strongly built, with intelligence in every move. His size ranges from 17 inches to 20½. His coat is fairly fine, flat on the body, and smooth or a bit wavy. Colors are liver and white with roan ticking, or orange and white with roan ticking. His tail is naturally short, and some Brittany Spaniels are tailless. The eye is deep amber and very expressive. Willing in temperament as well as intelligent, he is an easily trained, agreeable household companion.

Considering his size, the type and density of coat, and his way of working, the Brittany might well be called a setter rather than a spaniel; both types of dog have, in fact, gone into the creating of this breed. Originating in France, the Brittany Spaniel first came to the United States in 1931 and has become so popular here that the parent club of the breed runs its own field trials. He is a capable dog in many ways, and it is nothing for one of these dogs in the course of a week to compete in the field, at the obedience rings, and in bench shows. Not a few have made good in all three types of competition, for the Brittany Spaniel is a gun dog that can do almost anything very well.

Clumber Spaniel. The Clumber Spaniel is dignity personified—an excellent pet for anyone who wants

CLUMBER SPANIEL

a quiet, handsome dog. Although he is slow-moving in comparison with other spaniels and presents a long, low, heavy appearance, he is never clumsy. His head is massive in all dimensions; his expression is extremely intelligent.

There is a wide range in sizes: the females of this breed go from 35 to 50 lbs. and the males from 55 to 65. The coat is straight and silky, very dense but not long, with abundant, long feathering. The colors called for are lemon and white, as well as orange and white; the fewer the body markings, the better. Perfection of markings is sought, with solid lemon or orange ears, evenly marked head and eyes, and some ticking on the muzzle and legs.

This beautiful breed, outstanding for its individuality, is one of the longest established of all the present-day spaniels. The Clumber's distinctive personality and appearance is due to the introduction, back in the early history of the breed, of Basset Hound blood. The breed had its first show class in England before 1860. It has been a very popular breed in that country and as a hunting dog is perhaps better suited to shooting conditions in England and on the Continent than in the United States where fast-moving spaniels are preferred. But the Clumber is a certain finder of game, a well-nigh faultless retriever when trained for the work, and has made good as a gun dog in various parts of the United States as well as in England.

Pointers. One of the most generally popular of all the sporting breeds, our modern Pointer is an individualist and a great pet, adored

POINTER

and adoring, as well as a superlative competitor and a born showman. His short coat is easy to take care of, the usual color combinations being liver and white, orange or lemon and white, and sometimes black and

white, while others have these colors with ticking (flecks).

The Pointer stands well up on his feet, which are well padded to make the dog able to work in the field without going lame. Clean-limbed, lithe, and muscularly set without coarseness, the dog is built for speed and endurance. Adaptable to all conditions, he is better off when kept where he can have ample exercise frequently. In all the colors, the darker the eye, the better. The tail should be straight, strong, tapered, and carried level with or slightly above the line of the back.

Averaging about 60 lbs., the Pointer's weight is so distributed that he appears to weigh much less. The field trial Pointers weigh considerably less, although those used as shooting dogs vary little in size from the bench show or pet dogs.

The Pointer is one of the oldest purebreds among the gun dogs. As far as can be determined, he is the first dog ever used to stand game in the manner in use today. Although for many years it was accepted that English Pointers came from Spain and Portugal, it now seems that they came into use throughout eastern Europe and the British Isles about the same time. Records as far back as 1650 establish the breed as having been known well in England.

The pet hunting-companion of thousands of amateur sportsmen in this country, the Pointer has walked off with premier honors in the country's greatest field trials and has done a tremendous amount of winning in the show ring, topping some of the country's biggest events.

German Short-haired Pointer. The German Short-haired Pointer, brought to this country a little more than ten years ago, is an extremely intelligent-looking dog that has more than pleased the hundreds who have bought the breed as a pet.

Males weigh from 55 to 75 lbs., while females will go from 45 to 60 lbs. In height they stand from 21 to 25 inches. The coat is water-resisting; the colors are solid liver, liver and white spotted, liver and white spotted and ticked, or liver and white ticked. The feet are webbed.

Not only does the German Short-haired Pointer make a fine pet, but he excels in the hunting field and in the exacting field trials, combining the qualities of a good pointer, a fine duck dog, a land or water retriever, an excellent night trailer, and a fine guard dog that fears nothing. Little has been found in bird dog work that this breed cannot do well.

This all-purpose dog is a comparatively recent development for the hunting field, having been in existence in his present form for approximately 60 years, and seems to have been created from using the old Spanish Pointer, the English Foxhound, and the Bloodhound. He made such a mark in the sporting fields of Germany for his all around work and ready adaptability that his fame soon spread and sportsmen of the United States began to import the breed. In his time of stay in this country, the dog has more than made good on his promise and for the last few years breeders have been unable to keep up with the public demand for the breed.

Wire-haired Pointing Griffon. An intelligent dog, the Wire-haired Pointing Griffon stands from 19½ to 23½ inches tall and has a very harsh coat that is not too long and sheds water readily. Short-backed and strong-limbed, he is a powerful dog. He is steel grey with chestnut splashes, greyish-white with chestnut splashes, or white mixed with chestnut. He is never black in coat.

The Griffon's head is long and his harsh coat forms a mustache and eyebrows; his muzzle is square. The eyes are expressive, and the iris is yellow or light brown. The coat is hard and stiff, never curly, and the downy undercoat is its protection against cold weather and accounts for its quick drying after water work.

The tail is carried straight or gaily, has a hard coat without a plume, and is generally cut to one-third its length.

Although the Wire-haired Pointing Griffon was developed in the greatest period of breeding, the last quarter of the ninteenth century, it is but slightly known in this country, even among veteran dog-lovers. This is hard to understand because the breed has made a fine record in the hunting fields of Europe and the members that we have had in this country have more than made their way as consistent hunting dogs.

Originating with E. K. Kortahls in Schooten, Holland, the breed went wherever the developer did, with the prime progress in France so that most authorities label it as a French breed. The first classes for the breed in England were provided in 1888, and the first registration in this country was Pocahontas, by Medard out of Flora, entered in 1901.

Weimaraner. Companionability is the outstanding characteristic of

WEIMARANER

the Weimaraner, whose disposition is as charming as its coat is beautiful. Developed before 1810 by the nobles of the Court of Weimar in Germany, who wanted an all-around hunting breed that would be differ-

ent from other breeds of the time, the Weimaraner's lovable qualities, ability to work, and color have remained unchanged to this day. Because these nobles were jealous in their love for the dogs, they became house pets, living as companions when not in the hunting field, and quick in response to human wishes.

The "grey ghosts", as they are called because of their silence in movement and the short, glossy grey coat that runs from silver to taupe, are comparatively new in the United States. At the beginning of 1946 there were less than a hundred of them in the country, but wherever they have gone they have created a sensation because of their unique, striking appearance, their velvety coat, and their winning temperament. The latter makes the onlooker think of them first as pets and only afterwards as candidates for success in the competitive field.

They are fearless, alert watchdogs and have proved ideal as guardians of children and small animals. Standing from 22 to 26 inches at the shoulder and weighing, when adult, 55 to 85 lbs., their grace is such as to mask their size, and their soundness of engineering shows up in the fact that they can go all day in the field and still be at it when they are fourteen or fifteen years old.

Their work in the hunting field is a joy to behold, whatever the type of game, condition of cover, and ranges of temperature may be. In obedience trials their intelligence shows up with amazing strings of victories.

Chesapeake Bay Retriever. A sturdy dog possessed of much stamina, the Chesapeake Bay Retriever

stands from 21 to 26 inches and weighs 55 to 75 lbs., carrying his weight very well.

Coat colors range from a dark brown to a faded tan or deadgrass, the latter running from tan to straw-color. The coat is thick and short, less than two inches long, with a very dense fine woolly undercoat which provides protection against icy waters. There may be a wave to the coat, but it is not supposed to be curly.

The rear quarters are as high or even higher than the forequarters and both should denote much power, as it is needed to breast heavy currents, and the back must be short, well-coupled, and powerful. The expression is intelligent, with medium eyes of a clear yellowish color, set well apart.

The tail is of medium length, ranging from 11 to 15 inches, medium-heavy with feathering. The shoulders are sloping with full freedom of action; the chest is strong, deep, and wide. Nature, aided by breeding, has engineered a dog able to do his job and congenial as a pet.

The Chesapeake Bay Retriever is one of the few breeds to be developed in the United States, and while there is no authentic record, it is generally believed that this breed owes its origin to two Newfoundland puppies that were rescued along with the crew of a brig wrecked off the coast of Maryland in 1807. Because they proved to be grand retrievers, the residents of the area bred their own dogs to them, and later various outcrosses must have been used. The fame of the dogs spread far and wide because of their ability to handle up to 200 and 300 ducks a day in the cold waters of Chesapeake Bay.

Labrador Retriever. Coming originally from Newfoundland, rather than from Labrador as their name implies, Labrador Retrievers are very beautiful dogs, with all the intelligence suggested by their breadth of skull and a great desire to please at all times. These qualities make them very desirable as pets.

The majority are black, although there are also many fine yellow Labradors. The coat is short, dense, and free of feather. The tail is the tapering, round sort usually described as an "otter" tail.

The Labrador stands more than 21 inches high at the shoulder and gives the impression of speed and power, both of which qualities he

LABRADOR RETRIEVER

possesses to a marked degree. He has a world of stamina and can work in any kind of weather.

Extremely fine water dogs, the Labradors made a hit with English sportsmen early in the Nineteenth Century. They were then bred for the smooth, short hair they now have, because it had been found that with the longer coats the dogs were held back in their swimming by the ice that formed on their coats.

Some early authorities credited the breed with having no equal in the finding of wounded game, and to this day the breed is hard to beat at any type of retrieving. Labrador Retrievers have won a great many of the country's spot field trials and in addition have proved themselves fine shooting companions.

This is one of the few breeds which combine qualities in such a way that the same dog can acquit himself well in the field trials and come back to the bench show and win. It has not been uncommon for Labradors to win best-of-show titles in the United States and England, and several have won dual championships.

Golden Retriever. In the United States there are few dog breeds that have made more headway in recent years than the Golden Retriever.

A physical beauty, the Golden Retriever has a rich golden coat, not as dark as the Irish Setter, and sometimes with cream touches. The coat is flat or wavy, with good undercoating that resists water and cold. The tail is straight—not curled at the tip or carried over the back.

The Golden Retriever is an excellent pet in addition to being a powerful dog with good speed and staying powers—one which has become a power in the field trial world, a winner of best-in-show titles in conformation shows, and a star in the obedience trials.

Originally these dogs were known as Russian Trackers. They first appeared in England in a Russian circus act in 1860. Their intelligence was such that English sportsmen reasoned that the talent could be used in the field. The breed was scaled down from the "Tracker's" size of nearly 30 inches at the shoulders and 100 lbs. in weight, so that now they run 20½ to 24 inches and scale 55 to 68 lbs. Possessed of remarkable scenting ability, this was intensified by crossing with the Bloodhound. Golden Retrievers made their first American appearance before World War I. In the last few years interest in them has increased considerably.

Flat-coated Retriever. The standard for Flat-coated Retrievers calls for a bright, active dog of 60 to 70 lbs., with intelligent expression, speed, and power. Their black, slightly wavy coat lies close but is very dense, which makes possible their standing the rigors of icy water. The chest is deep and rather broad, but not so as to interfere with efficiency of action in the water or on the land.

This breed is scattered in small numbers through shooting sections of the country, but for some reason never has been pushed, with the result that here is another dog with fine potentialities as a pet and as a great working-hunting dog that is little known to the general public and has no specialty club to back up and promote the breed.

Oddly enough, while the Flat-coated Retriever is one of the least known of the pure breeds in the United States, it traces back to two breeds indigenous to North America, the Labrador Retriever and the Newfoundland. These account for

the color and the coat. As far as we know, the first dog of the present type to be shown appears to have been shown at Birmingham, England, in 1860.

Flat-coated Retrievers have proved to be excellent water dogs, performing all phases of that work in good style, while some of the breed have more than made good on upland game. Their all-around value lends credence to the theory that both the Gordon Setter and the Irish Setter have been crossed in here at one time or another, with an infusion from the Russian breed now known as the Golden Retriever.

Curly-coated Retriever. The Curly-coated Retriever is a very charming dog that makes a good

CURLY-COATED RETRIEVER

pet for adult or child. Although in England he has appeared in shows since before 1860 and has done a lot of good work in field trials, in the United States his devotees prefer him as a companion rather than for competitive honors.

As his name suggests, his coat is

a mass of crisp curls; it is most attractive in black or liver, almost of a solid color, and can stand the most rigorous going, either in water or on land. Extremely intelligent, he lives up to his appearance of an active, enduring dog, for he will virtually live in the water all day, and the more work he gets to do, the better he likes it. His way of going belies his weight, which ranges from 70 to 80 lbs.

The Curly-coated Retriever is believed to have come down from some cross of the English Water Spaniel which has existed since the Sixteenth Century. Somewhere along the line the old Retrieving Spaniel entered into it, as well as the St. John's Newfoundland, and very probably in the Eighteenth Century the Poodle brought the tightly-curled coat into the breed. At any rate, the Curly is considered the oldest of the Retriever breeds. And it is one of the few hunting dogs which has also been bred and used for guard duty; most of the other hunting breeds care only for their work afield or some adaptation of it. The Curly-coated Retriever is a breed that recommends itself as a pet, watch-dog, or hunting-companion for anyone located where water would be a part of the hunting scene.

THE HOUND GROUP

The Hound Group as a Whole. The nearly 20 breeds that are officially classified as belonging to the Hound Group, or Variety Group Two, have behind them a glorious record for the part they have played in a progression of civilization. Perhaps the antiquity of these breeds, as much as anything else, accounts for the public's speaking of dogs in general as "hounds".

While not all of these breeds are geared to live in small apartments or the smaller suburban dwellings, their very natures make them ideal as pets for the family that has the space to care for their needs. It is an indisputable fact that most of the hound breeds go back for centuries in their native lands, and because of their close living in the service of man, there has grown up a very close bond between man and the hound breeds.

In this grouping of dogs are found those breeds that by nature hunt game by scent or sight and thus have rounded up for man's table, much food. Starting with the dogs of the desert, which are believed to have been the first breeds put to practical use by man, all of which were hounds, history records the development of the other breeds which make up this group which is all utility and grace.

In size, these dogs range from the Dachshund and the Beagle, which are small enough to fit into the tiniest apartment, to the Irish Wolfhound, which in overall measurements is probably the largest breed known today.

The folk tales of all lands speak of hounds, singly and in packs, that added much to the history and literature of those countries, proving that from the very start, there were qualities in these breeds that made for that ideal companionship that man has valued in a silent partner. That relationship is what makes the hound work out so well today as a pet.

Africa, the desert lands, much of Europe, and the British Isles have given us most of our hound breeds, while here in the United States we can claim development of the American Foxhound and the Black and Tan Coonhound, and the refinement of many of the other breeds imported from other lands.

On the competitive side, be it the bench shows, the obedience trials, or the field trials, these various hounds have held their own in public favor as well as acquiring the top honors in the phase of competition elected.

Beagle. The merry Beagle, like the Cocker Spaniel, enjoys nationwide popularity, and owes the general favor to its all-around value, its

companionability and adaptability, its evenness of temperament, and its small size. Few breeds possess greater intelligence and it is unspoiled by being made a household pet, which cannot be said of all the working-hunting breeds, some of

BEAGLE

which go soft and lose the urge of the hunt.

In general appearance Beagles are miniature Foxhounds, seeming larger than they actually are because of their solid, compact build. At a glance one can see that they are able to take the wear and tear of a day-long chase. The coat is of medium length, close and hard and able to hit the toughest cover. The breed comes in two sizes: one class includes those under 13 inches at the shoulder, and the other consists of those between 13 and 15 inches. Both sizes are allowed to compete in dog shows and field trials, in both of which their overall entry for a year ranks very high.

Smallest of the present-day hound breeds, the Beagle goes back many centuries, although the actual origin of the breed is lost in the maze of ancient history. It is believed, however, that the Beagle stems back to the scent hound that seems to have been popular in the days of Xenophon, and moved West when the ancient Romans borrowed this and other sports, and thence on to England, although records show there were some hound packs in England long before that time.

The Beagle trains well to hunt either as an individual or in a pack, and in either case never loses his merriness that is mixed with honesty of purpose.

Basset Hound. The Basset Hound has been called the "quaintest" of dogs. He is low in appear-

BASSET HOUND

ance, running from 11 to 15 inches at the shoulder, with a long body and very heavy bones. He weighs between 25 and 40 lbs. The most popular Basset Hound in the United States is the crooked or half-crooked front leg type, with short forelegs that end in massive paws. The coat is medium-fine, but of enough strength to be of value in bad weather. The skin is loose and elastic.

The Basset Hound has been bred for centuries as a strictly sporting dog, well disciplined for hunting either in packs or as an individual, but because he is so intelligent and kindly of disposition, the Basset is not only a wonderful pal for the hunting field, but a grand companion for the home. Easily controlled and very affectionate, he is more or less a one-man dog.

Back of the Basset Hound is the old French Bloodhound and the St. Hubert Hounds, which accounts for the super-scenting ability of the Basset, an accurate, steady trailer, with plenty of tongue when on the scent. The breed was brought to England from France in 1866. Because of their short legs, Bassets are excellent in dense cover and their steadiness is invaluable when it comes to securing wounded game. They are used mainly for hunting rabbits, foxes, and pheasants, and, when trained for it, have been found to be of great value in raccoon hunting.

American Foxhound. The development of the breed we know as the American Foxhound is wrapped up with much of the early history of the United States; in fact, it goes back to the exploring days and the settling of various parts of the new United States. In all this time, while the breed has had many packs in the hunting field, it would not have progressed into a definite breed status without having proved its value as a personalized or pet dog as well as its worth in the field.

In size American Foxhounds range from 22 to 25 inches at the shoulder and are covered with a close, hard coat of medium length

AMERICAN FOXHOUND

which can stand almost all types of cover. They are fast on their feet, but their speed is guided by an intelligence that knows what it is doing and why, and their stamina is amazing.

The first words on the importation of hound stock to the Americas comes in the diary of one of the followers of De Soto, and from there on we find entries in the "history" of the Foxhound which indicate that a full pack came from England in 1650 and formed the base of present operations, which have gone beyond the early use to hunt Indians.

The Walker Hounds came to America in 1742, and 30 years later George Washington was among the subscribers that brought over another pack, and every few years more famous packs were brought in, mainly from England. The crossing

and recrossing of these lines, plus an evidence that there was a cut-in on the line left here by De Soto's men, resulted in the fine dog of excellent voice that we know today as the American Foxhound, a source of pride to many an American family.

English Foxhound. While the main basis of the American Foxhound comes from the English packs imported between 1650 and 1850, the English and American Foxhound breeds are now quite distinct. However, it must be admitted that while less than 10 percent of the packs used in the United States could not be registered in the very tightly watched Stud Book of the English Foxhound, we have enough of the English breed in this country to give a good view of what is considered a top hound abroad.

Many claim that the English Foxhound is the finest of all combinations of grace and strength, and indeed the strong point of the breed standard calls for symmetry, which we interpret as being balance and quality. It is mainly used as a "pack" dog here in the United States and few are held as individual house pets, although their intelligence and many years of close association with humans could well make them excellent as pets.

In color, the English Foxhound is mainly some combination of black, white and tan, but coloring is not considered nearly so important as having the short, dense, hard coat with a gloss. The breed is strong on pedigree and there is no trouble in tracing the ancestry of a true English Foxhound back before 1800.

Black and Tan Coonhound. The latest breed to attain the recognition of the American Kennel Club

BLACK AND TAN COONHOUND

as a pure breed is the Black and Tan Coonhound, which actually has a long history back of it for its excellent work in its chosen field. Untold thousands of people in the United States have known, watched, or owned these dogs and valued them for their sense, stamina, voice, and disposition, and many are the American youngsters who have grown up with one or two of these practical, exceptionally friendly dogs.

Measured at the shoulder the males of the breed are 25 to 27 inches, with females reaching 23 to 25 inches. Correct dogs are in proportion to general conformation so that they seem neither leggy nor too close to the ground.

As might be expected, this Coonhound gets its name from the rich

black coat that has tan markings of depth above the eyes, on the sides of the muzzle, chest, legs, and breeching, and black line markings on the toes. The coat is short and dense and thus able to stand the toughest of going when on the hunt.

It is primarily a working-hunting dog, able to stand the heat of summer and the worst of winter weather, as well as the most difficult terrain over which his course may be. A powerful, alert, and agile dog, the Black and Tan Coonhound is ever eager, aggressive at work but not a trouble maker, and always willing to be friendly with anybody and anything. Most impressive is his ability to cover great distance with a tireless, rhythmic stride that is a joy to watch.

Harrier. The Harrier is a breed not too well known in the United States today, although there is every evidence that they have been known here for as long as any of the hounds that hunt by scent.

In general color and conformation, as well as coat, the Harrier is like the Foxhound, although it usually stands 19 to 21 inches at the shoulder.

Early records of the Harrier as a breed indicate it was as much a pet dog as it was a huntsman, and its temperament is such as to lead one to believe it would be an ideal household companion.

In one sense it might have been

called "the poor man's Foxhound", for more than fifty years ago there were a great many packs in England that were thrown together, not by a club, but by individuals who brought their one or two dogs and ran them as "scratch packs". These packs were hunted on foot and could be so used today because the Harrier, a seemingly smaller and less speedy edition of the English Foxhound, can well be hunted on foot.

The origin of the Harrier is rather clouded, although one needs not too much imagination to see that the breed is very much like the hounds described by the Greek historian, Xenophon, about 400 B.C., as being used to chase hares. However, it is well authenticated that there was at least one pack of Harriers operating in England in about 1260, and that it was held together for at least 500 years.

Bloodhound. By name, the Bloodhound is known to more people than any other dog breed, but in actuality there are not too many dog lovers that really know the dog, its ancestry, tradition, and nature. This is unfortunate, for it is truly a great dog. Few breeds are more docile in nature or possessed of a finer protective instinct. Too large to be accommodated in fairness in a city apartment, they still make a fine member of the household.

They range in size from 23 to 27 inches at the shoulder and weigh from 80 to 110 lbs. In color they are black and tan, red and tan, and tawny.

Bloodhounds have been of much service to mankind over the centuries they have been known, and

BLOODHOUND

their work in following trails has been celebrated in many a fictional account that is more than matched by actual reporting of their deeds. Some of the really great Bloodhounds developed in the United States have caused more convictions than ace human detectives, with one dog credited with more than 600. One dog was known to have followed a scent that was more than 100 hours old, and another led police officers nearly 150 miles with success.

The name Bloodhound comes mainly from the fact that in the 12th Century dignitaries of the Church kept them, in fact, are credited with keeping strains pure, and so they were called "blooded hounds", which was corrupted into Bloodhound. It is a sad and serious looking dog that trails its quarry well, but never attacks it upon discovery. Contrary to opinion, it was not the true Bloodhound that trailed slaves, but mongrels schooled by owners for that purpose.

Basenji. The Basenji is a fascinating dog, loving and being loved by

BASENJI

children and of a size that is adaptable to even the smallest home. Built along the lines of a Fox Terrier, his standard of perfection calls for a 16-inch height for females and 17 inches for males. The preferred color is red, and as the coat is fine and silky, it shines like polished copper; there are also lighter reds, fawns, and chestnuts. Other characteristics are the erect ears standing right up from the head, deeply furrowed wrinkles of the forehead, and the tightly-curled tail that lies to one side of the back. Few breeds have greater intelligence, which is exemplified by their fine work in the

obedience tests, and on their jaunts into the hunting field.

Oddly enough, this is one of the last three breeds to have been recognized by the American Kennel Club, yet is one of the oldest in the world, for records show that specimens were presented to the Pharaohs of Egypt, where they were prized for speed, intelligence, hunting prowess, and their silence in the field. Actually they do not bark, but rather have a sort of yodel or chortle, and are popularly known as the "barkless dog of the Congo".

They were discovered again in 1895 by an English explorer, but it was not until 1937 that they were successfully introduced into England. They were brought into the United States in 1941. Since then they have made fine strides as is deserved by an appealing breed that is bright and cheery and that can be a perfect house dog, even to lacking doggy odors.

Dachshund. Although the Dachshund is most closely associated in the mind with Germany and much of its development must be credited to that country, the breed is universal in its appeal and there are few lands into which one may journey where fine specimens will not be found as pets. Part of the reason for the world-wide popularity of the Dachshund rests in its alert and appealing gaze, its intelligence, plucky spirit, and ready adaptability to all conditions. Another factor that has made the Dachshund an outstanding pet, especially in large cities, is the small size, the ease of

DACHSHUND

obtaining proper conditioning exercise, its native health and stamina, and its instinctive cleanliness. In addition, the Dachshund is an exceptionally playful dog, displaying an almost human sort of gayety and a special understanding and tolerance when playing with small children. With its boundless devotion to humans of any age, and by its very need and gratitude for affection, the Dachshund easily wins the love and human companionship on which it is so dependent.

There are three types of coat, which is again a point in its favor as a pet, for the owner can obtain the coat-type that suits his fancy. The best known is the smooth, short-haired type of coat, which is dense and resistant, although shining and glossy always, needing very little care. The wire-haired variety has a tough, spikey coat which is hard and has a good undercoat that enables it to buck any kind of cover in search of game. The third variety is the long-haired, which is not un-

like the coat of the Irish Setter.

There is a fourth recognized variety of Dachshund, the Miniature, which has a maximum weight just under 9 lbs. at maturity. It is almost small enough to put in an overcoat pocket.

In color, the Dachshund has the solid red of various shades; the black with tan points; and the chocolate with tan points. This again gives the potential purchaser a range to choose from.

In spite of its small stature, the Dachshund can accommodate itself to the country and handle itself well in the field. Its ability to hunt has never been bred out of it in the many years that it has been mainly a city-dweller. Even in exacting field trials, Dachshunds have quickly reverted to the style of their forebears and turned in a grand job.

Rough stone sketches give rise to the belief that the Dachshund or a near relative of the present-day dog existed back in the days of the Pyramids. It is well known that the type did exist in the fifteenth century when it was valued, as now, for hunting the badger.

Apparently the smooth-coat type came first and then breeders, anxious to meet certain game conditions, developed the wire-haired and long-haired coats. The wire-haired variety was a result of crossing with the terrier types of dogs to give a coat protection against briars and brush. The long-haired type came from other crossings, probably in the nineteenth century, with spaniel types, to produce a heavy, long coat that would protect against water and cold weather. Always the breed has been a worker and close companion of man and his family.

Greyhound. In a sense the word Greyhound is a misnomer, for few members of this graceful breed are

GREYHOUND

grey, although it has been stated that at one stage of civilization, grey was the chief color. Since ancient times the Greyhound has been revered by young and old, rich and poor, and although at times in various countries the possession of these speedsters by anyone other than royalty was against the law, they have grown up in close association with humans and have been house dogs more than kennel dogs.

The coat is short, smooth, and firm and may be of any color, although general preference today seems to run to whites or white with slate markings. Weights run from 60 to 70 pounds, so well distributed that they move fast or slowly with ease and grace and create an unforgettable picture.

The Greyhound may well be called one of the original breeds, for it has definitely been traced back to the tombs of the Fourth Dynasty of Egypt, roughly about 4000 B.C. Ancient records also place it as existing as a more or less native dog in nearly all tropical and semi-tropical countries for thousands of years, and exactly in the form that we know the breed today.

It made its way into what is now Western Europe and the British Isles as far back as the eighth century and there was used on such game as foot speed was needed, such as deer, stags, hare, fox, and so on. Of recent years there has been little use of the dog in this way, but its talent has been translated into entertainment through the medium of racing after a mechanical rabbit. As a show dog he rates with the best.

Whippet. Although a relatively young breed, having been brought out about a hundred years ago, the Whippet has a horde of staunch admirers in the United States and England. With a grace of temperament that matches his perfection of motion, he fits into the household and personal life of any family. Although credited with being the fastest domesticated animal of his weight alive, a point that can be neither proved nor disproved, the Whippet needs none of these titular honors to aid him in his winning of the human heart. His small size adds to

WHIPPET

his advantage as a house pet. Few animals are more unobtrusive, and yet this same dog that can lie at your feet in perfect peace is always alert to the protection of his family and can transform himself into a dynamo on the race track, in the hunting of game, and is expert at the business of ratting.

The Whippet stands 18 to 22 inches at the shoulder and seldom weighs over 20 lbs. The coat is smooth, close, and firm of texture and almost any coat color is acceptable, whether the dog is a pet or competes in races or shows. Although bred primarily for racing and rabbit chases, the grace, beauty, and style of the breed have made them a show favorite wherever they have gone.

In truth a miniature Greyhound,

this breed was bred down from his "big brother", crossed in with terrier breeds, and refined by using the Italian Greyhound.

Saluki. The Saluki is, in effect, a Greyhound with feathered ears, tail, and legs, and with a softer, silkier body coat. Revered by the ancients, it has been a family dog, rather than one of great kennels, and to this day is ideal as a companion and guardian of children.

Being a dog of the desert, the Saluki had not only to help keep the family larder well supplied, which it did with ease because of its speed and its far sight, but it had to act as protector of the family campfire and quarters. Today it is still a good watch dog, but never of the aggressive type, which means that it will warn of, and help repel,

SALUKI

intruders, but it will not go out of its way to create trouble.

Its range of coat color is such that even the most choosy person can find a member of the breed whose color will please him. Coats may be white, cream, fawn, golden, red, grizzled and tan, or black and white.

The Saluki can and will hunt any game that needs speedy pursuit, anywhere in the world. Soft to humans and tough on the trail, the Saluki is among those purebreds that are unchanged since their breed began.

Borzoi. Borzoi is the official name of the dog known for many years as the Russian Wolfhound, truly an aristocrat among dogs.

BORZOI

A speedy, yet powerful dog, the male Borzoi will stand 28 to 31 inches at the shoulder and weigh from 75 to 105 lbs., while the female will be two inches shorter and some 20 lbs. lighter. White is generally the predominating color of the coat, marked with lemon, tan, black, grey, or brindle. In texture the coat is silky, never woolly, and is either flat, wavy, or slightly curled, and quite long.

Long the pet of Russian royalty, who kept great kennels of the breed, with favored animals living in the household, the Borzoi today remains a fine pet for those with either the space to house them or the time to take them for proper exercise. Despite their size, their quietness of nature makes them able to fit into nearly any scheme of living.

It is likely that the Borzoi was a northern development of the general Greyhound family, which dates back to ancient times, and spread north and west from the desert lands. Evidently the Borzoi breed was developed first because of speed afoot for the procurement of food, and later the nobility used them for sport. In the Seventeenth Century Borzois were used as a courser of wolves, hare, and other game. In time the craze on the part of breeders for changes nearly ruined the breed, which is now coming back into the form that more nearly resembles the ancient breed—an aristocrat with speed, power, great courage, and sense.

Afghan Hound. The amazing appearance of the Afghan Hound has made it appeal to everyone who has seen it, with the result that there are far more Afghan Hounds maintained as pets in the United States than are entered in the show rings of the country. It is a strong, alert dog, with a graceful outline possessing a world of power and speed. Males stand about 27 inches at the shoulder and females at 25 inches, with an average weight of about 60 lbs.

Distinctive points are the top-knot of long silky hair and the high tail carriage, which had high value in its native Afghanistan where the waving tail could indicate to the huntsman where his dog was working a thicket. Another outstanding

AFGHAN HOUND

point is the unique set of the hip bones which allow a sort of "free-wheeling" that enables the breed to negotiate hilly country with ease.

It is believed that no breed can trace its ancestry as a pure breed further back than the Afghan Hound, for this picturesque dog of the desert is already authenticated as belonging to that period between 3000 and 4000 B.C. The breed is mentioned on a papyrus discovered in excavations, placing its recognition among royalty back in the Sinai area where Jehovah delivered to Moses the tables of the Ten Commandments.

Modern history of the breed really dates from World War I when British Army officers brought some

specimens back to England and also spread them through India, Persia, and Arabia. Its exotic appearance made it click with all strata of society and quickly it was adopted in the United States, where increasing numbers may be found in all sections of the country.

The hind quarters, flanks, ribs, and fore quarters are well covered with silky, thick hair, quite fine in texture. The ears and feet are well feathered, and the coat is a perfect insulator, for it can stand the greatest desert heat and the most bitter cold.

The Afghan hunts by sight, rather than by scent, and wherever it has been used has made a remarkable record since 5000 years ago, in many different lands. During all these centuries it was brought up with its family and so valued that the men of the desert would trade almost any possession to obtain a fine specimen.

While many Americans first buy an Afghan because it is "different", they soon learn that this dog is highly desirable also because of its companionable quality.

Irish Wolfhound. Here we have a "king size" dog, for this is the tallest of all dogs, standing from 28 to 34 inches at the shoulder, and spreading his weight of some 120 lbs. over so long a frame that he is like a freight train in passing and could readily put his forepaws on the shoulders of a man seven feet tall.

Despite his size, the Irish Wolf-hound is not ungainly or unable to get around.

As a guardian of the family he has no peer, but because of his size no potential dog-buyer should seek

IRISH WOLFHOUND

him out unless there is plenty of space available for the dog to range.

The coat of the Irish Wolfhound is rough and harsh, resistant to weather conditions, and usually grey in color, although other accepted colors are brindle, white, black, fawn, or red.

It is possible to trace this breed back more than 2000 years, and basically the dog of today is the same one that caused such a furor among those who long ago sought favor from the kings of Europe through gifts of great value. The dogs had to be fast and game, because they not only handled the Irish wolf, but they were unequalled in the hunting of the Irish elk, which was six feet high at the shoulder. Although the Irish Wolfhound was bred originally to feed his hu-

man associates by his field prowess, he has lasted as a companion because of his charm of manner.

Scottish Deerhound. Literature and Art have given us a fine line on the Scottish Deerhound, one of the most graceful and dignified of breeds, the finest tribute, perhaps, being that of Sir Walter Scott, who wrote of his Maida, "The most perfect creature of Heaven." Many of the paintings of Landseer depict the Deerhound.

As they were hunted in olden times mainly in pairs or singly, and were valued as "table providers" and guardians of Highland Chieftains, the breed grew up in close companionship with man, with a great desire for human companionship, and so were treasured as highly as pets as they were as working-hunting dogs.

From those days of the Middle Ages to the present time they have been household pets, and although quite large, they are so at home with humans that they can move through the smallest home without trouble. Possessed of a great loyalty, tractable and easy to train, intelligent and alert, the Scottish Deerhound makes an ideal family dog where there is the chance to obtain adequate exercise.

The Deerhound stands from 28 to 32 inches at the shoulder and ranges in weight from 75 to 110 pounds, which weight it handles easily and with such speed as to be a fine hunter against the swiftest of game. The hair in body, neck, and quarters is harsh and wiry, about three to four inches long, with softer hair on the head and breast. Dark blue-grey is the preferred color, after which come the dark and light greys and brindles, followed by yellow, sandy red, and red fawn.

The breed goes back to the sixteenth century, and although highly rated as a hunting dog, it never would have made its big place in history, but for its disposition and loyalty.

Otterhound. The Otterhound is another breed whose origin is shrouded in the mists of history,

OTTERHOUND

perhaps even more so in the fogs created by researchers' disagreements. To the casual observer and the seeker after a "different" dog to have as a pet, the fundamental fact that stands out is that here is a breed which was developed many years back for a very practical purpose, and any dog so bred which has lost its original job can be quickly converted to that association with

man that is known as owner-and-dog home companionship.

Otterhounds stand 24 to 26 inches at the shoulder and weigh as much as 65 lbs. They have hard, tough coats, of an oily nature, that enable them to shed water and stand extreme cold. In color they range from the preferred blue and white to a black and tan. They have no superior as swimmers, being aided by webbed feet. The head is broader in its proportions than that of the Bloodhound, and while Otterhounds lack, perhaps, the smartness of appearance of many breeds, they make it up in working ability, and their sense and willingness to work show up in the dogs' expression and add to their attractiveness as the companion of the family, to which they give undying devotion.

In disposition Otterhounds are much like the best lines of Bloodhound, and indeed there are authorities who believe that the Otterhound is merely a wiry-coated Bloodhound. There are references to such a breed as far back as 1200 A.D., but little proof that this was the dog we know today. We do know that the breed was developed and trained to rid the streams of otters, which prey on fish. One pack is credited with having killed more than 700 otters in a twenty-year period.

Norwegian Elkhound. Norway's contribution to the sport of dogs is the Norwegian Elkhound. Once one of the most ancient of all breeds, an all-round sporting hound of top grade ability, and a splendid home companion. Nature did most of the developing of this clean-cut, fearless, kindly dog, and all evidence points

NORWEGIAN ELKHOUND

to the fact that this dog, as long ago as 5000 B.C., was enough of a companion to his humans as to be buried with them.

In the United States, he is best known as a companion of rare quality; intelligent, readily adaptable, needing little room, fast to learn, sweet of disposition.

At the shoulders he stands 18½ to 20 inches, and makes a most attractive picture with his thick, hard and rich coat of more than medium length. The color is grey with black tips to the long covering hairs, somewhat lighter on chest, stomach, legs, and underside of tail.

The Norwegian Elkhound is medium in overall size, very compact, with the striking feature of short tail, set high and curled tightly over middle of back. The expression of the face is one of great intelligence, always alert and with a fearless but kindly gaze in the eye. His build is such as to allow him literally to bounce in his hunting work, at which he more than earned his keep in his native land.

In the United States, where hunted, he has done extremely well, but his main forte, at least in public, has been the obedience tests, where he is always to be reckoned with. For stamina and elasticity of action he has no superior.

THE WORKING GROUP

The Working Group as a Whole. There are thirty breeds or varieties that make up the Working Group, or Variety Group Three, and between what nature has done and what man has changed or bred for specific utilitarian purposes, the world has been given a group of

dogs that strikes the greatest responsive chord in the human heart.

These dogs were great as workers long before the "window dressing" of shows was developed as a meeting place to see who bred the best, and it is as workers and for what they have done for mankind down through the centuries that they are best known. Depending upon the family quarters for housing, however, each has those superb qualities within them that make them ideal as household companions and pets. The working breeds may have little reason on the whole to live up to their name in the complex civilization of today, especially in the United States, but their development as personal aides to man and as guardians of his family and his goods has brought out in them that quality of interdependence with their humans that makes them welcome in any home.

There are nearly as many native lands for these dogs as there are breeds, and the literature of the home countries is filled with tales of the deeds and value of their working dogs, while the art of these countries has depicted their nobility and beauty. Basically, all these breeds can trace their ancestry back for centuries, although some are seen today in a form of relatively recent development.

In size the working dogs range from the Corgis at 12 inches and the Shetland sheepdogs at 13½ inches to the Great Danes and other breeds that will tower more than 30 inches at the shoulder. Weights have gone well over 200 lbs. in the massive St. Bernards.

Coats are of all colors, textures, and lengths, and somewhere along

the line will be found a dog that esthetically meets the most exacting demands. Little wonder that the bench shows of the nation find a sizeable share of the attendance watching these members of breeds which for centuries have guarded the flocks and herds of all lands, contributed to the safety of children, and often laid down their lives for their families. Today many still serve as guards for home and properties, others spend their lives as eyes for the sightless, and many a grand page of history has been written by the thousands of working dogs who have done yeoman service as dogs of war. Here, indeed, nature has provided utility and beauty at once.

Collie (rough). Few breeds are better known to the general public than the Collie, and there is hardly

COLLIE (ROUGH)

an old family that has not had one, or at least visited with farm relatives where one or more of the breed went about equally at home in helping with the livestock or romping with the children.

Of late years there has been rather less employment of the natural working talent of the Collie, but his fame as a playmate and guardian of children has increased through the years. Besides his ability there is the appeal of his looks, for few members of the dog family have a more aristocratic appearance, or possess so notably a combined questioning and understanding expression.

The coat is abundant, except on head and legs, the outer coat being fairly harsh for weather resistance, and the inner soft and furry. Color is called immaterial, but it is noted that the sable and white, the blue merle, and the black and tan with a white collar are most popular and striking. Height ranges from 22 to 24 inches and weight from 50 to 60 pounds.

The breed apparently originated prior to 1800 and has steadily grown more beautiful with the many refinements breeders have brought about. The old tales of the original crosses that produced the Collie have many flaws and must be discounted, but it is known that chief credit must be given to the Scotch shepherds who wanted a dog of intelligence that was at once fast, quiet, and able to take all types of weather.

The Collie made a hit with Queen Victoria and from then on his success was assured.

Collie (smooth). The Smooth Collie is unknown to many American dog lovers, but there was a time when it ranked with or above the well-known Rough Collie. In characteristics they are much the same and either is splendid as a house companion and a playmate of children.

The Smooth Collie has often been considered as a different breed, but apparently was developed from the same stock as the Rough Collie. Where the Rough stood out as a sheep dog, the Smooth was the cattle drover's dog. In size it is similar to the Rough, but it has a short dense coat of good texture, with a good undercoat.

On both sides of the Atlantic, the Smooth Collie has shown signs of needing stimulation as a breed in recent years, possibly because it is a far less showy dog than the Rough.

Shetland Sheepdog. It would be hard to imagine a breed with more

SHETLAND SHEEPDOG

universal appeal than the Shetland Sheepdog, which is, in effect, a Collie in miniature, and able on a slightly smaller scale to do the same type of work. Their devoted natures, the sweet look in their eyes, and their intelligent expression endear them to all who see them and it would be almost impossible for American breeders to supply the demand of the general public for this "apartment-sized" working dog.

The "Sheltie" stands 12 to 15 inches at the shoulder and is strongly built, as befits a dog that can handle sheep agilely and smartly. Excellent as watchdogs, they are valuable for farm and city alike, showing the background of their native training.

It is true that changes are being made in this breed, which did not come into real show recognition until 1915 and was then held up by World War I, but while there can be debate on the wisdom of changes physically, it can be certain that none of the lovability of the breed has been destroyed.

On the side of intelligence, one has but to look at the high percentage of Shetland Sheepdogs that have made good in the highly interesting and competitive field of obedience trials in the United States, where often a "Sheltie" and owner that have never competed before step in and make a very high qualifying score.

They are a joy to watch in action, for every move is full of grace, and handled properly this could well be America's dog of tomorrow.

Old English Sheepdog. The Old English Sheepdog is affection-ately known as the "Bobtail", after one of its most distinguishing characteristics, for the breed either has no tail at all or one of not more than an inch or so. The dog has many pleasing points to recommend it,

OLD ENGLISH SHEEPDOG

either as a dog for work, or as a household pet, being equally at home with adults or children.

The very appearance of the Old English Sheepdog carries an appeal to all, and nine times out of ten, when youngsters see such a dog, they want it for their own. The breed is even-tempered, has a real sense of humor, and can make itself at home in a large house, a small apartment, a train, or a car.

The coat is profuse and of good hard texture, shaggy but free from curl, and under this outer coat is a kind of waterproof pile. The color may be any shade of grey, grizzle, blue or blue-merled, with or without white markings. The dog stands from 20 inches up, although sizes over 26 inches are objected to.

The breed is not one of the most ancient, but it can be traced back to sometime before 1800. It was first known in the West of England, but there seems to be some doubt as to what combinations led to the making of this breed, which first won fame as a drover's dog. Later it drew more of a following as its adaptability to all situations began to be known.

The Old English Sheepdog, with a soft mouth, trains easily as a retriever, and makes a top-grade sledge dog. Despite its profuse coat, it is easily taken care of, and that adds to its charm and value as a house dog. He has done well in the show ring and can hold his own in obedience.

Briard. With a long and honorable record in many fields, the Briard is probably one of the best all-around working dogs that we know today. Like all dogs that go back to ancient days and which have been bred to work with and for their families, the Briard is equally at home with the day's work or with the children of the household.

The breed is calm and has authority in his action and gaze. The barking is rare and comes only to give warning. The nature of his background makes the Briard an ideal dog in the house, where he adapts himself to conditions readily. Really playful for a large dog, he adores small children, guards them

well, and displays an infectious gayety that charms all. While he gets on with everyone, the Briard is a one-family dog.

An adult Briard will stand from 22 to 27 inches. He is always alert, active, and strong, and wears a long, slightly wavy coat that is rather stiff and strong. All solid colors except white are permissible, but the general run are black, dark and light grey, tawny, and combinations of any two of these colors.

The Briard can be traced back as far as the twelfth century. Starting as a defender against marauding animals and men, he went on to work for centuries as a guardian of flocks and herds. Later his retentive memory led to the creation of special tasks for Briards as police and war dogs. In the latter field they did liaison work between command posts and outlying units, and World War I took such a toll of the best blood that it took many years for the breed to come back to the fore.

Komondor. The heavily-coated Komondor is little known in the United States, mainly because the Hungarians have not been too anxious to let them get out of the country for fear that if they were made commercial, the sheep and cattle country of their land would be stripped of that companion dog which has so faithfully guarded the master's possessions for centuries on end.

It is of note that the official standard of the breed stresses the strength and protective sense of the Komondor, showing that these qualities were uppermost as breedings went on. Self-reliant, able to take care of himself against wild beasts in the olden days, he used his strength to take care of his master, his family, and his possessions. In Hungary, aside from his work he is valued as a member of the household and those who have owned the breed in the United States are keen for their adaptability to home conditions.

The Komondor stands 23½ to 31½ inches at the shoulder and over this frame is a long, soft, woolly coat of dense hair, all white and of varying lengths. This mats considerably and is rated of value because the mats are of more protection to the dog when engaged in a fight to protect its charges, be they human or animal. Few dogs are more alert, more protective and devoted, or more courageous. Let it be said that they do not go out of their way to seek trouble, but can handle it well should it come to them.

The breed goes back at least ten centuries in its native Hungary, and its chief task has been as a guardian, rather than as a driver, of the sheep and cattle.

Pulik. The Pulik is a comparative newcomer to the United States and few are acquainted with it, but each new person it meets becomes a new friend and can see why its fanciers are so enthusiastic. The dog comes of a long line and always has won respect for its companionship. Primarily a one-family dog, it is wary of strangers and is a true guard

PULIK

dog that can fit into any living circumstances because it is easily cared for, with plenty of stamina and more than average intelligence.

It stands about 17 inches at the shoulder, and has a long profuse coat of fine texture. Colors are white, black, or varying shades of grey or cream.

The breed is believed to have first appeared in Europe over 1100 years ago, having come from Asia, and has always had respect as a versatile and easily trained dog. In the main his work has been as a herder of sheep and those who have seen him work have been amazed by his footwork. The Pulik is popularly known as the Puli.

As well as being an all-around farm dog, the Puli has been the subject of official experimentation by the United States Department of Agriculture.

German Shepherd. The German Shepherd is a dog of dignity, reserved toward strangers until he knows whether they are friendly or

GERMAN SHEPHERD

hostile. Once given, its friendship stands for life, and instinctively it takes to young children and, for a dog of size, will readily adapt itself to the smallest home. In recent years it has been valued chiefly as a guardian of the home and a delightful companion.

At the shoulder, the German Shepherd stands 23 to 25 inches and weighs from 60 to 85 lbs. It has a double coat to guard it against all kinds of weather, the harsh outer coat being of medium length and straight, while under this is a dense woolly coat. Color runs from a jet black to a rather light grey, with many variations in between.

Called by many the "police dog" because its first rise in public favor was due to the stories of its remarkable work in war and police duties

in Germany, this breed is not a police dog with the general implication of toughness. Rather it is a dog with such mental traits that it can be trained to do any type of work well, and we find that its record of service with the American Armed Forces in World War II was such that in 1946 orders went out to purchase sound stock for future Army work.

Few breeds have behind them, either in their own line or that of their ancestry, a finer record of working service or a more devoted following than the German Shepherd which was developed by careful breeding from the best points of older herding and farm dogs. Because of the necessity of close association with man, both as a worker and as a home companion, the founders of the breed and those who have followed it have, in the main, given equal thought to the proper temperamental qualities and to the physical structure.

Built to move at an effortless trot that allows it to work all day, the German Shepherd has found no field in which it cannot star, but most famous has been its record as a guide for the sightless. Police work has fallen naturally to it, and on the competitive side it has been outstanding both in obedience trials and bench shows. Some of the breed have done remarkable work in the hunting field.

Belgian Sheepdog. There are six varieties of the Belgian Sheepdog known in their native country, and of these two are relatively well known in the United States. Best known is the Groenendael, a long-

BELGIAN SHEEPDOG

coated black type, which is actually the youngest in point of development. Next best known is the Malinois, which is short-haired and of a brindled fawn color. The breed usually stands from 22 to 24 inches at the shoulders and will weigh about 53 lbs. in good condition.

Those who have had much contact with any of the varieties of the Belgian Sheepdog are lavish with praise for its devotion to the master and its ability to fit in with his moods. These dogs come by their devotion to family as do all the breeds that have been bred to work, and the Belgian Sheepdogs have a long record back of them of handling herd duty in excellent fashion. Like all breeds that have been developed for the work of herding sheep, traits and lines lead back to

the oldest strains, notably the Moorland dog.

The size and build of Belgian Sheepdogs, coupled with their stamina, devotion to duty, and speed, led to their great use as war dogs when Belgium was engulfed in World War I. Many thousands were trained and put into action, where they acquitted themselves very well, especially for messenger duties. Following World War I the breed started to make some headway in the United States, but since the depression of the early thirties has been at somewhat of a standstill, although those in obedience work have upheld the adaptability and intelligence of the breed.

Doberman Pinscher. From the very start the Doberman Pinscher

DOBERMAN PINSCHER

was highly desired as a companion of the family and the bulk of sales today are into homes of people who want utility in the form of a guardian and companion, and the elegance that makes people turn to admire so streamlined a possession.

The coat is smooth, short, hard, very thick, and close-lying. The coloring most popular is the black and tan and the rich red, but some are chocolate and others are blue. The Doberman stands 24 to 28 inches and will weigh 65 to 75 lbs. in condition.

The Doberman Pinscher is a "tailor-made" dog of fairly recent origin, but the breeding that led to its development and recognition in about 1900 has proved worth while, for year by year it gains more friends all over the world. Herr Doberman, who originated the breed, did so after many years of experimentation to get a guard and house dog, able to do anything well, and he bred in not only physical characteristics but the intelligence desired in an all-purpose dog.

Entirely devoted to its family, the Doberman Pinscher has carried its spirit of service beyond the hearth and many Dobermans lay down their lives in the service of the country, notably working with the Marines in the Pacific Theater of World War II. Their sleek excellence has carried them to many notable show wins, while their German records for intelligence in tests have been matched by the hundreds that have done more than well in the official obedience tests of the United States. Truly this is an all-around breed.

Boxer. The Boxer needs little introduction to the American public, for, while its numbers do not place it in top brackets in the matter of registrations or licenses, it is so impressive in appearance that the ma-

BOXER

jority of families would wish to have one. Its popularity has come about during the past ten years, in part due to the publicity attendant on its many show wins, but mainly because the breed is kindly at heart while possessing a face that serves to scare off intruders.

The appearance of the Boxer and its attraction to and for children has made the breed a great house pet and has in addition led many famous artists and illustrators to use the breed in cover designs and commercial advertising.

The smooth, shiny, short coat appeals to the housewife in that it does not shed on furniture or rugs. The range of color is fawn that runs from a light yellow to a dark deer red and the brindles ranging from a golden yellow background to almost black, with clearly defined black stripes. Many have attractive white markings on the chest, feet, and head.

The males of the breed should stand 22 to 24 inches and the females from 21 to 23 inches. Weights should run from 60 to 70 pounds. The breed is not that of recent origin, but rather of re-development in the past one hundred years, as serious breeders of work dogs went back to develop once more a dog similar to those used many centuries ago. The Boxer can definitely be traced back to the old Molossus family, of which the Tibetan Mastiff won earliest fame.

In Germany, where his development mainly rests, the Boxer has earned much fame as a police and war dog, which meant stamina, speed, intelligence, and courage.

Rottweiler. The Rottweiler is a strongly built dog, standing from about 22 to 27 inches at the shoulder. His coat is black with sharp markings on the muzzle, cheeks, chest, and legs, in tan or mahogany brown. The hair is short, coarse, and flat, with an undercoat on the neck and thighs.

Although the Rottweiler is little known in the United States, even to inveterate showgoers, few breeds are more intelligent, more adaptable to all conditions, and more understanding of people.

He is a direct descendant of the dogs used by the Roman expeditions through Europe to drive the needed "meat on the hoof", and was developed in the area around Rottweil, Germany, where the dog became both a guardian and a driver of

ROTTWEILER

cattle, and attracted much fame for his dignified ways and his ability to do all things well. After many centuries of fine work as a drover's dog and other utilitarian purposes, changes in laws and the invention of modern appliances nearly drove the breed out of existence. However, in about 1910 when the use of dogs for police work was really getting under way, it was reasoned that here was a "natural", and so the Rottweiler joined the German Shepherd, the Airedale, and its own descendant, the Doberman Pinscher, on the force. This work brought out more of the character of the dog, and in the United States we find the dog's ability showing up with fine scores in obedience trials.

Great Dane. The Great Dane has often been called "the King of

Dogs", partly because of his size, but more because of the regality of his appearance, his pride of bearing, and his nature. He has weight and size, speed and endurance, courage and nobility. He has come a long

GREAT DANE

way from his origin for work and yet has never lost that flair for doing that which he may be assigned. Given his preference, the Great Dane would prefer to live at home with his human family, regardless of whether that home were a country estate or a small city dwelling.

The males must be at least 30 inches at the shoulder, but it is preferred that they be 32 inches or more, and the females should stand not less than 28 inches, with the preference going to those 30 inches or over, providing that proportion is maintained. Weight must be in proportion, for the Great Dane is not a clumsy, bulky dog.

The color range is wide enough to suit anyone, for the fawns run from a light golden yellow to a deep golden yellow; the brindles have the base of light fawn to deep golden yellow with strong black cross striping. In addition there are blues, blacks, and harlequins. The latter are pure white with black patches well placed through the body, large enough to get away from a dappled effect and not so large as to make a blanket.

Great Dane authorities claim no great antiquity for the breed, although one might read descriptions in early writings and see rough sketches that could readily be interpreted to mean that the breed existed around 3000 B.C. The real interest lies in the fact that serious breeders are continuing to develop a large dog of rare quality of mind and temperament.

Mastiff. While in general the name Mastiff covers many big breeds

MASTIFF

of the past, as we understand or use it today it refers to the Old English Mastiff.

He is a huge dog with a well-made frame that makes him more active than one would suppose. Although used at times as a war dog and guardian, he was valued more for his companionship and devotion to his master. In later years in England and since the introduction of the breed to the United States, he has been noted as a home companion, and for those with the area sufficient to exercise his huge frame, he is an ideal purchase as a family pet.

The outer coat is somewhat coarse and lies flat over an undercoat that is dense, short, and close lying. Colors are fawn, apricot, silver fawn, or a dark fawn-brindle. In all cases an impressive relief is furnished by the dark muzzle, ears, and nose.

The males must stand at least 30 inches at the shoulder and the females run from 27½ inches up. Weights run from 140 to 200 pounds and it is so distributed as to keep the dog from being clumsy.

The Mastiff is described in Caesar's account of invading England in 55 B.C., and later they came back to Rome to fight in the Circus. Others of the breed were used in England to keep off wolves and other savage game. Yet through all their fighting career, the Mastiffs won more fame for their devotion to master and family.

Bull Mastiff. Accepted first as an excellent watchdog and in many cases picked for estates where there were children to guard, the great affection of the Bull Mastiff for children and its love for adults has made him welcomed as a household pet.

He is a powerful dog, but not bulky. The males stand 25 to 27

BULL MASTIFF

inches at the shoulder and will weigh 115 lbs., while the females stand 24 to 26 inches and weigh 100 lbs. The weight is so distributed that the dog is active and alert, possesses no fear but starts no trouble. The coat is short and dense, giving good protection against the weather. The colors are fawn or brindle.

The Bull Mastiff, as we know him today, goes back something less than one hundred years, and although he has been accepted as a distinct breed in the United States only since 1933, the last few years have seen him add steadily to his friends.

The breed was developed from the Mastiff and the old style Bulldog, which little resembles the Bulldog we know today, and the proportion of the two breeds may be said to be 60 percent Mastiff and 40 percent Bulldog. The breed was created because of the trouble of handling poachers on large estates, where keepers' lives were in danger. The Mastiff was tried first, but his bulk kept him from being fast or quiet enough, while the old style Bulldog was a bit too aggressive and quite apt to become a killer. What was desired was a dog that would down the poacher and bring him to court, rather than to injure him. The cross of the two breeds made the ideal dog for the work.

Pembroke Welsh Corgi. The Pembroke Welsh Corgi is an intelligent dog and has well proved itself

PEMBROKE WELSH CORGI

as a working dog from the start. Like the Cardigan, it is a fine dog for children and is the right size for the small home; it is consequently much in demand. It stands no more than 12 inches at the shoulder and weighs from 18 to 24 lbs. Any color other than white is acceptable, although an almost fox red seems to predominate. The coat is of medium

length, dense, and weather-resistant. The tail is but a stub.

Apparently the Pembroke Corgi stems from the same family that gave the world the Schipperke, the Keeshonden, the Norwegian Elkhound, the Pomeranian, the Samoyede, and the Chow Chow.

The Pembroke Welsh Corgi is a much younger breed than the Cardigan Welsh Corgi, but at that is older than most of the breeds we know in the United States today, for records show that the dog was known in Pembrokeshire as far back as 1107 A.D. Research indicates that the direct ancestors of this lively breed came to Wales in that year with Flemish weavers.

World interest in the Pembroke got a great boost with the ownership of some fine specimens by England's Princess Elizabeth; after that the charm of its own temperament proved its worth to high estate. It has done well in the American bench shows, and those that have gone into obedience trials have turned in some star work.

Cardigan Welsh Corgi. One of the oldest breeds in the British Isles, which has given the world many of its best dogs, is the Cardigan Welsh Corgi, and yet the dog has not been long recognized in the United States, nor is it as well known as its fine qualities should rate it in public esteem. Yet it should be highly appealing to those dwellers of city apartments and small suburban houses, for not only by nature is it a fine, clean house dog, devoted to its family, but it is small enough to fit in anywhere.

By the standard of perfection it should stand about 12 inches at the shoulder and should weigh from 15 to 25 pounds. It is foxy in appearance and measures about 35 inches from the tip of its nose to the end of its moderately long, somewhat fox-like tail.

The Corgi is believed to have been known in Wales for more than 3000 years and is a member of the same general dog family as produced the Dachshund, as might be guessed by the proportions of the breed. The fact that the breed has been little known rests in the fact that the hillmen of Wales knew no reason why they should advertize these dogs that had served them so well for centuries.

The Cardigan Corgi started his service to the early Celts of Cardiganshire by helping beat out game and acting as guardians of the children. Later he proved his worth in driving cattle on the Common Lands, nipping at the heels of the cattle and thus taking over as much land as possible for the dog's owner. At all times, the dog has been considered worth his weight in gold.

Eskimo. As a breed, the Eskimo dog has treated man far better than man has treated him, and although

he is not the safest dog in the world to cut loose to roam the streets, with his own human family he is devoted, at home wherever he may be and most considerate with small children when treated decently. He

Eskimo

is intelligent, fearless, alert, and enduring.

In size he ranges from 20 to 25 inches at the shoulder and packs from 50 to 85 lbs. on his tightly-knit frame. His coat consists of an outer guard-layer of hair some five inches in length, and an inner woolly coat that is thick and dense and sheds water and cold. It must be added that like other sledge breeds there is little or no doggy odor. The coat color runs black, black and white, white, wolf grey, blue grey, tan and buff, or in combinations of these colors.

The Eskimo is a member of the so-called Spitz family and is thought to have originated in Eastern Siberia, whence he roamed with his masters to range the entire top section of the North American continent. This is another of the famous sledge dog breeds that have won honor for their service to mankind in the hauling of needed supplies—food, medicines, and machinery—where other forms of transportation could not get through. The Eskimo's usefulness to human beings goes back at least 2000 years and includes not only duty as a sledge dog, but also as a pack animal, and in summer he takes on the pulling of boats. Added to that is his prowess, because of his fine nose, as a hunter's aide.

A team of these dogs has been known to go, with a "working" sledge, 100 miles in 18 hours, and 20 miles an hour is not unknown with them, although their usual pace is rated by the weight they haul.

Alaskan Malemute. Nobody seems able to trace accurately the

ALASKAN MALEMUTE

origin of the handsome sledge dog known as the Alaskan Malemute, but even the oldest tales of the breed lay stress on the personality of the dog, its use as a combination work and pet dog, and the strong attach-

ment between them and their humans.

They have become a popular sledge-dog among sportsfolks who enjoy this form of winter recreation, and with their great fondness for children, have become favorites with the youngsters who have gone along with the family for this sport.

In weight they range from 50 to 85 pounds and stand at the shoulder from 20 to 25 inches. The Alaskan Malemute is a true "picture" dog with a thick, dense, and coarse coat that is not too long and is lined with a thick, woolly, and oily undercoat. The thick fur around the neck is for protection against the weather. The tail is well furred and carried over the back as a "waving plume". The colors are black and white or a wolf-grey and the markings are usually in a mask or cap form.

The breed was first found in the territory we now know as Alaska, and the earliest reports show that even then the natives were using them as draught dogs, and the reports went on to mention the great care taken of the dogs by their masters, which probably gave the foundation for the temperament that makes them so close to their owners today and therefore such satisfactory companions.

Few breeds are as powerful for their weight and inches as the Alaskan Malemute, and with their power goes great speed, which accounts for their many wins of races and the records they have set.

Siberian Husky. Like all other sledge dog breeds, the Siberian Husky is an alert, intelligent, tractable dog, easily trained for the own-

SIBERIAN HUSKY

er's desires. Having had for many years to work for his living in close contact with man, where the life of each was dependent on the other, the Husky is a "natural" as a pet. He can accommodate himself to any changes in physical surroundings and loves the companionship of children.

The Siberian Husky stands from 20 to 24 inches at the shoulder and will weigh from 35 to 60 pounds. While all colors including white are allowed, as well as all markings, the commonest are the silver and wolf greys, tan, and black with white points. The coat is thick, soft, and double, with the undercoat downy and the outer of a smooth, soft texture. This outer coat is of medium length.

The breed originated in Northeastern Siberia, where the Chuchi natives used them as sled dogs, guards for possessions and children, and other purposes. This explains their all-around abilities and their devotion to youngsters. The first to come to Alaska were imported in 1909 for racing purposes, and quickly won many of the top stakes of Alaska, Canada and the United States, and set many records.

In the rare times the Husky takes part in bench shows or in the obedience trials, he makes a hit with the onlookers and generally comes out with a share of the winnings.

Samoyede. Few are the breeds that at work or play move about so silently, or possess such a carefree air. Weighing from 36 to 55 pounds

SAMOYEDE

and standing 18 to 22 inches at the shoulder, this breed has been known gaily to haul tremendous loads by sledge. It is doubtful if any breed has lived closely with its own people for a longer time than the Samoyede, a schooling that can be said to make them pets of value for any family.

They are beautiful with their pure white, cream, or white and biscuit coats that cover their bodies with a thick, close, soft, and short undercoat which has harsh hair growing through it to form an outer coat that is protective against the elements. That it does protect against everything is proved by the fact that dogs born in Siberia have crossed the equator with no ill effects and other dogs from the Antarctic expeditions have returned to England to help in the starting of fine kennels.

The Samoyede is gentle, companionable, excellent as a watchdog, and though it never starts trouble it can well take care of itself. Independent, intelligent, it seems to wear a perpetual smile, adoring and adored by children. Like all other Arctic breeds, it has no doggy odor.

Research indicates that these are the direct descendants of the primitive dogs that with their peoples were driven ever northward from Iran by stronger tribes and finally landed up by the White Sea and there, for centuries, man and dog lived, dependent each on the other. Little wonder then that the Samoyede gets on so well with people.

Giant Schnauzer. Another of the breeds of purely German development is the Giant Schnauzer, one of the three Schnauzer breeds all of which stem from the same basic stock. (Two of the Schnauzer breeds, the Giant and the Standard, are working dogs, while the third and smaller one is a terrier.) As is the case of all dogs bred for a specific purpose of work, the Giant Schnauzer works out well as a home companion where there is sufficient space and displays a playful, affectionate disposition.

The Giant Schnauzer will stand from 21 to 26 inches and has a black, black and tan, or pepper-and-salt colored coat which is close, hard, and wiry, and of medium length. He is most enduring and does not mind any sort of weather condition. It is evident that the medium or Standard Schnauzer was the basic breed from which this one was produced by using several crosses of breeds to attain the size, coat, and drive.

This dog is powerful, possessed of much stamina, and has proved his intelligence by having been accepted for the rigid work of the German police. This work followed his use as drover's dog, back in the days when all meat was driven over the road, and his subsequent service as guardian for stockyards, breweries, and butcher shops. There his strength and intelligence won the chance for police work.

He came to America a little more than twenty years ago and has made slow but steady progress, which is speeding up now that some are making good in obedience trials.

Standard Schnauzer. Of the three accepted Schnauzer breeds, the first was the medium or Standard Schnauzer, which has recently been

STANDARD SCHNAUZER

moved from the Terrier Group to the Working Group. It is not known exactly how far back in history the Standard Schnauzer goes, but it is known that as far back as the fifteenth century he was valued as a household pet, a position he has retained until this day. Dürer painted one into his portraits before 1500, Rembrandt painted several, and one appears in a canvas by Sir Joshua Reynolds in the eighteenth century. Standard Schnauzers have made great progress in the United States and England, in both of which countries they have been mainly used as companions and guards for children.

The Standard Schnauzer is a squarely-built dog, compact, alert, intelligent, reliable, and of high spirit. He stands 18 to 20 inches and wears a hard, wiry coat that comes in pepper-and-salt and other mixed colors, light or dark, or black. Very noticeable are his bristling whiskers and eyebrows that accentuate a quizzical expression.

In addition to being a great house pet, the dog has earned his living as a guard dog and rat catcher, and it is said that before World War I at least 90 percent of the farm produce wagons in German market places were guarded by dogs of predominantly Schnauzer blood. There they were known as the dog with the "human brain" and some of their feats have surely earned them that title. They are found to be good also at retrieving and have starred when given the chance in obedience tests. Their presence in the show ring is also felt and they have won many honors.

Bouvier De Flandres. Once seen, the Bouvier De Flandres are never forgotten, for they are striking in an odd way, in that their coat is always slightly tousled as though not fully groomed. This coat is harsh and not long. On the head it is shorter, except around the eyes on each side of the muzzle and under the chin—creating an effect of beard, mustache, and eyebrows. Colors range from fawn to black, through pepper and salt, brindle, and grey.

The first look will show you the

impressive power of the breed, which stands from just under 23 inches to just over 27 inches. The eye is clear and dark, showing the breed's vigor, stamina and great intelligence. There is no doubt that breeders, both in its native Belgium and in the United States, have carried on with the breed as a working type, preserving the temperamental and physical characteristics that have made these dogs famous. But since the majority of the earlier breeders of these dogs were farmers, butchers, and cattle merchants, most of them small in their line, the breed also grew up to be a home companion as well as guardian, and these traits are there to this day, so that they are appreciated by young and old alike in those homes which have been fortunate enough to own them.

The Belgian breeders have so remembered the working start of the breed that they have a demand that before any Bouvier can win the title of Champion, he must also win a prize in competitions as a police dog, defense dog, or an army dog.

St. Bernard. The very nature of the St. Bernard makes him adaptable to all types of living conditions, but he is better off where there is ample room to exercise him to keep his huge body in top condition. Long famed as a benefactor of mankind, in the present day the "Saint" is primarily a pet dog, able to get along with old or young, and liked by all classes of people in many countries.

St. Bernards stand from 25 to 28 inches at the shoulder and weigh from 150 to 200 lbs., and some have gone as high as 250 lbs. In color they

St. Bernard

are various shades of red with white, and white with light or dark brindled patches.

No breed is more famed through song and story than the St. Bernards, especially through the record of the dogs from the Hospice of St. Bernard in the Alps, which are officially credited with saving more than 2500 lives. Similarly, no breed is more impressive, whether you are looking at the smooth or rough-coated variety.

Their exact origin is in question, especially since the St. Bernard Hospice suffered fires that destroyed records. However, it is known that they are of the Molossus family and that it is likely that they were brought back from the East by Roman soldiers and wound up in Switzerland. Oddly enough, while they were brought in to strengthen other breeds, they in turn weakened in time from inbreeding and disease, and in about 1830 the Newfoundland was crossed in and strength was restored without spoiling the characteristics of the original breed. Today their intelligence shows up in fine work at the obedience tests.

Bernese Mountain Dog. One of the most ancient of all breeds, yet one of the least known in the United

BERNESE MOUNTAIN DOG

States, is the Bernese Mountain Dog, a very hardy animal which is very impressive in looks, not unlike the Collie in size and appearance, and exceptionally faithful to its own people.

On the whole Bernese Mountain Dogs are one-man dogs, give all their affection to the one person they select, get along well with the rest of that family, but do not make advances to strangers or casual visitors.

Since about 1907 their nature and appearance have made them desirable as household companions and show dogs, very popular in their native land. Their coat is soft and silky with a bright sheen, wavy but not curly, and quite long. The color is a deep black with tan or russet markings on the forelegs and between the black and white of the chest markings. They stand between 21 and 27½ inches and look every inch the fine working dogs they once were and might easily become once more because both the physical and temperamental qualifications remain unchanged.

There is no doubt that this great and powerful worker earned its right to retirement from working, for it had back of it more than 2000 years of faithful service, much of it as draught dogs in Berne, Switzerland, and the surrounding territory, to which it was brought by invading Roman soldiers. Eventually its work ceased and the breed was forgotten save in isolated places and might have been lost to the world, were it not for a fancier who picked up some good specimens before the turn of the century.

Newfoundland. The Newfoundland is another of the dogs that is well known to nearly every American family, not only for its wonderful work in the water which has made it world famous, but for its grand qualities as a companion, guard, and friend—a supreme household pet. From the time of its introduction to the United States it

NEWFOUNDLAND

has been accepted as an ideal dog for a child, and the ambition of many a family has been to have one of them as a companion for the children.

The majority are a dull, jet black, but the white and black are famous through the famous painting by Sir Edwin Landseer, and are usually called the Landseer Newfoundland. In size and weight they are alike, dogs standing about 28 inches at the shoulder and weighing up to 150 pounds, while females stand 26 inches and weigh 120 pounds. The coat is coarse in texture, flat and dense, oily in nature and capable of resisting water.

The exact background of the Newfoundland is uncertain, but most probably the breed was bred by crossing the Great Pyrenees, which the Basque fishermen brought to the coast of Newfoundland, with the native dogs. At any rate, there resulted a dog suited to the island, so coated as to stand the icy waters and with webbed feet to make travel over the marshes easy, great strength to enable him to help pull nets and boats, and so intelligent and devoted to humans that his record of life-saving is nothing short of phenomenal.

There are not very many Newfoundlands in any one place, but they are being bred in many countries and, in all cases, stem down from the fine stock made popular in England. Always they acquit themselves well, either at work or in their now larger field, that of a companion and guardian of children.

Great Pyrenees. Approximately referred to as "animated snow drifts", the Great Pyrenees is a dog of immense size, keen intelligence, kindly expression, and a look of majesty about him. In the United States he is a great pet, especially adored by children. The big dogs, all white or mainly white with a touch of grey, tan, or badger, have been spending their lives guarding and getting along with little things and living close to their masters and families, and it is no transition for them to step into city, village, or country home and immediately adapt themselves.

The Great Pyrenees will run 90 to 125 lbs., and stands from 25 to 32 inches. He looks even larger because of his double coat that can stand all types of weather. The inner coat is heavy, fine, and white and the outer

GREAT PYRENEES

is coarser, long, flat, thick, and wavy but not curly.

Protector and companion of the shepherd, he has for centuries herded and guarded flocks in the Pyrenees Mountains, taking all kinds of weather in his stride, and has also spent much time guarding the large estates in his native France, where his intelligence, courage, and stamina have stood him in good stead. It seems strange that his recognition in the United States dates from 1933 only, for actually the first of the breed to come here were brought over in 1824 by General Lafayette, who from experience knew well their value in the new land, in protecting flocks. The breed has gone far and will go further.

Kuvasz. One of the most interesting dogs of all times is the Hungarian breed, the Kuvasz, a large pure-white dog standing up to 26 inches at the shoulder, which by the very nature of the two main tasks he has faced in the centuries of his existence has developed into an ideal dog for the home that can accommodate him, making a fine companion devoted to the master and his children. The coat is rather long on the neck and croup, becoming a little shorter and slightly wavy on the sides.

The Kuvasz is another of the many large working breeds whose ancestors came out of Tibet. First known task of the breed was the

KUVASZ

protection of royalty and for hundreds of years there were kennels of these dogs maintained to protect kings and nobles of the court, and so worthy were the dogs that kings valued them above their own henchmen, and few dared launch an attack on an estate guarded by any of these dogs.

Later some specimens got into the hands of the herders, who used them to guard and drive cattle and sheep. As time went on they were bred down somewhat in size until they got to the present 26-inch height. History tells us that in ancient times when the dogs were companions and guards of royalty, they were about as huge a dog as the world has seen. Large as the breed was, many nobles trained their dogs for hunting and they were able to do well on the big game of the day. They are still free movers, and even though quite large, they are very light on their feet.

THE TERRIER GROUP

The Terrier Group as a Whole. Known as Variety Group Four, the Terrier Group is one of the most interesting of all, comprising as it does some twenty breeds. Two of these breeds have two varieties: the Bull Terriers, which come in White and Colored varieties, and the Fox Terriers, with their Smooth and Wire-haired varieties. (The Boston Terrier, even though his name would seem to place him in the Terrier Group, belongs to Variety Group Six, the Non-Sporting Group, and the Yorkshire Terrier, which one might also look for among the breeds of the Terrier Group, belongs to the Toy Group, or Variety Group Five.)

Most families in the United States are familiar with one or more of the Terrier breeds. All of them are of such a size that they can be kept in a small house or city apartment, and at the present time the Terrier's purpose in life is that of a pet, a house companion, a role they fill very well because of their alert, trim appearance and their merriness of disposition. However, they were all originally bred for specific needs, and they were all, at one time or another, working or sporting terriers. The name "terrier" means "to go to earth", and these dogs have long records back of them, mainly in bolting the fox and other animals, and in their native lands many are still used for their original purpose.

It is well known that, given the freedom, they will revert to type and do quite well, and one of the greatest show dogs of all time, a Smooth Fox Terrier, will revel in going to earth after what small furred game he can find on the grounds where he lives.

Six countries gave us all the recognized breeds within the group. Tibet gave us the Lhasa Apsos, and from Germany came the Schnauzers, the Giant and Standard varieties of which are listed as Working Breeds while the Miniature has been left in the Terrier classification. Ireland produced the Irish Terriers and the Kerry Blues, while Wales gave us the Sealyham and the Welsh Terrier. Scotland is the native home of five breeds: the Cairn, Dandie Dinmont, Scottish, Skye, and West Highland White. England, producer of many fine breeds and refiner of many others that came there from other countries, is the home of the Airedale, Bedlington, Border, both varieties of the Bull Terrier, the Smooth and Wirehaired Fox Terrier, Lakeland, Manchester, Norwich, and Staffordshire.

In England more Terriers are owned and shown than any other variety, and that love of these pert dogs has been passed on to the United States where they rate highly and at times seem to dominate the show aspect of the sport. They also have proved their intelligence through the fact that the majority of the breeds have sent some fine workers into the field of obedience trials.

Most of the breeds are of a fiery nature—not trouble makers but alert to all things, keen in detection of trouble, and thus excellent watchdogs, which adds to their value as pets. The range in Terriers is so wide that the potential purchaser can look through the list and surely find something that suits his needs and his surroundings.

Airedale Terrier. The Airedale often has been referred to as the King of the Terriers, and there was

AIREDALE TERRIER

a time when it was the most popular of all terrier breeds in the United States, according to official registrations. As in the case of many of the breeds, it is possible to stretch the imagination and find likenesses of the breed in ancient paintings; however, we do know that the breed was created by the practical and sporting men of Yorkshire, using various mixtures crossed with the Otterhound, which made for a real sporting or working terrier. Backed by this fine sporting record, as well as prime work in police details, the Airedale always has been an ace as a pet, and for every dog that appears in official competitions, there are hundreds serving as companion to young and old, alertly guarding home, family, and goods.

Most distinctive is the hard, dense, wiry coat, lying close over the body and legs, with some of the harshest being crinkled or a bit wavy. Head and ears are tan, with the ears slightly darker. The under part of the body, as well as the legs, are tannish, while the sides and upper part of the body are grizzled or black, and here and there one finds a red mixture.

Largest of the twenty terrier breeds, the Airedale stands about 23 inches at the shoulder, and although not bulky, is a powerfully made dog, well able to take care of itself and its family. It is a highly intelligent dog that has proved itself splendid in the hunting field on big game and in the obedience test classes that interest the one- and two-dog owner of the country. In addition it has made an enviable record in war duties, where its power, intelligence, and courage have been real assets to the cause they served.

Irish Terrier. The Irish Terrier is one of the most popular of terriers, although he has never been bred so extensively as some of the other breeds. Ever alert and always the well-turned-out gentleman, the Irish Terrier makes a snappy appearance in his red coat. Few breeds have a finer record of loyalty to their family or as much stamina and courage, and few are more adaptable. Of a size and disposition to make themselves equally at home in

the field or in the city dwelling, the Irish Terriers stand in the top ranks as family pets.

The coat is dense and wiry in texture, with a broken appearance, but lies close to the body and is

IRISH TERRIER

short enough so that the body lines are always in full view. Under this coat is a short protective undercoat, which gives the Irish Terrier the chance to stand all types of weather. Golden red, bright red, and red wheaten are the preferred colors; rarely is there any white.

The Irish Terrier in perfect trim will weigh from 25 to 27 lbs., and stand about 18 inches at the shoulder. This arrangement keeps the breed active and lithe, fast on the feet, and free of any clumsiness. The outline is racy and altogether the breed makes a most attractive appearance that matches its lovable personality. Never asking quarter, the Irish Terrier never goes out to seek trouble, and is equally at home romping in the fields with the adult members of its family or on the floor with children. During World War I, the breed added to its fame as a war dog and was highly rated by the commandant of the British War-Dog School.

The origin of the Irish Terrier is much in debate, but there is evidence that this is one of the oldest of Terrier breeds.

Welsh Terrier. The Welsh Terriers seem born to associate with children and that alone would rec-

WELSH TERRIER

ommend them as household pets. However, there are many other points that make them sought as family companions, among them their hardiness and the ease with which they can be groomed. As a breed they are somewhat more quiet than most terriers, but they cannot be imposed upon for they are alert to their rights. Their gameness is proved by the way they have handled the otter, the badger, and the fox.

They stand about 15 inches at the shoulder and ought to weigh about 20 lbs. A good description of their build is to say that they are set up like a well-made hunter. The coat is

black and tan, or grizzle and tan, and is very close, wiry, and harsh. The head is relatively broad, with a flat skull, and the eyes are set wide apart, which sets them off from many of the related terrier breeds.

The Welsh was purely a hunting and home dog until toward the close of the last century, and since then he has made great strides in English show circles. While the first came to the United States in about 1888, it was not until 1901 that show classification was provided for the breed, and since that time they have come on fast as show winners, obedience stars, and general American favorites.

Old paintings and prints lend weight to the claim that the Welsh Terrier is the oldest of all the terrier breeds, for they show a rough-coated black and tan terrier of about the size we know today. Unchanged in physical conformity for hundreds of years, the Welsh is unchangeable in disposition, and can be relied upon to keep its head at all times.

Lakeland Terrier. A gay breed, lacking in fear and always friendly, the Lakeland Terrier is able to differentiate between friend and foe and to serve as a good watchdog. For a relatively small dog, the Lakeland is impressively powerful, being efficiently engineered, as was needed for its centuries as a real worker.

The Lakeland's coat is dense and harsh with a fine undercoat that makes the dog able to withstand any rigors of weather. In color these dogs are mostly black and tan, grizzle and tan, or blue and tan, although the wheaten specimens have proved most attractive to the public.

LAKELAND TERRIER

The weight runs about 17 lbs., although 15 lbs. may be acceptable. At the shoulder the Lakeland stands from 13½ to 15 inches.

It is told that long before any notable hound packs were formed the farmers of the lakeland district in England would make up packs of these Terriers and some Hounds and set out to destroy the foxes that were raiding the sheep folds. Thus developed a breed that was noted for its hardiness, gameness, and intelligence.

Although the Lakeland Terrier is one of the oldest of all working Terrier breeds, it is little known in the United States, mainly because no one has tried very much to push the breed into the spotlight. Before the end of World War II there began to be more activity in the breed,

and wherever the breed made its appearance on the street or in the shows, there was an instant demand to know where they might be purchased for household pets, especially by people who lived in city apartments or who for other reasons had little space.

Border Terrier. Few Border Terriers in the United States know what the show rings are like, but all of them do know what it means to be held in high regard as family pets, a role they fill splendidly, whether in a city apartment or on a country estate.

The coat is red, wheaten, grizzled with tan, or blue and tan, with a close undercoat beneath a harsh and dense outer coat that guards against all types of weather. In weight they will run from about 11 lbs. to 16 lbs. The head is rather broad, with a short and powerful muzzle, and in this feature the Border is not unlike a junior edition of the Otterhound.

The Border Terrier makes up for its lack of size by its intelligence and courage, and is one of the oldest of all Terrier breeds, having been developed as a purely working Terrier many years ago on either side of the Cheviot Hills. As is the case with all working types of dogs, the Border Terrier was raised close to its breeders and therefore got a running start as a pet in the household.

The breed came about through

the need of the farmers of the section for a game terrier to hunt and kill the hill foxes that ravaged stock, and while Borders are long enough of leg to follow a horse, they are small enough to follow the fox to ground. Although popular with the farmers of England and Scotland, and thus exhibited proudly at country fairs, the breed was little known outside its native section until about 1920 when a breed club was formed to protect the hardy little fellows, and from then until the start of World War II its fame spread through the major shows and city-dwellers picked them up as pets.

Norwich Terrier. The Norwich Terrier is another of the Terrier breeds created for a specific working purpose, but because it has a hard close coat that needs no trimming and does not collect dirt, it has proved ideal as a house pet.

This game little dog stands no more than 12 inches high at the withers, and 11 lbs. is rated the perfect weight. The coat color is red, black and tan, red wheaten, or grizzle. The hair is hard and wiry and lies much closer to the body than that of the Cairn Terrier. Longer and rougher on the neck and shoulders, it often forms a virtual mane in winter time.

In spite of its small size, the Norwich has proved itself over the years an excellent adjunct to the hunting packs. It has been only a few years

that the breed has made appearances in the American show rings, and yet it first came to this country after World War I, when it was known as the Jones Terrier in honor of a famous English breeder and huntsman, and many tales were told of the little fellows' ability in the hunting field and their gameness in tackling anything up to the size of a bear. As the Norwich Terrier, it has been accepted as a purebred in the United States for some ten years.

The first to come to this country were placed in the hands of many Masters of Foxhounds and since that time they have been kept of pure strain by several hunt clubs, which have found them invaluable in going to ground when the Foxhounds have driven their quarry into its hole.

Smooth Fox Terrier. Game to the core, alert always, and highly

SMOOTH FOX TERRIER

intelligent, the Smooth Fox Terrier is one of the top pet dogs of the world and also a front-ranker when it comes to dog-show wins. In show condition, the Smooth Fox Terrier will weigh about 18 lbs. and will stand not more than 15½ inches at the withers; the head should measure approximately 7 inches.

It is likely that no breed of dog is as widely spread through the world as is the Fox Terrier, and this applies to both the Smooth and Wire-haired varieties. Clubs have been formed in nearly all countries to promote and guard the breed, and it is possible to go into any land and find hundreds of them filling the role of pets quite as well as the breed once filled the role of Sporting dog.

Although few people realize it, the Smooth variety was classified as a Sporting dog for many years—a tribute to his keen nose, amazing eyesight, and his stamina in the field. His chief work afield was as an aide to Foxhound packs, for when the pack would drive the wily fox to its hole, the Smooth Fox Terrier would drive him out.

There is still much debate as to the origin of the two varieties of Fox Terriers, and while for years there was cross-breeding of the two types, this is non-existent today. In temperament there is little difference between the two varieties, so that it is probable that the original devotees of each were after the same type of dog, the difference being that one group wanted a dog protected by a wiry coat, while the others preferred not to mask the

classical outlines of the Smooth variety.

Wire-haired Fox Terrier. The Wire-haired Fox Terrier stands equally high with the Smooth as a household pet, being of a size that

WIRE-HAIRED FOX TERRIER

enables him to fit into the smallest city apartment with ease, yet able to take good care of himself on a huge estate. Snappy in appearance, he readily makes friends for the breed by his liveliness and fine personality. A great dog in the show ring, as records of England and the United States will attest, his real fame is as a pet of young and old alike, while few breeds have made a better mark as watchdogs.

Built like his Smooth cousins, the Wire-haired has a broken coat, and the more wiry and harsher the coat is, the better it is considered. At no time should the coat have a woolly touch or appearance, as this takes away from the attraction of the dog and generally indicates that the dog has not had the care that should be lavished on so valued a pet. The coat must be long enough to show a great difference all over from the

Smooths, but at the same time it should never be long enough to create a shaggy appearance.

English in origin, the Fox Terrier dates back to the late eighteenth century, and is bred according to standards laid down in England in 1876 and adopted in the United States nine years later, changed only in regard to the weight which was lowered two pounds. The Wire-haired Fox Terrier will scale the same weight and stand the same height as the Smooth, and like the Smooth variety has white in predominance in the coat. Both are made attractive by the tan or black markings that come in various proportions.

Kerry Blue Terrier. A splendid pet, the Kerry Blue comes in all shades of blue from the almost silver-blue to the practically black-

KERRY BLUE TERRIER

blue. The coat is soft and wavy, and the body is well covered but not so much as to make it matty to any degree. Few breeds are more attractive or distinctive than the well-groomed Kerry Blue.

They stand about 18 inches at the shoulder and will weigh in good condition from 32 to 38 lbs., although their compact build and wavy coat creates the impression of a much heavier dog. They are strong, durable, fast in action and thought, and possessed of a disposition that makes them fit into any set of circumstances. It is said that a Kerry never gets old.

As might be expected from the name, the Kerry Blue originated in the mountains of County Kerry, Ireland, where they have been pure-bred for well over a hundred years. Although primarily serving their owners in this country as pets, the breed was created for and served all this time in its native land and in England as a dog of utility. They have been used successfully for hunting all types of small game and birds, and are noted as excellent retrievers from both water and land. They also have been used with great success as herders of sheep and cattle, and have an enviable record as watchdogs and guardians of the family.

It was only after their adoption as the National Dog of the Irish Republic that the breed came into fame as a show dog, and they have been campaigned with fine results both in the United States and in Europe. Their first show start in the United States came in 1922, and of recent years the Kerry's success in trailing down show wins has matched his trailing of game on his native heaths.

Scottish Terrier. Much in the limelight because of the late President Roosevelt's "Fala", the Scottie's high place in registration rankings

SCOTTISH TERRIER

proves that the breed has for many years been extremely popular among pet-lovers. Scotties are grand companions for house or street and fit well into any mode of living.

In prime condition these attractive dogs will weigh around 20 lbs. and stand about 10 inches high at the shoulder. The coat is about two inches long and is harsh and wiry in the outer coat, with a dense undercoat that makes the breed impervious to weather changes. While the black coat is the best known to the general public, there is much favor for the steel or iron grey, the brindled, and the wheaten.

The expression of the Scottish Terrier is keenly alert, and seems a mixture of questioning and laughing at its human owners. Head and tail are always carried well up and proudly, and add to the impression of great strength in small size.

Although there has been much discussion as to the age and origin of what we know as the Scottish Terrier today, it is only in the last seventy years that we have had an agreement on what constituted the breed and that a written standard of perfection has been followed. The breed made its first official appearance in the United States in 1883 and has forged steadily ahead ever since, thanks to its great popularity with all members of the household, a carry-over from its long association close to the families in Scotland that would not do without one.

Cairn Terrier. The Cairn Terrier is a thoroughly charming dog adaptable to all countries and weather, being exceptionally hardy, a highly desirable quality in a pet. The Cairn can be found in the smallest of city dwellings and on large estates, at home wherever he goes, and still re-

CAIRN TERRIER

taining the old Sporting Terrier instincts that made him highly prized in his native Scotland.

The matured Cairn will weigh about 14 lbs. and stand between 9 and 10 inches at the withers, with a body length of about 15 inches from the front of the chest to the back of the hind quarters. The coat is surely weather-resistant, being of a profuse, harsh variety on the outer coat, with a soft and furry undercoat. The coat comes in all colors except white, and it is desirable that ears, muzzle, and tail-tip be darker than the rest of the body.

The Cairn is a most alert-looking dog, with shaggy eyebrows that give him a quizzical appearance that is fascinating. The distinctive Cairn head is broad and short, with a foreface a little longer than the distance from the well-defined stop to the occiput. The ears are set wide apart and are small, pointed, and erect. The head furnishings are plentiful and rather softer than those on the rest of the dog.

In hardiness, personality, gameness, and intelligence the Cairn Terrier rates high and is highly recommended by authorities as a household pet, although he made his name as a real working Terrier and as such has proved his excellence in obedience tests.

Sealyham Terrier. As is the case of all these truly working, sporting Terriers, the Sealyham grew up with families and thus was a pet from the very start, a classification it has never lost. It weighs about 20 lbs. and stands 10½ inches at the withers, which makes for a compact dog without clumsiness. The body length

from withers to tail measures 10½ inches, which allows for the flexibility needed for the original task of doing battle underground. The coat is weather-resistant, with a soft undercoat covered with a hard, wiry

SEALYHAM TERRIER

top coat. White is the preferred color, although tan, badger, or lemon markings on head and ears are not uncommon. The Sealyham is a sound dog in all respects.

Captain John Edwardes developed the breed on his estate in Sealyham, Wales, out of a rather obscure ancestry, which never was questioned as to specifications, because from the start the dogs showed they had stamina and courage to tackle anything, and were small and fast enough to dig into game holes and do battle underground. The Sealyham earned an amazing reputation for hunting down fox, otter, and badger for more than fifty years before it ever ventured out of the purely working Terrier rating and made its appearance in the shows of Wales, from which it spread all over the world.

The Sealyhams' courage and intelligence show in their expression, and this as much as anything else has given them the high regard in which they are held in the United States, both as ideal home companions and as stars of the dog-show rings. Whenever owners have put them into obedience training they have found they had a dog that could match performance with the best.

West Highland White Terrier. The West Highland White Terrier is a hardy dog as befits his Scotch origin, and is ever the gay companion, able to adapt himself to any set of conditions. His main purpose in life seems to be to enjoy his family's companionship and to pay in kind by making them enjoy him. He will go for a walk in the country or in city streets with joy and be equally happy if his owner wants to go for a swim or a drive.

Ranging from 13 to 19 pounds and standing from eight to 12 inches at the shoulder, the West Highland is a pure white dog with a dry skin that does not have odors and is readily cleaned by brushing. The coat must be double, the outer one hard, free from curl, and about two inches long, while the undercoat is furry, close, and soft. The ears are always carried erect and come to a sharp point. The tail is about five inches long, covered with hard hairs and never worn over the back.

The breed had been in existence as a separate variety for well over 100 years before anyone thought of putting it into current dog shows. These dogs made such a hit with all who saw them that breeders never were able to keep up with the demand for them as pets, mainly because in addition to their alert, compact appearances, they were and are a dog equally at home in the house or out of doors, winter or summer.

Their fame spread to the United States and from the start of their importation, they caught on in public favor, which is indicated by the number of people who may be found watching the West Highlands at the American dog shows. Few dogs breed more truly and there is never any question that they are satisfactory, attractive dogs from the Scotch highlands that have made good all over the world.

Lhasa Apsos Terrier. The Lhasa Apsos stands about 10 to 11 inches at the shoulder, and while wary of strangers, is gay and assertive. The few that have been seen in the United States have created many friends for the breed, especially among those people who like something a little different in dogs and want a small-sized pet.

The coat is dense and of good length, heavy, straight, and hard, with no hint of the silky or wooly. The head furnishings are heavy, with quite a fall over the eyes, and with whiskers and beard. The tail is well feathered and is carried in screw fashion well over the back. Known as the true Tibetan Lion-dog, the Lhasa Apsos is most desirable in the golden or lion-like colors, although the range of coat color covers sandy, honey, golden, slate, smoke, grizzle, black, white, brown, and parti-color.

The Lhasa Apsos comes from that land of mystery, Tibet, and can trace its ancestry back more than 800 years. Yet the breed is little known in the United States and not too well known in other countries. This may be accounted for by the fact that these Tibetan dogs originated and were mainly kept in the Lamaseries around the sacred city of Lhasa.

It is said that in the main these dogs were kept in the homes of the top classes in Tibet, and that, as special marks of esteem, the Dalai Lamas of Tibet have sent specimens to the ruling powers of China. They have not been kept as pampered pets, but are hardy dogs, able to cope with any situation, and have been trained to detect enemies, making use of their very quick hearing.

Skye Terrier. The Skye Terrier is one of the five Terrier breeds that Scotland has proudly presented to the world, and it is likely that it has been less changed since its origin, apparently four centuries ago, than any other of the terrier breeds. It is a most distinctive breed, and although in the main there is at present little hunting use for the Skye,

he has never lost his hold on the people who idolize him as a pet.

The Skye Terrier stands nine inches at the shoulder, with a body length from back of skull to root of tail of 23½ inches. With this goes

SKYE TERRIER

a massive head of 8½ inches and a tail of about 9 inches, making an overall for dogs of 41 inches, with females some two inches shorter.

The coat is double, the outer being about 5½ inches long, and hard and flat, over a short, woolly undercoat. It is said that in the old days this heavy coat was the dog's best insurance against the wild game for which the dog was used. In color the coat is dark or light blue, or grey, or fawn with black points.

The Skye is unbelievably fast when he needs to be and is game to the core, with very keen hearing, scent, and sight, all of which made him so much in demand as a hunter when good dogs often meant the difference between a filled or empty larder. It has been said that long before his days as a hunter were passed, the attraction of his appearance and personality were such that no lady of high birth would be seen out walking unless accompanied by a Skye Terrier.

Possibly because of the long coat that more or less disqualified him as hunting changed, his main function now is that of household companion.

Dandie Dinmont Terrier. The Dandie Dinmont has a definite reserve and dignity that sets him apart

DANDIE DINMONT TERRIER

from the usual run of snappy, noisy Terriers. He does not start trouble, but can finish it, and is an excellent watchdog and guardian of home and family. While the breed is still used to a great extent in its native land as a working Terrier, the majority of the breed are family pets, and this includes the show dogs, which have made a hit in the United States and England. Seldom does the supply of purchaseable stock catch up with the demand for Dandie Dinmonts as pets.

The head is large and broad, but not out of proportion to the long, strong body that is most flexible.

Averaging about 18 lbs. in weight, the breed varies from 14 to 24 lbs., with a shoulder height of 8 to 11 inches, and the body length from the top of the shoulder to the root of the tail is roughly twice the shoulder height. The coat is of a pepper or mustard color and comes about 2 inches long; it is a mixture of hard and soft, which gives protection against the elements.

Bred down from selected representatives of the rough Terrier hunters of the Cheviot Hills of Scotland, the Dandie Dinmont was recognized as a distinct breed as far back as 1700. Sir Walter Scott and others wrote of the Dandie, and the noted artist Gainsborough included him in some pictures. The Dandie Dinmont once seen is never forgotten, as few breeds of dogs possess more outstanding points to recommend them. The long, weasel-like body of the Dandie was purposely bred to aid in his work of going to ground for all types of vermin from rats to foxes.

Bedlington Terrier. The Bedlington is a unique dog, lamb-like in appearance but hardy, and thrives in any surroundings, for which reason it makes an ideal pet for either the country or city home; it is as a pet that the Bedlington has made its greatest fame. Although guarded as bolters of vermin and as fighting dogs in the early days, the breed has always been close to its owners and has progressed most since the formation of the National Bedlington Terrier Club in England in about 1877. This club brought the breed out as a show dog, which brought the Bedlington into public observ-

BEDLINGTON TERRIER

ance, and it became very popular in every country in which it appeared. Few dogs are so striking in appearance, or match the breed in personality.

The breed comes in blue, tan, liver and tan, sandy and tan, sandy, liver, or blue and tan, standing about 15 inches at the shoulder and weighing 22 to 24 lbs. It is so built that its action is like that of the Greyhound, light and springy. The coat is unlike that of any of the other Terrier breeds, being thick and somewhat wooly, furthering the appearance of a lamb, with an absence of hair on the rather long ears that are fringed at the tips. The head is narrow, deep, and rounded, with a high occiput and a distinctive topknot that sets the dog off in a striking fashion.

Bred in the mining shire of Bedlington in Northumberland, England, the breed apparently goes back

to 1820. The Bedlington is a game dog able to hold its own as a working Terrier against badger and other game. In olden times the breed built quite a reputation as a fighting dog, but now is used almost solely as a household pet, beloved by young and old, and with a keen devotion to its family.

White Bull Terrier. Bred in the days when life was coarse and rough, the White Bull Terrier became known as a courageous fighter when called upon. This reputation seemed to hurt him somewhat in the eyes of those who wanted pets, but later years have proved that few breeds fit better into the home than the Bull Terrier, which may run as low as 25 lbs. or as high as 60 lbs. in weight, although most seem to run between 45 and 55 lbs. The head is long and

WHITE BULL TERRIER

distinctive in that there is no stop and little brow. The small eyes are set on the oblique, giving an oriental appearance.

The Bull Terrier dates back more than a hundred years in its native

England and came from the old white English Terrier, which no longer exists, crossed with the Bulldog, and evidently the matings were crossed in with the Pointer. Originally of many colors, breeders worked for many years to produce the all-white dog that we know today, and there are also many of the colored variety. Because he was owned and trained by gentlemen to fight only on just provocation, the White variety became known as the White Cavalier, a name that has stuck to this day.

Colored Bull Terrier. There is little difference, except in color, between the White and Colored Bull Terrier, as both have a tight, dense, short, flat coat that takes on a high gloss. In the Colored variety, any color other than white is acceptable, or any color with white so long as the white does not predominate. The Colored Bull Terrier is not often seen in the show rings, most of them being kept home as pets, where their devotion to young and old is remarkable, as is true of their white cousins.

Staffordshire Terrier. The Staffordshire does well as a pet of a family, and has one characteristic not found in many breeds, namely, that it will quickly adapt itself to a change of surroundings and a new owner. The coat of the Staffordshire is short, close, and very stiff, with a high gloss. The standard allows

for any solid or parti-color, but all white, or a mixture that shows over 80 percent white, black and tan, or liver is not desired.

Argument always will persist when it comes to naming the direct ancestors of the Staffordshire Terrier, but no one will question the gameness, speed, and stylish engineering of the breed. They will run from 35 to 50 lbs. in weight and stand from 17 to 19 inches at the shoulder, which makes for well-distributed power. It is easy to see that with such a build these dogs could have been developed for fighting in the days before this sport was outlawed in all civilized countries. However, although the early association is as a fighting dog, it is wrong to rate the dog on that basis today, for on the whole they will start no more fights than any other breed.

The basic parents of the Staffordshire must have been the old-fashioned Bulldog and one of the truly game Terriers, possibly the Fox Terrier. It must be remembered that the old Bulldog looked nothing like the English Bull of today, and, as a matter of fact, a comparison of the ancient pictures with that of the present Staffordshire shows that this breed looks more than any other like that Bulldog that won fame as a bull-baiter. It is quite likely that the Staffordshire was the main ancestor of the White Bull Terrier we know today.

Manchester (Black-and-Tan) Terrier. The Manchester Terrier is the same dog that used to be known as the Black-and-Tan Terrier, one of the oldest of all Terriers, and one which because of its grace, speed,

MANCHESTER (BLACK-AND-TAN) TERRIER

and intelligence has been used in the creation of many of our newer "manufactured" breeds. Few dogs are more acceptable as pets, for they are quiet, clean, and very intelligent, as well as having a special "class" look that makes dog-lovers want to have them about the house. In weight they range from 14 to 22 lbs., so distributed as to give a racy appearance, without being too whippety.

The black of the coat is glossy and alive, while the tan should be of the mahogany variety. The tan markings are even, as though painted there by an artist. There is one over each eye and one on each cheek. The lips of both jaws are tan-lined, the lower tan area extending to the throat and ending in a "V". The insides of the ears are tan, as well

as the forelegs to the knees. In all markings the tan and the black never run together.

Manchesters were created in the Manchester district in England, a noted center for rat-killing and rabbit-coursing, and came about through the crossing of a famous Whippet bitch and a famed rat-killing dog. The result was so pleasing for a dual purpose dog that the fame of the Manchester Terrier spread through England. The name was changed to Black-and-Tan and later back to the original name.

For the past twenty years the breeders of the Manchester have been getting good results in their campaign to bring the breed back to the popularity level it enjoyed in the old days, when every neighborhood had its quota of Black-and-Tans.

Miniature Schnauzer. Generally the Miniature Schnauzer comes in a

MINIATURE SCHNAUZER

dark grey pepper-and-salt coat of harsh, wiry hair, although the black dogs of the breed are becoming quite popular in the United States. The ideal height is 12½ inches and altogether the dog makes an appealing picture, with the result that it is in high favor as a pet, especially among those who wish a distinctive dog, set apart from all others. The wiry whiskers, which accentuate the rectangular muzzle and the prominent eyebrows create an unforgettable picture. Few breeds give such an alert appearance, and this is matched by a physical and temperamental agility that makes the breed beloved by young and old. Of an excellent size to be played with by children, and small enough to need but little room, the breed is very popular as a member of the household.

It has been a distinct breed for fifty years, having come down from the Standard Schnauzer crossed with the Affenpinscher, a small black German toy breed. The Miniature Schnauzer was originated as a yard and stable dog, and is an excellent ratter, but does not follow the habits of the English Terriers by going to ground after small game. The breed is highly intelligent and has made a good mark in obedience tests as well as in the show rings of the country.

The Miniature Schnauzer is the only one of the three Schnauzer varieties remaining in the Terrier Group, since the Standard size was moved over into the Working Group with the Giant. It is a breed of German origin, and although great antiquity is claimed for the Schnauzer, it seems more likely that this compactly built dog came from crossing the black Poodle with the wolf-colored Spitz and then with the old German Pinscher lines that included some of the Wurttemburg droving blood.

THE TOY GROUP

The Toy Group as a Whole. The Toy Group assemblage consists of 16 breeds, which are toy only in size, for they have all the heart and drive of their bigger cousins, and within their heads is rare intelligence that makes them able to cope with any problem. It might be considered by the uninitiated that these breeds were all developed down from larger breeds to make an apartment-sized dog. Actually, the majority of these breeds are "naturals", and own a longer claim to fame than the bulk of the big breeds.

It might well be that they drew their early popularity because they took up so little room, a feature much in their favor in these days of small houses and city apartments. This Variety Group Five might as well be named the Pet Group as the Toy, were it not for the fact that, under right conditions, there isn't a breed in the world that can't be made a good pet.

Although the casual dog lover might consider that because of their small size the sixteen breeds need coddling and are hard to raise, that they are delicate and must be pampered always, it is well to drop this misconception. True that some of the breed individuals are soft and need this babying, but that is never a breed fault, but rather a fault of the owner. Actually, these small dogs prefer to be rated as "all dog" and allowed to go their way as would their big cousins.

In the one common meeting ground for all breeds of dogs, namely, the obedience trial classes, more than half the Toy Group breeds have had representatives in open competitions, and at no time have they had to hang their heads in shame. Two-pound Chihuahuas and five-pound Pomeranians have more than held their own, and in all instances these dogs have proved as able to take it as any of the dogs from ten to fifty times as large.

In the days before dogs were able to have the benefit of the skills of the veterinary scientists, it was generally a case of the survival of the fittest, and thus we can accept the antiquity of most of these small breeds as assurance that if we take one into our home as a pet, we are not taking on any invalid.

Pekingese. To the general public, the Pekingese is perhaps the best known of the Toy breeds. The regal appearance of these little dogs, their intelligence, and their occasional perverse stubbornness have endeared

PEKINGESE

them the world over. Few dogs are more adaptable to living conditions, for they take everything in stride. One look at the fronts which are massive for the size of the dog, and at their heavy manes and tapering hind quarters, and you know why they are often called Lion Dogs.

A limit of 14 lbs. is set on their weight, but they are so built as to give the onlooker no thought of small size, but rather of character. The coat is long, straight, softly coarse, with a heavy undercoat. Character is added by the oriental expression of the short and broad muzzle, the dark eyes, and the manner that shows that this is every inch a dog rather than too dainty and mincing. For the Pekingese is a dog with a mind of its own, fearless and to a great extent possessive. Usually the Pekingese rules the roost and bosses other dogs in the family. He has plenty of stamina and is not hard to raise.

There is no question but what they always have been pets from their earliest days in China, which were at least as far back as the eighth century. There they were the dog of royalty, held sacred, and the theft of one was punishable by death.

It is odd that their introduction to the western world came about through the looting of the Imperial Palace at Peking by the British in 1860. They were held rather closely there until the first show appearance in 1893, after which they were in great demand, just as they have been in the United States ever since they were first seen here.

Pomeranian. The Pomeranian does not trace his ancestry and his reason for existence back to royal favor, as do others of the Toy breeds,

POMERANIAN

but rather to the working breeds, for undoubtedly he is of the Spitz family, which comes down from the sledge dogs of Iceland and Lapland, and eventually became the little dog we know today. Doubtless he was bred

to his present size by people who, because of his intelligence and love for humans, wanted to be able to take him into any living quarters.

The Pomeranian has two coats, the undercoat being soft and fluffy while the outer is long, straight, and gleaming all over, and especially heavy around the neck and fore quarters where it makes a heavy frill that adds to the dog's attractiveness. The tail turns back over the body and is covered with a spreading, fanlike profusion of hair. The colors are orange, red, cream, sable, brown, or black.

The breed is most attractive in all respects, with a disposition that endears it to all and an ability to fit into any circumstances. The standard calls for a classification for those under 7 lbs. and one for those over that weight. Despite their lightness, they are hardy, possess a world of stamina, and their intelligence is proved by the many honors won by the breed against the best dogs in the country in the obedience rings.

The Pomeranian is well built, handles himself well, and is most pleasing to watch either in repose or action. He is most alert, an excellent watchdog, and thus matches his beauty with utility. The Pomeranian's record in the major shows of the country is one of which fanciers may well be proud.

Papillon. Years of living close to its folks have developed the Papillon as an alert, affectionate breed of high sense, adaptability, and an unbelievable hardiness. Good-tempered and loyal, the Papillon is at the same time a spirited little dog and can therefore be a delightful companion

PAPILLON

for children of any age or disposition as well as of adults.

While once they were of a solid color, today they are more attractive with a white ground color, set off by patches and ticking of other colors, sometimes of two colors and sometimes of three.

They are actually another of the Toy Spaniel varieties, slender, graceful, and dainty in action, but not sissified. The head has a light hair covering, while the body is more heavily dressed and the tail is like a long, flowing plume.

The Papillon, fancied by royalty for centuries, owes its start to Spain, later development to Italy, and the perfection of today to France. First known as one of the "dwarf spaniels", later development of the ear set and fringing that resemble butter-

fly wings brought about the name of Papillon (the French word for "butterfly") which is now official.

As small as the Papillon is, he is an excellent ratter.

Japanese Spaniel. One of the oldest of all breeds, the Japanese Spaniel is another that always has been maintained as a pet, being equally at home with children or adults.

The coat comes in a distinctive black and white, or a red and white, and is silky, long, straight, and profuse, free of wave or curl, with a rather thick ruff. Weights run about 7 lbs. These dogs have a distinctive oriental cast of expression and are aristocratic in appearance. There is nothing of the weakling about the breed, and few dogs make more charming house companions. They

JAPANESE SPANIEL

are adaptable to any surroundings and naturally clean.

It is generally understood that the breed came first from China and reached Japan when the Emperor of China presented a pair of these dogs to the Emperor of Japan. They were kept as royal pets and the rare times they were given to noted foreigners it was because of some rare service rendered to Japan.

Commodore Perry brought the first of the breed out of Japan when he opened trade from there to the world in 1853, and while we know that he gave a pair to Queen Victoria of England, no one knows where those that came to America were first located. However, from then on quite a number came to this country, being smuggled out in great numbers. The demand was high because of the attractive looks and fine personality of the breed.

English Toy Spaniel. There are actually four varieties of the English Toy Spaniel, the difference being in

ENGLISH TOY SPANIEL

the color of the attractive long coat. The King Charles variety is black and tan; the Prince Charles is a tricolor of white, black, and tan; the Ruby is a sort of chestnut-red; and the Blenheim is chestnut-red and white. The coat of all types is soft, silky, long, and wavy, with a heavy mane and considerable feathering

on the ears and feet. These dogs weigh from 6 to 12 lbs.

The English Toy Spaniel is highly intelligent, very alert, and has a captivating charm of manner. Although considered solely as a pet for many years, there was a time when the breed was valued also for its work on birds, and even today, given a chance, a member of the breed will revert to type and prove that the hunting instinct has not been bred out.

Where the English Toy Spaniel first came from is a matter of some dispute, although it is generally agreed that he came to England from the Orient, with stopovers in Southern Europe. There seems to be some relationship to the Japanese Spaniel, for both have a short nose, and there is also a resemblance, in the compactness of this breed, to the Pug, which is a Chinese dog.

He is definitely known to have been in England as early as the start of the seventeenth century when he was a larger dog than he is at present, and this suggests a relationship between the Toy Spaniel and the Cocker Spaniel.

Maltese. How the Maltese came into existence history does not tell us, but every written word on the breed, every work of art depicting these dogs, shows them as pets. So adored was the tiny mite that the Greeks even built tombs for their Maltese pets.

In weight they are not supposed to exceed seven pounds, and here again is a breed of which one says, "The smaller, the better." The coat is pure white, long, straight, and silky, with no undercoat. It hangs

MALTESE

down evenly on each side with a distinct part extending from the nose to the tail.

Although sometimes incorrectly classed as being of the general Terrier family, they really belong among the Spaniel types. In spite of their small size, they are alert, extremely intelligent, and as hardy as the people of their native Island of Malta.

The breed has spread out generally, although most of its fame, aside from its native island, is confined to England, where the nature and tiny size of the breed made it a great favorite. In the United States the Maltese has captivated the hearts of more people than can find stock to buy. The one member of the breed that has taken to obedience schooling has proved the intelligence of the breed.

Yorkshire Terrier. The coat of the Yorkshire Terrier is of a fine silky texture, perfectly straight, nearly long enough to sweep the ground, even on both sides, and very glossy. It is of a deep, steel blue color from the back of the skull to the root of the medium-length tail, golden tan on the head, and bright tan on the chest.

At one time weights varied from under 3 lbs. to 15 lbs., but of later years there has been uniformity in type and size, nearer the lower level of early days. Under its gorgeous coat, the Yorkshire has a well-made body, and if its coat is done up out of the way it can romp with the best of them, for it has a great deal of playfulness, courage, and intelligence, and is not so delicate as the size might imply. The Yorkshire Terrier exhibits much of its Terrier ancestry, although it has become such a pet, with its long silken coat,

YORKSHIRE TERRIER

that it is necessary to guard against any reversion to type.

It was in the late 'Eighties that the name Yorkshire was given to the breed officially because it was there that the breed was brought into being by weavers who had come down from Scotland, bringing with them various breeds, of which the Skye Terrier was the leader and evidently the chief ancestor of the Yorkshire. It was a dog made by the working classes, partly because of their love for beauty matched with fine temperament, and partly because they knew that something so beautiful would be an easy sale to the wealthy.

Toy Poodle. The Toy Poodle, while being much smaller and held

TOY POODLE

as a distinct breed from the Miniature and Standard varieties, is surely related and doubtless came into being through the desire of non-hunting lovers of dogs to refine down this highly intelligent breed to a dog that could be accommodated in the smallest of living-quarters. Like its larger cousins, it is a great pet and when given a chance evinces their ability to do things well.

The breed should stand 10 inches or less at the shoulder, and is well-built, being refined in appearance, able to handle itself well, and with a world of pride in its bearing.

The coat is profuse, of a good, hard texture, in any solid color, although the preferred shades are white, apricot, cream, blue, or red.

While it is admitted that the present-day Toy Poodle is a direct descendant of the Standards and Miniatures, it is equally well known that the Toy variety was familiar on the European continent for centuries before the start of the eighteenth century when it became known in England. As far back as the fifteenth century European artists painted these dogs into their pictures.

It is said that the Toy Poodle, although regarded as a "dandy" and maintained entirely as a pet, was used for one utilitarian purpose, in that it was one of the breeds that served as ancestors of the truffle dog of England, evidently for its great scenting ability and sagacity, which was crossed with the Terrier's staying powers and ability to go to earth.

Brussels Griffon. Few breeds are as loaded with personality as the Brussels Griffon, which more than makes up for his lack of antiquity. In size he is truly a Toy Dog, but in spirit, in the cocky way he carries himself, in hardiness, speed of foot, and thinking ability, he is a very real and gamin-like dog. Little wonder that so many want the breed as a pet that breeders cannot keep up with the demand. The Brussels Griffon virtually walks into the hearts of all who see him.

The breed comes roughly in two sizes, the smaller being about 7 lbs. at the maximum and the larger running from 7 to 12 lbs. The coat is reddish-brown, the whiskers sometimes being black. One type of coat is wiry and dense, and never has a touch of wooliness or silkiness, nor should it ever be long enough to appear shaggy. This rough-coated

BRUSSELS GRIFFON

type is not unlike the Irish Terrier in texture and color of coat. There is also a smooth-coated type, not unlike the Pug dog. In fact, it is said that at one time the Pug, a native of China but then popular in Holland, was crossed in with the base breeds that made the Belgian favorite, which perhaps accounts for the similarity of structure between the Pug and the Brussels Griffon. The latter is far better known than his ancestors, which were the Affenpinscher, now coming into greater favor than he has known for many years, and the so-called Belgian Street Dog.

That the Brussels Griffon is bright can be attested by the fact that those which have gone into obedience work have made good, and do their

work in a strutting fashion, knowing that all eyes are on them.

Affenpinscher. Long before the Affenpinscher was seen in the American dog shows, people had been hearing about an old breed that had been dubbed the "Monkey Dog". This dog traces back to the seventeenth century and got its nick-name because of the prominent chin with hair tuft and mustache, the bushy eyebrows, the piercing eyes with the quizzical expression, and the black-bordered eyelids.

The ideal member of the breed runs about seven or eight pounds in weight and will stand about 10 inches at the shoulder. The coat is hard and wiry, longer in some places than others, and really weather-resistant. Black is the favored color, but pepper and salt mixtures, black with tan markings, and other dark colors are allowed.

The Affenpinscher is as alert as he looks, moves briskly, and is without fear. Although small, he is compactly built and gives the impression of being much larger than he really is, and of being able to fend for himself. He is a great companion and truly a comical sort of a dog by nature. Very intelligent, he can be trained to do almost anything within reason.

He is the progenitor of the Brussels Griffon, which has far outrun him in world wide popularity, but with the passage of time and the admission of more Affenpinschers to the United States, it is expected that the breed will climb the ladder of general favor within a few more years. The breed is one of Germany's many products, most of which have been in the working and sporting fields.

Pug. The Pug is one of the Toy Group that needs no explanation of its value as a house companion and

Pug

all-around family pet. From time to time it has taken on a new wave of popularity stimulated by its charm of manner.

The breed is square and cobby, a truly compact dog with a wide chest, strong legs, and a short, blunt muzzle. It weighs from 14 to 18 lbs. The tail is curled tightly over the hip, with a double curl considered perfect. The coat is smooth, short, soft, and glossy, and very easily taken care of, which adds another point to the Pug's favor in selecting a pet for the home. The coat color is silver, apricot-fawn, or black. There is plenty of stamina in these little dogs, a great deal of personality and intelligence, and boldness in action.

They have done well in the show rings of the world as well as in obedience tests—another proof that brains and beauty can go together.

Quite often the Pug is credited as being a native of Holland, which is where he came into his first fame, but actually the breed came from China and was brought to Holland and England by Dutch East India sailors. It was England that really perfected the breed as we know it, although American breeders have helped along with the work that has seen the dog come back into public favor faster than breeders can meet purchasers' demands.

Toy Manchester Terrier. There are probably more people who call the Toy Manchester Terrier the Toy Black and Tan than call it by the official name. Whatever the name, the dog is smart in appearance, and for the past 20 years has been making the climb back into favoritism with the public that it enjoyed when first known some 150 years ago.

It is a graceful dog, fast on its feet, fond of people, and easy to keep. Its dense, smooth, close, thick coat is not at all soft and has a glossy, satiny appearance.

It is mainly black, with deep mahogany spots evenly and cleanly spaced over each eye, on each cheek, and on the chest just above the front legs. This mahogany color also lines the upper and lower lip and the inside of the ears. The tail is not very long, but tapers, and is carried on a line with the back, which arches. This arching back indicates some relation to the Greyhound family.

Weight is not supposed to exceed 12 pounds, although many prefer a dog nearer 7. At one time there was a great fad of breeding them as small as possible, with the result that they went down to three and four pounds, which created the story of a lack of hardiness. This tale drove the breed down in favor, but it has come back with the breeding of the slightly larger dogs, and the potential purchaser need not fear acquiring a weakling merely because the dog is of a Toy variety.

Italian Greyhound. No breed kept solely as a pet goes further back in time than the Italian Greyhound, which, practically in the form known today, existed as far back as

ITALIAN GREYHOUND

2000 years ago. It is true that it owes some of its refinements of the present time to its popularity with royalty and the privileged classes in England, having been brought there early in the seventeenth century.

And during all this time it won favor as a pet because of its size, grace, and marvelous temperament. There is no evidence that at any time it was anything other than a pet.

The smaller dogs are preferred, providing they excel the larger in type and conformation, the two classes being divided at 8 lbs. and under, and over 8 lbs. The skin is fine and supple, with thin hair as glossy as satin. Acceptable colors are red, blue, cream and white, all shades of fawn, and mouse.

One of the interesting tales about the Italian Greyhound is that concerning Frederick the Great of Prussia, who took his pet Italian Greyhound into battle with him. During the Seven Years' War, there was a time when Frederick hid under a bridge with the dog, whose silence saved Frederick's life and turned the tide of the battle.

It is believed, but never proved, that the Italian Greyhound was bred down from the "Gazehound" of ancient days—dogs that hunted by sight alone.

Miniature Pinscher. For those who like the sleek lines and grace of the Doberman Pinscher but who lack the space to take care of so large a dog, the Miniature Pinscher provides the same qualities in Toy form. There is nothing delicate about these little dogs, who are great watchdogs and fine at bluffing other dogs twice their size. The Miniature Pinscher is alert, intelligent, and loyal to the core.

They stand about 11½ inches at the shoulder and weigh from 6 to 10 lbs. The solid reds are most popular;

MINIATURE PINSCHER

other permissible colors are a rich black with tan or rust markings evenly placed, as in the Doberman; a brown with red or yellow markings; solid blue; and blue touched with red.

The coat is thick, hard, and short, lying close to the body and very sleek. This makes them easy to care for, although their hardiness is the greatest thing that recommends them as pets for city or country, large home or small.

In the show ring the Miniature Pinscher makes quite an appearance with his hackney-pony type of gait, and there is little wonder that he does so much winning. His competitive fame is not confined to his beauty, for when his owner elects to try the tests of obedience, he finds that the dog loves to work and can turn in a superlative performance.

It is not a new breed, although the real advance of the dog started about 1895, with a lively jump from ten years later until World War I. He began a real surge in the late Twenties, and since 1940 has been coming on at a rapid pace in public favor.

Chihuahua. The Chihuahua may be small, but he is mighty in ability to think for himself and makes a desirable pet because he neither needs nor wants too much babying. The breed comes in both a smooth or short coat and a long coat, although the latter is but recently making itself popular in the United States, where the breed is reaching a higher point of perfection than in its native Mexico.

Weights run one to six pounds in the smooths and two to eight pounds in the long-coated type, with two to four or five pounds preferred in each. In the main they have terrier characteristics, and are graceful,

CHIHUAHUA

alert, intelligent, and very fond of people.

The color range is wide, going from a pure white to a solid black, and many have splashes of different colors. The Chihuahua, once only the pet of royalty, is now the household companion of people in all walks of life and can make himself at home anywhere.

Those members of the breed that have gone into obedience competition have starred against the best of their day, and many a time one of the breed has gone to sleep in the sterling cup he has won in beating dogs up to fifty times his weight.

The Chihuahua descends from the Techichi, so favored by the Toltecs, who evidently existed with their dogs before the Mayan civilization in Central America in the fifth century. It is believed generally that the breed came about through the crossing of the Techichi with a small hairless dog such as is still found in parts of Asia.

Mexican Hairless. Although likely to have been once a breed on Greyhound lines and sizes, the Mexican Hairless has been bred down until today it is the size of a really small Fox Terrier. The skin is smooth and soft, with no wrinkles and definitely hot to the touch. There is a coarse tuft of hair on the skull and sometimes a few hairs on the tail.

The Mexican Hairless is a muscular little dog and always seems tense as if eager to be off, somewhat like a high-strung athlete or horse. Not too many are seen in the United States, although numbers were com-

MEXICAN HAIRLESS

ing over the border before the start of World War II, and it is likely that interest in the breed will again stimulate activity.

The Mexican Hairless is related to the other hairless breeds, chiefly the two hairless breeds of China, and is believed to have come to Mexico with the Aztecs. What their original purpose was has never been revealed, but the superstitions growing up around them of healing-qualities preserved them as pets of the family for many centuries, and it is as pets that we know them today.

THE NON-SPORTING GROUP

The Non-Sporting Group as a Whole. The Non-Sporting Group, or Variety Group Six, is rather a misnomer, because it implies a lack of utility, either in a working or sporting field. Actually the bulk of the breeds involved could well be assigned other groups and could come out well, either in competition or at the work expected of the breeds within that group.

Primarily, these eight breeds, of which Poodles have two size varieties, might be classed in these days as pets, which is no slighting of them, for the best function of the dog is as a morale builder around the house. Every one of these breeds can well be raised in the small suburban home or the city apartment, and yet, so sturdy are they all, that they can adapt themselves to the wide spaces of the country estate or farm and never be at a loss.

The Boston Terrier is well known to all dog lovers, and is the only American-developed dog that was designed purely for pet purposes. The Bulldog has had a change since its early days, and it, too, is a pet for thousands and might well be a leader in some purely pet classification. The Chow Chow has pet rating and yet in its ancestry it can point to work in both the sporting and sledge fields, and is one of the most ancient of breeds.

The Dalmatian, best known to the public today as a home companion, has at various times been more than a pet, and once had a distinguished record in the sporting field, being a hunter of no mean ability. The Keeshond rates in the broader working field and has a fine standing as a guardian. The French Bulldog's rating today is solely as a pet, and a good one all through, but few dogs could be better employed as ratters. The Schipperke is the smallest of the group, one of the smallest breeds out of Toy classification, and yet is all dog, and has a great history as an "alarm clock" and watcher over the safety of his family.

The Poodles, both Miniature and Standard, are the most misplaced in this Non-Sporting classing, for here is a breed that for centuries earned its living and much of its family's through its prowess in the hunting field. Even today, where clipped for the occasion and given a little training, it surely distinguishes itself in the hunting field, being an especially fine water retriever. Its flair for the spectacular, its clownishness that lends to acting, made it into a circus dog of repute and via that medium it came into the home as a genial companion.

One day the official listing of these breeds in the Non-Sporting group may change, but never will the character of the dogs be altered, nor their genius for taking over the home, large or small, be changed.

Boston Terrier. Here is one of the few dogs of purely American manufacture, and so well did the earlier fanciers of nearly 70 years lay their foundation, and so well have breeders carried on the lines since, that the impish looking, satiny-coated Boston Terrier, has long rested in the top brackets of public popularity. Few dogs are better known to young and old, and none excel it as a companion of the family.

BOSTON TERRIER

It is a lively, very intelligent, smooth and short-coated dog that appeals to all people because of its neat appearance and the ease in caring for it. It comes in three weight classifications: under 15 pounds, 15 to 20 lbs., and the heavyweights from 20 to 25 pounds, which is a far cry from the first specimens that tipped the scales at 32 or more pounds.

They are preferred in a dark brindle with flashy white markings, but some come in a black with white markings. The tail is very short, set on low and never carried above the horizontal. The ears are small, carried erect, and add to the smart appearance of the dog that for years rated as the most popular in the country on the basis of official registrations and local licenses. The foundation of the breed

rested in a dog that was a cross between an English Bulldog and a white English terrier, possessing a squared head. The breed had some trouble getting started in official circles, but as the type began to be standardized, authorities noted the public appeal of America's first purposely-designed pet dog, and in 1893 official standing was given the Boston Terrier.

They well merit their description as the American Gentlemen.

French Bulldog. The French Bulldog is surely an individualist, and another of those dogs developed purely for companion purposes, as its actions and bearing shows. Bred as companions, the Frenchies are excellent as watchdogs and guardians of the children, and so adaptable that they are as much at home in a one-room apartment as in a mansion.

FRENCH BULLDOG

As a rule they are quiet, although they love to play, and another claim on family affection is their natural cleanliness which endears them to the housewife. Although definitely brought down from the English

Bulldog, the smaller specimens of which had been sent to France, the "sourmug" expression is missing, and instead we find an alert, impish look.

The most distinctive feature of the physical side of the dog is the so-called "bat" ear, which is set high on the head and has a rounded top. The coat is fine, short, smooth, and shiny, and all colors are accepted, although the dark brindle is by far the most popular. There are lighter brindles and some are of a fawn color, although these are relatively rare. The lightweight class runs under 22 pounds, and the heavyweights will range up to 28 pounds.

The French Bulldog is so built that he appears much larger than he is, being of heavy bone, compact, and with an impressively powerful appearance for his size. He is extremely active and highly intelligent, and there is little wonder that he took hold on public fancy so well after his first public appearances in the United States.

Bulldog. The name Bulldog came about first because of the ancient sport known as "bull baiting", which has long since been outlawed. The old members of the breed were far different from the bench-legged dogs we know today, but the same courage still exists, and the level of popularity of these "sourmugs" has never varied from olden days to the present time. The name Bulldog

seemed synonymous with British courage and finally with the spirit of sport, so that many schools, colleges, and military units adopted the breed as their mascots.

When bull baiting was outlawed in 1835, it seemed that the Bulldog

BULLDOG

day was gone, and indeed it started to pass into obscurity, but some hardy fanciers persisted in saving good strains, and bred out the viciousness that was part of the bull fighter's heritage, and before long the Bulldog became as popular in the home as it once had been as a fighting dog.

In maturity, the breed will run from 40 to 50 pounds, with a short coat that is flat, fine and glossy. Colors are many, with the red brindle perhaps the best liked, followed by other brindlings, solid white, red, fawn or fallow, piebald and then other colors.

The Bulldog is thick-set, with wide shoulders, massive short-muzzled head, low slung body, with an appearance of power-plus. The gait is more or less of a "roll". It is not as slow a breed as one would think and those that have gone into obedience work have proved able and agile, some being nearly as fast as a terrier. The turn to pet days has brought out the intelligence of the breed, which had been soft-pedaled in its fighting days.

Dalmatian. Here is another breed over which one can start an unending argument as to its origin,

DALMATIAN

but no one can dispute that it is an early breed and that from the first known history, it was not only a dog of fine utility, but a wonderful companion to the master's family. Today he is respected as a clean home dog, and a striking mascot.

One thing that has clouded the Dalmatian's origin is the fact that he was a dog of the gypsies and so stayed little in one place. The name comes from the province of Dalmatia. He stands 19 to 23 inches and weighs from 35 to 50 lbs.

The Dalmatian's coat is short,

hard, fine and dense, sleek and glossy, easy to care for, and most attractive in its black or liver spottings that are distinct and range in size from that of a dime to a half dollar. The ground color is white and the spots set the dog off effectively.

He is a fun-loving dog, but easily trained for any serious purpose, and although today he is 98 percent pet dog, the Dalmatian can hunt well and in addition to his bodily excellence that has seen him through to many show wins, his work in the obedience tests has proved the intelligence of the dog. Few breeds are more adaptable, either to changes of duty or to living conditions.

The Dalmatian is unspoiled and unspoilable, a completely natural dog that has never been "monkeyed" with, and as a result, easy to raise, sound in body and temperament, alert always, an excellent guardian of the young. There is speed in the lithe limbs, and a world of stamina, and history records that whether as a hunter, a guard, a ratter, a draft dog, or a shepherd, he has never failed.

Poodle (standard and miniature). The Poodle is another of the breeds over which controversy can rage in regard to its origin and its antiquity. He comes in three sizes, the Toy variety being discussed in the section relating to all Toy breeds. Of chief interest to us here are the Standard and Miniature sizes, which, although now almost entirely functioning as home pets, have behind them a great working-hunting background.

Few breeds have the intelligence

POODLE (STANDARD AND MINIATURE)

record of the Poodle, which goes back centuries as a hunting dog, being especially adept at retrieving, and many is the family that owed its "meat on the table" to the ability of the Poodles at retrieving. Those that are still used to hunt in the United States do as fine a job in water work as one would want to see.

Circus performers soon sensed the intelligence and the adaptability of the Poodle and for years they have been part of acts that called for quick thinking and a certain sense of clownishness. There is elegance, rather than daintiness, to the trimmed Poodle of the day—a born aristocrat that gives the impression of laughing at humans.

The Standard Poodle stands over 15 inches at the shoulder, and the profuse coat gives an impression of much greater size. The range of color is wide and for that reason appeals to more people. Blacks and whites are the most popular, but the browns, silvers, blues, and apricots have their following. The coat is of harsh texture, even length, frizzed or curly, and not at all open. The clip may be of many types, and some for purely working purposes have an overall clip that appears like a retriever.

The style and grace of the Poodle and his flair of showmanship has led him to as many show wins as a breed could want to have. On the side of work he can point to an enviable record in the field of obedience training. Even under a green handler, Poodles are hard to keep out of the ribbons in these exacting tests that call for intelligence, speed of action and reaction, adaptability to conditions, and soundness of temperament.

The Miniature Poodle differs from the Standard merely in size, being under 15 inches at the shoulder, and because he takes up less room, is fast coming to the fore in public demand, and at least in shows and obedience is able to hold his own against his big brother and other breeds.

Chow Chow. Because he was beloved by rulers of empires and for centuries was owned only by the mighty, the Chow Chow became a great pet, desired by many, and for that reason was weaned away from his work as guardian, sled dog, and hunter, and became a household

CHOW CHOW

companion, a field in which he still ranks high all over the world.

The Chow Chow's coat is dense and abundant, straight and off-standing, coarse to a certain degree on the outside, with a wooly under-coat that helps protect against all types of weather. Any clear, solid color is allowed, although the reds predominate by far, and are followed by the blacks and the blues. The black tongue is unique.

The ruthlessness of Chinese emperors in destroying all that was dear to their predecessors hampers one in tracing the exact ancestry of the Chow Chow, but it is definitely known that as far back as 2000 years ago the dog was the official hunting dog of China. There is every reason to believe that the Chow was one of the primary breeds of dogs and that

he was the ancestor of many of our sledge dogs and of other breeds that carry their tails curled over the back.

It is believed that the first of the breed went into England in about 1780, and they quickly took hold and demand ran high, although steady importation did not start for another 100 years, and by 1895 they were popular in the United States.

It is likely that the largest kennel of hunting dogs in the world was that of the 2500 couples of Chow Chows maintained by one of the T'ang emperors about 700 A.D., along with a staff of 10,000 huntsmen. Given a chance today, the Chow would revert to type and be a good hunter.

Keeshond. A lovable breed that originated in Holland, the Keeshond is known mainly as a barge dog, presumably guarding his family and the cargo of the barge as it went through the canal system. He bore many names until the Patriots named one pet of their leader, Kees de Gyselaer, after the man. To this day, the Keeshond has been a dog of the people, at home any place in the world so long as his own people are there.

He is an alert dog, highly intelligent, and can be taught to do anything. His coat is wolf grey and always looks in the best of shape. It is harsh and off-standing, with a dense ruff and a thick, soft under-coat. The tail is tightly curled, with a double curl at the end quite desirable. He stands 17 to 18 inches at the shoulder. The Keeshond steps smartly as he moves, and there is every evidence of speed, stamina, and elasticity.

The breed is Arctic in origin and related to the Samoyede, Chow Chow, Norwegian Elkhound, and Pomeranian. That he goes back as a distinct breed to before 1800 is proved by paintings. As in many other cases, he nearly became extinct, but in 1920 fanciers started to bring him back and quickly the old tales spread and the dog came back to stay and is now popular on both sides of the Atlantic.

Schipperke. The most exacting demand for a small dog that is "all dog" is met by the Schipperke,

SCHIPPERKE

which originated many centuries back in the Flemish provinces of Belgium. He is a grand house dog of great intelligence. Weighing from 6 to 18 lbs., and so unconscious of his small size that neither owner nor friends regard him as small, the "Little Skipper" has cemented the position he held hundreds of years back as "house dog without a peer".

His coat is abundant, harsh to the touch, short on the ears, the front of the legs, and the hocks, with an attractive neck ruff. The head is somewhat fox-like and the eyes are exceptionally bright, with an ever-questioning expression.

He is short and fast, adaptable to all conditions, chock full of personality and stamina, about as smart as a dog can be, and game to the core. Ideal with children and adults, extremely loyal, clean, and resistant to disease, the Schipperke has much to recommend him besides his record which has seen him survive wars and act as messenger, as well as his being probably the first dog to have a specialty show run for him. This was in 1690 when a show was held for the Schipperkes of the Guild workmen at the Grand Palace in Brussels.

Small as he is, the Schipperke makes a good hunter, being excellent on rabbits and at times has made good as a 'coon dog. He has a world of stamina and it is not rare for the dog to live to be fifteen or more years old.

He started as a pet of the workmen of Belgium and then was taken up by royalty, rather than the reverse which is the usual order. In the United States the demand for the dog exceeds the supply.

CHAPTER III

CARE OF DOGS

KEEPING YOUR DOG HEALTHY

Main Factors Which Make for Good Health. Besides proper feeding, which is of course fundamental in maintaining your dog's health and which is discussed later in this chapter, it is necessary to see that your dog is clean at all times, is provided with the right sleeping quarters, gets enough exercise, and is free from worms and fleas. Careful grooming and training, both of which are discussed after the suggestions for feeding, also contribute to your dog's well being.

We shall now consider factors which keep a dog in good health; and at the end of this chapter we shall take up the question of illness and the care of sick dogs.

Keeping Your Dog Clean. You can prevent many sorts of infection and many major and minor ills by keeping your dog clean, with shiny coat and clean skin.

BATHING. It is not surprising that most dogs dislike being bathed, for too many baths are harmful to dogs. The few dogs that do enjoy baths like them because of the attention they receive at the time and not because they feel they need a bath. Your pet can be driven to insane scratching by being washed so often that the necessary protective skin oils have been dried out. There is need to bathe your dog only when he has rolled or in some way got into something foul-smelling. Then be sure you use a soap (in cake or liquid form) that cleans, deodorizes, and is made with more oil than drying agent. Your pet supply house, the veterinarian, or the drug store will have the proper kind of soap. Be careful, of course, not to get soap in your pet's eyes and to rinse off all the soap thoroughly.

After the bath it is important to see that the dog is not exposed to drafts or cool air and to keep him indoors, unless the weather is hot, until he is perfectly dry. It may be quite a few hours before the skin and undercoat are really dry, even after the surface coat appears dry enough. Most dogs are fairly susceptible to colds, bronchitis, pneu-

BATHS AT REGULAR INTERVALS KEEP YOUR DOG IN GOOD CONDITION

monia, and the like, if not properly cared for, and many a fine dog has been lost because of having been bathed, perhaps unnecessarily, in cool or cold weather without sufficient protection afterwards from colds and their complications.

BRUSHING. The best way to keep your dog clean is simply to get a good dog brush—and these come in styles suited for each type of coat —and brush your dog vigorously from one end to the other. Done daily, it takes but little time, cleans the outer coat, and forces the dirt that has clung to the skin to work off into the coat and thus into your brush. Brushing also helps remove dead hairs, so that your dog will shed less hair around the house, and stimulates the flow of natural skin oils. Your dog will appreciate being brushed, for it relieves him of the task of scratching himself, which he does not only to relieve an itch but to remove dirt that bothers him. Besides making your dog more comfortable, brushing prevents minor skin troubles that can develop into major ones. Fifteen minutes of brushing each day will also give you additional pleasure in the looks of your dog.

If you want to whiten your dog's coat, you can still avoid baths by brushing in and then brushing out the type of powdered dog-chalks that are used in competitive shows to make dogs gleam.

DAILY BRUSHING WILL KEEP YOUR DOG'S COAT HEALTHY AND CLEAN

Providing Healthful Sleeping Quarters. A dog will adapt his own habits to the conditions under which he is going to live with you. From the standpoint of health, regardless of whether you have a puppy or a grown dog, you will want to give him sleeping quarters, at least for the night, that are out of drafts and are warm and dry. In doing so you decrease the chances of colds and the more serious troubles that develop from them. But "spoiling" a dog is a matter for the individual owner to regulate, and if it includes what many owners do—permitting the dog to sleep on the bed—it is strictly the owner's privilege and neither he nor the dog will suffer any ill effects from this habit. Most dogs, however, prefer merely to sleep in the same room with a chosen member of the family than actually to sleep on the bed. If your dog sleeps in your room and you are a fresh-air fiend, you will have to remember, of course, to keep your dog out of drafts.

If you want to provide your dog with a bed of his own, you can give him an old chair with a solid back and place it out of drafts, or you can buy one of the excellent dog beds (they come in all sizes and last a grown dog a lifetime) that are available in any large store dealing in pet supplies. This, too, must be placed in such a way that neither drafts nor dampness can reach your pet. It might not be difficult for you to build a dog bed that answers the same requirements as those sold in stores. At any rate, be sure your dog doesn't have to sleep on the bare floor, although he may seek this on hot nights to get whatever coolness there may be.

YOUR DOG WILL APPRECIATE HIS OWN SLEEPING QUARTERS

The bad habit of wandering around at night or whining and waking folks is a matter of training and will be taken up in the Training section of this chapter. Suffice it to say here that the average dog will not disturb you at night unless there is something physically wrong with him, or unless there are noises foreign to that which should be associated with your home—and his.

Exercising Your Dog. A dog must have exercise to keep his system working well and you free from doctor bills. For that reason, as much as any other, you should select a dog that can best be fitted in with your scheme of living. If you live in the city and have little time, get a small dog that is not of the normally working type, for it will therefore need less exercise to keep itself from getting soft, flabby, or sick.

Regardless of where you live, it will be best if you or some member of your family can take the dog out for a walk the first thing in the morning, and again later in the day. Possibly youngsters of the family can exercise the dog after school hours, or an adult in the evening after work. Later at night, the dog should be taken for a brief walk that will tend to hold him through the night with no mishaps.

Make the walks interesting for him by talking to him, or in some way paying attention to him, so he will move along briskly in the joy

AN OUTDOOR RUN GIVES YOUR DOG FREEDOM AND EXERCISE

of being with you, for this smart walking is much better than a sluggish, moping pace that usually denotes a physical lack somewhere. Of course, if you can run with him, so much the better, but do not let him off the leash where there may be danger to life and limb.

If you happen to live in a place where there is a yard, or where you can take him to some safe park where you can play with a ball, you will be giving him exercise that will keep that spring in him better, and prevent the kind of flabbiness that comes even to those humans whose work is not exercise and who never find time to play.

Jumping exercises are fine for the majority of breeds, and of course, as in the case of the obedience competition, you would graduate the height of the jumps expected, according to the size and build of the pet. If you live in a city where there is a lack of usual jumping facilities, you can take a long stick or a cane and walk along and have your dog jump over it as he goes along. This is fun, at the same time.

There is another method of exercise that you can use in your own home and without disturbing the neighbors if you live in an apartment. It is a trick used by many trainers and handlers of show dogs. Get a box or table of the right height and teach your dog to jump onto this type of platform. But do not have him jump down. The idea is to make him gather and spring, and this will work wonders in developing the rear quarters of the dog, which in turn will make him move better and more gracefully.

One must always think of feeding the dog in relation to the amount of exercise that he is getting, for if overfed in relation to work, the dog becomes fat, usually in the wrong places, gets a shortness of breath, and the general effect is to open the system to infections that abound in the more thickly populated areas. Actually, if a person buys a breed that is geared to the size of the living quarters and the amount of time that can be given for exercise, there can be no troubles on this score.

Swimming is an excellent form of exercise for the dog, and if the owner has the chance to take his dog out for a swim at a place not too crowded by humans, the results will be very beneficial. Of course, if your dog happens to have some skin affection at the moment, let him stay out of the water for fear of further irritation. Do not allow strictures against bathing for cleanliness scare you away from allowing your dog to swim. There is no comparison, for in the former the dog is standing still and having things rubbed into him that actually are rubbing better things out, while in the latter he is getting a natural form of exercise that is good for all parts of his body.

Worming Your Dog. There can be no better advice on the subject of worming your house pet than to see your veterinarian. There is a different type of medicine for each type of worm and the dosage must be given in accordance with the age and weight of the dog. The wrong medicine at the wrong time in the wrong dog can wind up as "no dog at all".

If you take your pet to the nearest veterinarian, he will make a slide of the worms and find out with a microscope just what worms show up in the dog and will either take care of the matter for you or will prescribe the proper medicine and give you all necessary instructions. In some instances the "patient" is to be starved overnight before the treatment and then, after the treatment, he is to be given a laxative, usually milk of magnesia.

In general we have to contend with four main types of worms: the round worm, which is common in puppies and found in all types of dogs, hook worms, tape worms, and whip worms. There have also been cases of a fifth type—the heart worm, and this is one invader that the house-pet owner must leave strictly alone.

ROUND WORMS. The round worm is one of the best known, and most often seen, because it wanders up out of the intestines into the stomach and is quite often the cause of vomiting. If round worms increase too much in numbers, they can cause a serious intestinal blockade. They run about two to four inches in length and are about as thick as the lead in a pencil or perhaps a trifle thicker, tapering down at each end. Here is a case where fasting the night before treatment is advised, and the use of milk of magnesia suggested one hour or more after the worm dosage has taken effect. It is best to check this trouble again in about ten days. There are standard remedies that are effective for getting rid of the round worm, which is the type of worm most readily removed.

HOOK WORMS. The hook worm is a tiny but dangerous enemy. Caught early, however, it is easy to get rid of. Hook worms are generally picked up from the soil. They bore through the skin of the feet, or are licked off by the dog, and are sometimes even absorbed through foods that have gone bad.

The hook worm clings by tiny hooks to the dog's intestines and, if not otherwise nourished, will suck blood. If allowed to go untreated, they cause untold damage. More than once stud dogs have been made sterile and brood bitches have failed to produce puppies, at least living ones, because of the inroads of these violent attackers of dog life. Nursing puppies have been known apparently to choke up and die or else lose all interest in feeding, while older pups and grown dogs will become listless, anemic, and waste away so that it requires a great struggle to bring them back to what they might have been. It is wise in this case, to follow your veterinarian's advice in the matter of treatment and supplementary feeding to make up for losses, and to sterilize thoroughly the area in which the dog lives.

WHIP WORMS. The whip worm is not too easy to handle as most medications pass by its chief habitat, which is the caecum (the appendix in humans). It is a stubby body and a thin, long neck, and occurs in all sections of the country. The chief symptoms are a generally run-down condition, a nervous reaction not unlike the "running fit", pesty skin irritations, and quite often a miserable attack of diarrhea. In many cases the cure is an operation similar to our appendectomy. This is another reason why the layman should save time, money, and worry by having necessary worming done by a qualified expert.

TAPE WORMS. Known in man and beast for centuries, tape worms are long and flat, and come to the dog through the flea or louse, which has picked up the pest. A tape worm comes in segments and is generally first detected by small, dried segments that appear around the rectum, or which, still alive, appear to be crawling out.

The tape worm is hard to get rid of, for it clings to the walls of the intestines by suction. And even once your dog is rid of it, another may appear, for the tape worm passes eggs that are in turn picked up by other carriers and re-enter the dog. This calls for a careful check on your dog and a most thorough sterilization of the area in which he normally lives.

The tape worm causes not only generally poor health, but also creates anal irritation, which accounts for much of the dog's dragging himself along on his hind quarters. The coat will dry out, too, and extreme nervousness, even to the point of convulsions, may come about if the tape worm is permitted to linger too long. Again, it is obviously of the utmost importance to take your dog to a veterinarian.

Removing Fleas and Ticks. Even dogs that receive the best of care can sometimes get fleas. There are many flea powders that may help get rid of them, and these come with directions for their use. The main disadvantage, however, in using flea powders is that often they cause the fleas to jump off the dog but allow the fleas to remain alive, in which case they will still be around the house and will jump back into your dog's coat as soon as all the flea powder has worn off.

The best way to rid your dog of fleas is to buy a comb that is sold for this purpose, comb the fleas out of your dog's coat, and shake or brush the fleas into a vessel containing boiling water. These combs are made in such a way that the fleas will cling to them long enough for you to get them into the boiling water, which is the surest way of killing the fleas. This method also has the advantage of not causing any skin irritation as some flea powders might, and as strong soaps certainly will. Bathing and ordinary brushing do not remove fleas entirely although they may remove some of them.

Ticks should be removed very carefully with a pair of tweezers and burned. They should never be touched with the bare hand since they are carriers of Rocky Mountain Spotted Fever. If your dog spends a lot of time outdoors, and particularly if he has a long or shaggy coat, it is advisable to look him over for ticks once a day, especially in the summer. Ticks are more easily removed if they have not been on your dog's skin for more than a day. If not removed, in a day or two they will be considerably swelled up with the blood they have sucked. In looking for ticks, pay particular attention to the dog's ears, for this is a favorite place in which the ticks fasten themselves.

Sweaters and Coats. If your dog is of a short-haired breed and you live in a climate where the winters are severe, it may be advisable for the dog to wear a sweater or coat on the coldest days, especially if you live in a city and must keep your dog on a leash so that he cannot immediately warm himself by natural romping and exercise. The best sweaters and coats are those which protect the chest and abdomen as well as the back, for actually your dog's chest and abdomen are far more sensitive to changes in temperature than his strong, more heavily furred back. A light coat of some kind in wet weather is especially helpful for small, smooth-coated dogs that have an antipathy for going out in the rain. Some pet shops even sell rubbers for dogs, but these are unnecessary and probably very few dogs, if any, will tolerate them. It is usually wise, however, to wipe off your dog's paws after he has been out in wet weather, to prevent colds as well as to protect your floors and rugs from mud.

General Advice on Feeding. In the feeding of puppies and grown dogs, there are several factors to be considered. Among these are the age and size of the dog, its state of health, the time of the year, and the amount of exercise that it gets.

Each and every dog breeder and owner has his own individual theories as to the diet of a dog, and that theory must work out properly for the dog, or the owner would not continue to keep his dog on that diet. However, it is not wise for the new dog owner to adopt a diet for his new pet merely because someone else has been following that system.

It is presumed that the owner would not buy a new pet unless he found that it was doing well for its age and was in the best of health. Therefore the simplest way to start out on a new dog or pup is to ascertain what that breeder had been feeding his dogs, and what amounts, for if the dog has done well in a kennel with many other dogs of the same breed, it is certain to do even better under the same general diet when the dog has become the center of someone's household.

In the majority of cases, breeders will automatically give you feeding instructions for your puppy or grown dog as a matter of good business, because if your pup stays in the best of health and always looks it, your pet is one of the best advertisements in the world for him and his stock.

You must, however, take into consideration, especially on the amount of food to be given, what changes there have been in the exercise that your dog will get. If it is to be less than he has had in the previous home, then cut down on the amount of food given at each feeding, and if the dog will get more freedom and more exercise, he will need more food at your home.

If you have secured a young puppy that is just past the weaning stage, regardless of breed, you should feed him five times a day until he is almost three months old. You can then cut him down to four meals for the next month or six weeks and drop it to three feedings until he is eight months old. After that you will cut the dog down to two meals a day and run on that schedule until the fifteenth month, if he is one of the smaller breeds, and up to two years if he is one of the big, ponderous breeds. In other words, the time to drop from two to one feedings a day is when the dog has reached maturity, and the larger the breed, the longer it takes to get to maturity.

Regardless of whether you feed your dog five times or once a day, try to keep the feedings to a set schedule and you will find that your dog will get along much better. He is a creature of habit and comes to look for food at set times and will thrive better on regular food at regular intervals. However, you should forget the schedule for a little

A HEALTHY MEAL FOR LITTLE PUPS

time if your dog has been out for a romp or has gone through an experience of any kind that has left him keyed up or exhausted.

Another point of regularity that must never be overlooked is always to feed your dog from his own dish, even if this means taking the dish along when you have your dog away from home with you. Punish him, if need be, for taking food from any other container, because that is the simplest way to teach him not to eat contaminated or purposely poisoned foods, and thus this bit of regularity may save your dog's life.

Unless your dog actually appears sick, do not fret over him or baby him when he refuses good food, or noses through it and leaves the bulk of it. A dog can be "off his feed" as well as a human, and is better off if you pick up the dish after no more than twenty minutes' chance of eating. It does well to underfeed dogs now and then, and some top-flight breeders consider it good practice to have their dogs occasionally go without food for a day. In doing this, you have to use your head and know whether your dog is under- or overweight. Always be sure that your dog has clean, cool water, regardless of whether he is on a "fast" or not, but with small puppies do not leave the water dish always available, as they have a tendency to drink too much and that will throw the diet off balance.

EVERY PET SHOULD HAVE HIS OWN DISH

Suitable Foods for Puppies and Grown Dogs. The first thing to think about in making up a dog's diet is the nutritive value of the food, rather than whether the dog really likes it or not. Knowing what the dog can thrive on, what will make him always look and act well and full of stamina, is half the battle. And if you can slightly vary the diet, you will find your dog is less "picky".

Milk is an excellent food, whether it be whole or skim, evaporated milk that has been diluted, or buttermilk. However, some dogs are like some humans—milk does not agree with them, and when you find that it upsets their stomachs, take it off the diet list. It has been noted that dogs that do get a fair amount of milk are apt to stay free from arthritic afflictions.

Eggs, and nearly always raw, are another good food and help condition the coat, provided your dog can "take" them. Some dogs are so sensitive to eggs that they cannot eat any foods in which eggs have been cooked. Young puppies generally do better if the eggs are soft-boiled.

The base of the puppy feeding, for the first six months that it is on its own, should be milk and eggs, with small amounts of meat, not too fat, that can be raw or have had scalding water poured over it. In using the scalding method, you can mix in a small quantity of one of the many excellent dry foods, either meal or biscuit form. In doing this, either for the young or old dog, do not have the mixture sloppy, as the dog will get plenty of volume but little nutrition. Besides, he rather prefers food that he has to work on to that which he can lap down.

Cod liver oil should always be a part of the puppy diet, and it is as well, in cold or damp weather in the colder climates, to add a bit of cod liver oil to the grown dog's food. There are many good brands of baby foods in tin or glass on the market that make fine additions to the puppy diet. Tomato juice is excellent for young or old dogs and many breeders do considerable canning of tomatoes to add to the dog's feeding during the winter months.

Vegetables, especially of the leafy variety, are sound additions to the feeding of most dogs, although they must be used as "additions", preferably cooked with the meat or fish part of the main meal of the day. The heavily starched foods never should be given to the dog as the system does not take care of them readily.

Fish, either by itself or cooked up into a chowder and mixed with a good standard brand of dog meal or kibble, goes well with nearly all dogs, and if you have enough dogs to warrant it and can pressure-cook the fish, the bones will mash right into the fish and add to the food value. However, never give a dog fish bones by themselves or mixed into food unless they have been thus thoroughly mashed.

The question of giving dogs bones is always a subject for debate. Surely nobody would be foolish enough to give a dog a bone that is easily splintered, as it will lodge in the throat, or else go far enough along to produce an intestinal blockade. Never give a dog chicken bones. Too many of the so called "good" bones is like too much of anything else, and you will note that the dog's stool becomes too hard and dry, a sign that eventually this dryness will clog up the system's outlets. However, one cannot get away from the fact that a good hard bone is excellent for the dog to chew on, to develop his teeth and keep the gums from getting soft and flabby. Of course one can substitute some of the very hard dog biscuit, which will act as a tooth cleaner at the same time.

The dog is primarily a meat-eating animal, and develops more stamina when basically meat-fed than when not. Whether to feed raw or cooked meat is a matter of how well your dog does on either; the notion that the raw-meat eater is a dangerous dog is pure fallacy. Find out on which form your dog does best and stick to that as a rule. The cheaper cuts of meat, as well, as beef or lamb heart, kidneys, and liver are welcome parts of the dog's diet. Many of the commercial foods on the market—the dried meals and kibbles—have meat or meat derivatives cooked into them, and can be used as a basic diet for nearly all dogs. In most communities there is horsemeat available and many of the finest dogs of the country are raised on horsemeat and the prepared meals or kibbles. Since there is little or no fat in horsemeat, it is well to add oils in some form, either cod liver oil, salad oil, bacon drippings, or suet.

Much has been said on the use of table scraps, and it is generally agreed that the house dog may have these if there is not too much starchy food on the plates.

Dog biscuit should be kept on hand always and in a dry place to prevent spoilage. It is not only nutritionally fine for the dog, either by itself or put into other foods, but grand as a snack when the dog gets a bit hungry at night, or as a reward for something well done.

The better brands of canned dog food can be highly recommended, but the very cheap ones should be avoided.

The main thing to remember on the "what to feed" list is that you start with that food series on which you have seen your breed do well, and you keep generally to that line until you see that this or that item disagrees with your dog.

If your dog is inactive, cut down on anything that tends to fattiness, as well as on amounts given at each feeding.

The feeding of a female in whelp is covered in the chapter that takes up the matter of breeding dogs; in general it builds up almost entirely to a meat diet, with plenty of milk or milk-producing items added, with care taken not to permit her to get too fat, which is equally bad for her and the coming puppies. After the puppies have come and during the time that she is nursing them, she will appreciate and do well on an increased milk diet, and more odds and ends rather than a steady diet that is basically meal or kibble.

In very hot weather shift your feeding to the cool of the evening and cut down on heat producing elements, avoiding most of the fats and oils, and in the case of young puppies that are getting oatmeal, shift to a dry cereal with milk or a broth. In cold weather shift to the heating elements in foods, but do not feed your dog hot food.

Above all, keep the food and water dishes spotlessly clean so that infections and other ills can be avoided as much as possible.

Amount and Frequency of Feedings. The amount of food to give a dog must vary with the time of the year. His weight, age, and degree of maturity, and the amount of exercise he receives should all be considered carefully.

In all cases it is well to remember that it is better to feed smaller amounts more often than to heap the food container. At any age or size, rather than stuff your dog and allow him all he can eat, give him enough so that he will literally polish his plate and be wanting just a little more. It is more than likely that among house-pet dogs, regardless of breed, more have died from being fed too much than for any other reason. It is well to raise or lower the amounts fed at any particular span in accordance with how your dog looks and acts, and to give him an extra amount if he has been getting more exercise than usual, or else to give him an extra meal in the form of dog biscuit.

No hard and fast general rule can be set down for feeding dogs of all breeds, sizes, ages, and conditions, but a study of the work of hundreds of breeders over a long period of time would seem to provide a sound system, namely, an ounce of food for each pound of the dog's weight. There would be many reasons for going under or over this amount, but for the new dog owner it is a good rule to start with. Observation and common sense on the part of the pet owner should do the rest.

The same common sense that dictates amounts to be served each time will guide the pet owner as to how to make up a diet balanced to suit the dog's needs. While raw, red meat could be used in ever increasing proportions as the dog gets older, scientific study has revealed that the modern dog can get by on a practically meat-free diet.

A practical guide for the new dog owner in regard to the amounts to be given at each feeding will be found in the following:

TEN WEEKS THROUGH FOUR MONTHS. During the period that calls for four meals per day, which is roughly from ten weeks through the fourth month, make two of the meals of milk. If you have a purebred dog, you can know from the breed charts what the dog should weigh on maturity, and it is well to figure ahead on that basis.

Considering such breeds as will not weigh more than 15 pounds when fully developed, it is well to give them about four ounces of milk at two of the feedings and allow about one ounce of solid food at each of the other feedings—preferably scraped beef to give them a solid foundation and greater stamina.

Breeds that will weigh at maturity between 15 and 30 pounds should have at least six ounces of milk at each of two feedings and four ounces of solid food.

For maturity weights of 30 to 60 pounds allow 12 ounces of milk and 6 ounces of solid foods, giving two meals of each. For breeds weighing over 60 pounds and running up to 100, permit 15 to 18 ounces of milk at those two feedings and 8 to 10 ounces of the solid feeding. Where you have one of the really heavy breeds that will scale when fully grown between 100 and 200 pounds (and there are not many of these), the milk feedings should run 20 to 30 ounces each time and the solid food should be from 12 to 18 ounces.

FIVE MONTHS THROUGH EIGHT MONTHS. Here we should have our dogs cut down to three feedings, and at times let it go at two feedings. In any case one of these feedings should be milk, with which a light food could be given, preferably a cereal that suits the dog's system.

For the breeds under 15 pounds, allow 4 ounces of milk and 2 ounces of some solid feeding. To the breeds that scale from 15 to 30 pounds, permit 8 ounces of milk and 5 or 6 ounces of solid food. When we reach the breeds varying from 30 to 60 pounds, it is best to allow a pint of milk (16 ounces) and 8 ounces of solid food.

In feeding the dog of 60 to 100 pounds of matured weight at this age period, allow 20 to 24 ounces for the milk feeding and 10 to 12 ounces for each of the two solid feedings. For those breeds that scale up from 100 to 200 pounds, have the milk with light food weigh about 30 to 40 ounces, depending on how large that dog actually will be, although a quart of milk is a good average to strike. Here you would make the solid feeding run from a pound to 20 ounces.

NINE MONTHS THROUGH SIXTEEN MONTHS. In the very large breeds we would run the age limit to 20 months and at times to 24 months. At this stage we have cut our dogs down to two meals each day. One of these feedings should always be milk mixed with a light, easily digested food.

In the up-to-15 pounds classification, both the milk and solid meals should weigh 4 ounces. Moving to the 15 to 30 pound limits, the dog should have 8 ounces of milk and 12 of solid food.

The 30 to 60 pound classification, which covers very many breeds, calls for 12 ounces of the milk and light food meal and a pound for the solid foods. Moving above this to those breeds that should weigh up to 100 pounds, the lighter meal calls for 15 to 18 ounces and the solid food ought to weigh 20 to 26 ounces. In the top-weight breeds that will scale as high as 200 pounds, the milk and light food feeding should be 20 to 32 ounces and the solid foods from 30 to 42 ounces.

MATURITY. For the lighter breeds up to 15 pounds, allow 6 ounces of solid food with a light snack in the morning, and if indicated, give a few dog biscuits through the day. Let your dog of the 15-to-30-pound class have milk in the morning and a pound of solid food in the late afternoon. In the 30-to-60-pound group of breeds, our solid feeding should be about 24 ounces, and if the dog's condition warrants it, a light snack at another time of day will be all right.

The dog in the 60 to 100 pound classification should have between 30 and 36 ounces of solid food, and here again the snack idea is all right if the dog is down in weight or has been having sufficient exercise to run off the food. When we get to the top-weight brackets that run up to 200 pounds, the solid foods should vary from 45 to 54 ounces and might even run to 5 pounds.

Feeding Sick Dogs. If your dog is sick or injured, the veterinarian, at the time of treatment, will advise you what to change in the dog's diet. Under sick conditions, the dog, like the human, will prefer the liquids, or he will want and should have more lean meat, preferably raw beef in chunks or ground. Beef or lamb broths are usually good at such a time, with bits of meat floating about, but not the more substantial stew with vegetables, which would be too heavy for the ill one's digestion. Cod liver oil's efficiency in promoting bone and tissue growth is valuable in the case of a dog with a break or disabling tears in the skin.

Advantages of Careful Grooming. Whether one is a dog lover or not, he cannot help but turn and admire the dog that looks every bit the canine lady or gentleman; and the well-groomed house pet can attract as much attention as the greatest of show dogs.

DAILY GROOMING WILL KEEP YOUR DOG LOOKING SMART AND FEELING HEALTHY

Involved in the looks of the dog, of course, is the basic fact of health and cleanliness due to his being well-brushed rather than over-bathed. A dog feels like the proverbial "million dollars" when he is invigorated by a good brushing that has left him sparkling clean. In accordance with the demands of his breed, he strides or prances or moves like a little hackney pony, knowing that many eyes are on him.

He knows, too, that everything that could be done for his health and beauty has been done, and that his owner is very proud of him and enjoys the attention he attracts. Every dog owner can have that grand, proud feeling if he will put his home pet through the beautifying processes that have kept that "dog on the street" looking so smart, the perfectly natural "beauty parlor" treatments that all dogs need to keep in the best of condition.

You have started with a dog that is healthy and been kept that way through proper feeding, right exercise, good living quarters and the consistent brushing that has kept that sparkle of cleanliness and good living. You will preserve that beauty and health by grooming that dog in accordance with the standards of your breed.

Even if you do not want to enter your dog in any show where the judge will pass on the dogs according to their meeting the standard of perfection, you do have pride in your dog and you want him to look like a dog of that breed. Therefore you find out how the show specimens of that breed are trimmed to bring out the best there is in them.

Care of Teeth and Nails. Quite naturally you will have taken the usual care of the dog's teeth by making sure that food particles have

CARE OF YOUR DOG'S NAILS IS IMPORTANT

not been allowed to catch and ferment, thus possibly bringing on some illness. Then perhaps you will have noticed that the top specimens of the breed walk more briskly, seem more on their toes. You may find that your dog needs his nails trimmed back so that their overgrowth does not cripple the dog. At the least, the untrimmed nails will throw your dog off balance, develop the wrong muscles and produce a gait contrary to how your dog should go.

In some breeds you can do this with scissors or shears, but it is best to obtain a regular clipper that can trim the nails properly. Dogs that have plenty of exercise on hard pavements will need little trimming, but the average dog of today has little chance to keep his own nails back to proper length. Hold the foot so that you may see where the blood vessels come and do not cut into them. Pet your dog and make him understand that the action of cutting the nails will not hurt him. Most dogs, once they realize that they walk and feel better because of that clipping, will welcome you when you take care of them.

Trimming, Clipping, and Plucking the Coat. Having trimmed the nails so that your pet can stand right, you can set him up and see how the coat should be "barbered" if your breed calls for it. In the case of the smooth-coated dogs, there is little to do save to brush regularly with a medium hard brush of stiff bristles that will take out dead hair and dirt. This has its advantage from the housewife's point of view, for there will be less shedding around the house, and fewer dog hairs on clothing and furniture and floating around the rooms. As a rule, about the only other thing you have to do with the smooth-coated dog is to use scissors to trim off the hard whiskers that grow about the muzzle, and the extra hairs that threaten to cover the base of the ear channel and sometimes help to bring on cankers.

To know how best to care for the coat of your longer-haired dogs, you can go to a top-flight breeder of that breed to which you are devoted and learn from him how it is done. Actually, it is best that for the first few times, you pay to have this "barbering" done. Observe the tools needed and purchase them at a supply store.

Or, you have even a better chance of seeing how to do this work if you can attend a number of dog shows. There you can see how the finished product looks. You can stand near the section where handlers are grooming their dogs for the show ring, and putting on the finishing touches.

The terms applied to this "barbering" are "clipping", "trimming", and "plucking", and there are some breeds which require all three actions. Remember always that this beauty work is not at all sissified, as so many consider the show dog and all that goes to keep him in the show-window of the dog sport or hobby. Actually, while the final dressing may have added effects that do not appeal to you, there is the sound reason of cleanliness and good health back of this work for good looks.

The main effect of this trimming and clipping and plucking is to remove dirt from the outer coat, as well as dead hairs, and the sooner the dead hairs are removed, the faster will come the new coat, and the less scratching your dog will do.

It is a necessity in many breeds to pluck to get dead or superfluous coat out. There are regular plucking combs and knives in the market and in many places it is possible to buy plucking charts which will show you exactly how the coat of your dog is to be handled. The makers of the necessary tools usually put out such charts for each breed requiring their products and you never can go wrong by following them, although it is often wisest to get instruction from an expert in the line, lest your dog look as though he had run afoul of a lawn-mower.

Clipping is done for several reasons. In the nature of ordinary grooming this removes hairs where the coat should be down low and acts to prevent too much hair weight in places where bulk of hair would collect more dirt. Incidentally, the clipping also helps to reveal the classic outlines of your dog and thus adds to its beauty.

Another reason for clipping is to get down to the skin to take care of certain injuries or skin diseases. However, this should not concern the average pet owner, as in this case the work should be handled by the veterinarian who is treating the condition.

Under no conditions should you clip or permit anyone else to clip all the coat off your pet unless there is an overall skin trouble that demands treatment. To do so not only makes your dog look like a freak, but it leaves him open to many skin troubles that never would otherwise come his way. Do not make the mistake of thinking you have done your dog a kindness in hot weather by removing the coat, for that same coat, be it a longhaired or a shorthaired dog, acts as does the insulation of your home, keeps it cooler in the summertime and warmer in the winter. It is seldom the heavily-coated breeds that "pass out" in the hot weather.

Trimming is done mainly to get rid of individual hairs that are longer than the rest and have come in out of place or do not groom down as well as the rest of the coat. This action is more or less like the human going to the barber shop and asking for a trim instead of a haircut.

Brushes, combs, and trimming knives come in proper styles for all types of coats and it is ruinous to use the wrong utensils in grooming your dog. In the longer coated dogs, a vigorous brushing should come first more or less to remove dirt and make it easier to get out dead hair and foreign substances; then the comb finishes the task by completing the breaking up of any mats that may have occurred in the coat, and which, if allowed to remain, would necessitate the shears and an ugly looking spot in the coat.

It is important that you, the pet owner, keep the dog's brushes, combs, and other utensils as clean as you demand that your barber keep the tools that he uses on you.

UTENSILS USED FOR GOOD GROOMING

Clipping is done either by the electric types of tools used for finishing a man's haircut, or by the hand type. In general the former is preferred to the latter because of speed; however, there is the great danger of getting a "clipper burn", which either affects the skin or more or less scorches the coat and deadens the hair. Neither should be used by the amateur. In the hands of the expert, the hand clipper does a rather fast, over-all job of taking the coat down and preserving symmetry of outline and is useful in getting the coat to the length desired by the breed standard, which actually is in conformity with the comfort of the dog.

Plucking originally was done entirely by thumb and finger and to this day there is no doubt but what the best jobs of plucking are done by this old and laborious method. The term "stripping", usually applied to taking down the coat of one of the terriers, is merely another name for plucking, which actually reduces the length and amount of coat to the length desired for that particular breed. In any event, it takes longer than clipping but is much more efficient in the long run. It is especially efficient in removing the overabundance of under coat that often grows on our heavier-coated dogs, or those whose origin intended them to be outdoor working or hunting breeds that would need dense undercoat to protect against all types of weather.

A dog that has been properly plucked and then trimmed creates the smartest of appearances and makes a more comfortable pet as well.

TRAINING YOUR DOG

Housebreaking. The matter of housebreaking will be your chief concern if you have acquired a new puppy, perhaps away from its mother for the first time. If your new dog is older, the chances are that it knows what it is all about, and merely needs the chance to adjust its living habits to the new quarters.

There are two chief ways in which to house-train a puppy, and the use of one or the other depends largely upon where you live. If you happen to live in the country, or on the first floor of a city dwelling where there are handy dirt plots, you will use the outdoors method almost from the start.

It is natural that a pup will make errors, for after all while he has been in his original home, the mother has taken care of cleaning it up. Suddenly he comes on his own when he moves to your house. Excitement over the change may cause him to dribble, but you can beat that by watching carefully in the first few hours and as soon as an "accident" seems inevitable, pick up the pup and take him down onto the ground, and then as soon as he has finished, pick him up with many words of praise and bring him back into the house.

Do the same almost immediately after he has eaten or had water to drink, being sure to take him out through the same door, so that he will associate that door with the idea of tending to nature's calls, and before long he will warn you by going to that door.

Of course, you are apt to have a bit of trouble the first few nights even if you do live convenient to outdoor ground, and it is well to couple the paper treatment with the outdoors regime. Take your pup out the last thing at night before going to bed, and do not feed or water him late, for this would stimulate his processes. Puppies should have, of course, their own sleeping quarters, raised off the floor a bit to avoid drafts and their bad effects. Between those sleeping quarters and a door leading to the outside, keep newspapers on the floor, watch the pup carefully, and when you note his readiness to make an error, pick him up gently and hold him on the papers until he has taken care of himself. Then, after praising and petting him, take him back to where he was before. In a short time he will react to your praise and strive to earn more of it by going to the spot and doing the very things that evoked the praise.

You will gain nothing by trying to beat cleanliness into your dog, for you are bound to create a nervous wreck that will be no good to anyone. Dogs are creatures of habit, and it is therefore your responsibility to see that he is fed and watered at regular times, and that he has been exercised with the same degree of timing. It may surprise you to find how fast you can set the habits of a dog by that regularity.

If it happens that you have no sure means of bedding your pup down for the night without leaving him a chance to wander into trouble, you can give him his bed, raised off the floor, and then, set apart from it but within a fenced enclosure, some papers; the pup will naturally prefer to keep a clean bed and will use those papers and save you work.

If you are housebreaking your puppy by the paper method or by a combination of paper and outdoors methods you will find that no matter where you live before too long you will be able to time your dog's needs, pick up all papers, and use the outdoors method alone. In general, with patience and timing, you can housebreak your puppy in two to four weeks.

With the new older dog your problem again becomes one of regularity and careful watching to swing the dog back to knowing what is expected in this new home. Remember that there are few willfully dirty dogs. Keep your dog in his own area until he is housebroken and then give him increasing house privileges as he improves. Soon he will move from room to room only on invitation.

Curing Puppies of Whining. One of the big problems in having a new dog in the house is that of the dog's whining because of lonesomeness, which is like homesickness in us humans. If you constantly get up to see what is wrong or to quiet the little pup, you merely make trouble for yourself and everyone who can hear him. Pups are like small children, craving attention, and if the least yelp brings the desired attention, you can be sure that every time you respond to that yelp you are setting up grief for yourself and starting to create a spoiled dog who will expect the habit to continue.

One of the oldest tricks of guarding against puppy disturbance is to place a clock where the pup can hear it tick. This will more or less lull the pup to sleep, or its familiar sound will put him back to sleep when he awakens feeling he is in a strange country.

Discipline and Punishment. The matter of discipline is one to consider carefully. If you are one who must correct with the heavy hand, the whip, or loud shouts, you should not have a dog. Loud shouting at a dog merely rattles him into doing more wrong things. Any scolding or correction vocally must be done in a tone of command. Never be in the silly position of trying to "shout down" a little dog, nor must you correct your dog in the tone of "Please, Mister Dog, will you do this?" In all commands or vocal corrections use words as short as possible. The tonal effects will stay with the dog and that one word, always used the same way for the same thing, will strike a memory chord in your dog and he will immediately respond.

If you must punish a dog physically, be certain that you do it at the moment the dog does any misdeed, and not half an hour later, or after you have come home to find that something was torn up hours before. The dog's memory for any single action is very short, and unless you have caught him in the act of doing a misdeed, there is no use in trying to punish him. Leave him alone and consider it unfortunate that you were not on hand at the right time. Nine times out of ten the wrongdoings of the dog can be traced to the owner's fault—improper or lack of training, ignorance of dog psychology, mental or physical laziness.

Obedience is the root of all training and it must be taught by kind firmness, tact, a realization of your own share of mistakes, and regularity of training. Teach your dog one thing at a time, and move to the next lesson only after you are certain that he has learned the first one fully.

As you gain much by only punishing when it is deserved and when you have actually caught your dog in the wrong, since circumstantial evidence is worth nothing in dog discipline, so will you gain even more by immediately praising any good thing your dog has done, either on command from you or simply from past training. Your dog loves praise and will strive to earn more.

Habits in dogs, as in humans, may be good or bad, and in all cases are a matter of training or the lack of it, and the proper association of ideas and words. To have a well-behaved dog is your responsibility as a dog owner. Common sense should enable you to educate your dog to good habits.

Be consistent in all your teachings and never punish your dog for some trick that a few days before you permitted him to do because you thought it was cute and great fun. Above all, never punish your dog when your temper is out of control, for if you cannot control yourself, you surely cannot control the dog.

When your dog needs punishment, never whip him with his leash, your own hand, or anything that should be associated with the pleasures of companionship. When physical punishment seems really necessary, a rolled-up newspaper is generally considered adequate for a brief spanking (as distinguished from a cruel beating) and not likely to do any actual harm. The noise it makes from a not-too-vigorous slap across the top of the dog's hind quarters—a relatively harmless place—or on the floor just behind the dog, is usually enough, after one or two instances, to make the rolled-up paper by association a symbol of punishment and disapproval to the dog. After that the mere sight of it, or the sound of your slapping it against your own hand or on some object, will probably be enough to let the dog know that he has done wrong and make him feel punished. A reproving tone of voice accompanying the raising of the rolled newspaper will add to its effectiveness, without any actual blows.

If your dog runs away from you but returns on your call, remember that the last command was obeyed and he merits praise for the good act and forgiveness for the original bolting. Discipline at the wrong time will confuse the dog and he will lose his desire to respect your commands.

Protecting Your Belongings. Be certain to give your dog his own dishes, his own bed, and his own toys, and keep them clean at all times. If he has these things he will be more likely to leave your possessions alone. He will be, for example, far less apt to chew up slippers and stockings if he has some toy to chew that he cannot destroy and which can quickly be substituted as an alternative—with a quick, sharp *"No!"*—for the wrong object he has begun to chew; then pat him and praise him for playing with his own toy.

Curing Dogs of Jumping on People. The dog that jumps on people when they come to your residence is an annoyance, and yet it is the owner's and not the dog's fault, for that is the pup's way of shaking hands and making the visitor welcome. It is easy to break this bad habit by not allowing him to do it to you. The old trick of stepping on a dog's hind paws is worthless, for the dog can sidestep easily and you have taught nothing. To the accompaniment of a loud, sharp *"No!"*, raise your knee smartly and strike the dog in the chest. This will knock him back and often flat on his back. A few such experiences and the dog will stop, for they all learn by good or bad experiences.

Training to "Sit" and "Down". Teach your dog "sit" and "down" and use those commands often, but of course only when they mean something, and you will have cured many things. They are the sure way of keeping your dog from fawning all over your company when they arrive to visit, and the "down" is especially good in preventing your dog from running to the door and barking when someone knocks or rings the bell.

The "sit" is most easily taught with your dog on leash and wearing a chain slip collar which will tighten with the rapidity of your motion. Have your dog on your left, for that is where he belongs when he goes for a walk with you. On the command "Sit!", pull up sharply with the leash which is held in the right hand, and this shift of balance will almost always cause your dog to sit in self protection. However, if need be, use the left hand at the same time to press down on the rump. The instant that dog has the sitting position, praise him lavishly and he will think that he has done it by his own volition and will associate the command "Sit!" with an action that can earn him the much-sought praise.

The "down" also is best taught with your dog on leash, and should come after he has learned the "sit". With the dog in the sitting position,

TRAINING TO "SIT"

come out in front of him at the end of your leash, and hold this quite taut and rather close to the ground. With a sharp "Down!" and your hand raised just above the height of the dog's head, you have the dog in a position where he must move slightly forward in answer to the tight leash and must drop his head and forward part of the body to avoid your upraised hand. This combination will cause him to seek the most comfortable position and that, of course, is the natural "down".

There should be no trouble in putting over this lesson, which once learned will pay you back many times over. If you do have any trouble with the foregoing, go through the same routine of the sharp command to "down", and bring the upraised hand down smartly on the taut leash. The shock of this action will usually suffice after a few times to sell your dog the idea that it is best to seek the "down" position.

Under no circumstances praise your dog for doing this right, for there you give a command to "come" without meaning to, nor should you associate the dog's name with the command. Merely sharply order your dog to "down". Later, you will teach your dog to stay in the down position, and when you are releasing him from that, you may show your pleasure with praise.

In handling the general run of dogs, you will find that the "sit" and "down" taught properly will make your pet an unusually fine dog around your own home or to take visiting to a friend's house. You will, of course, before going visiting, have taught the dog property rights—that he may not chew other than what belongs to him.

TRAINING TO "DOWN"

Training to Collar and Leash. One of the most important items to consider in breaking in a new dog is the matter of collar and leash familiarity, so that you do not make a spectacle of yourself when out for a walk with your dog. The simplest way is to get the collar first, making certain that it fits and looks smart. Do not force the dog into the collar, but play with him and after you have it on (not too tightly) praise him for looking so smart and he will go about the house as proudly as a child with new shoes.

Give him two or three days to get accustomed to the collar before putting on the leash. Here it is best to let him become acquainted with the leash before it is attached, allow him to smell it and to know that it is a friendly thing. Then snap it onto the collar and allow him to wander a bit about the house, and pick it up quietly and walk with him to the door, so that he will associate the leash with the idea of going out.

If possible, it is best that two of the family go out with him the first few times that he has the leash attached, and treat him in one of two ways. If he is inclined to lag or drag back, have the person without the leash walk a bit ahead and encourage him to come along. If he is a "puller", then let the second person stay with you or drop a bit back.

One thing always to remember is that this collar and leash procedure is supposed to be pleasure and under no circumstances, as has already been said, should you use either in punishment, no matter how badly

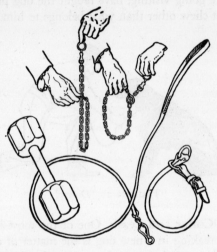

PROPER EQUIPMENT FOR TRAINING

the dog needs discipline. The leash is a working, pleasurable bit of equipment, not part of a crime school.

Take your dog for a walk, not the reverse, as nothing is so silly-looking or nerve-wracking as a tug-of-war between dog and owner, and remember that the dog has you at a disadvantage, having four legs to your two. Build up the dog's confidence in you by kindness and patience, and a desire to "do" for you because of devotion and the eager-ness for praise from you. This will give you a good start in the matter of leash-breaking as applied to walking outside. Here it is best to equip your dog with a chain slip collar of the right mesh that will slip up quickly to a tight fit if your dog is wrong. Keep your dog at your left, with the leash in the right hand, leaving the left hand free for reaching down to pet your dog for being good. This also leaves that hand free to carry bundles and to open doors.

Use a leash that is as long as you are tall, which allows enough play to correct the dog. Start out with your dog sitting at the left knee and move forward with the command "Heel!"; be sure you make it a command, and the one word will be associated in the dog's mind with being at your left. At the start always praise and pat your dog for being correct, and use the right hand for correction. If your dog lags, encourage it a bit and step up your pace so that he will think he is in danger of losing you. If he lunges ahead, snap him back with a quick snap of the wrist, and when he has come back to your left side, praise him quickly so that he will think he did it of his own volition.

Remember that the association of pats from the left hand and words of praise at the same time will make your dog want to ever be at that left side. Thus you have won your biggest step on the road to real obedience.

Training to Come When Called. The question asked dog experts most often by novice owners is "How can I make my dog come when I call him?" If you are a city dweller, you are most unwise and not a responsible dog owner if you allow your dog to be off leash and thus subject to traffic hazards and the picking up of disease germs. But if you live in the country or any place where your dog can safely be allowed out without a leash, it is best to teach your dog to come when called in the confines of your own home, or outside when you have a relatively quiet area in which to work. Because you have built up love and a desire to be with you by your earlier treatment of the dog, a good start has been made. Start in your home by the simple command "Come!", coupled with the dog's name. In most cases this will work at once, and as he comes to you, praise him lavishly and pat him. Then go off and leave him with the command "Stay", and keep doing this until he comes at every call.

If your house pet does not learn these things readily, try the exercise with your leash or with a 25-foot length of pliable clothesline. Sit or down your dog and go to the end of whatever you are using for a leash.

and if there is no response to "Come, Toby", then give a jerk on the leash and bring the dog in to you. Praise him as though he had done this of his own volition and it will not be long before he will be doing it on his own accord and free of a leash.

Obedience Training Classes. With the basic lessons in good home training you can build up any training that you wish to have your dog follow. The home pet owner of today, indeed, has better luck than those of the past in training the individual dog to be a better member of the community. For there are many communities that have an obedience training class in which the owner is taught to train his own dog in the rudiments of obedience. Where there are no such classes in the city or town, there may be one not too far away. The costs of these classes are very small, as generally they are run by other pet owners who merely charge enough to clear expenses. Most sessions last about ninety minutes and are held once a week, with no obligation on the part of the pet owner save that he train his dog by homework for about fifteen minutes a day, which is enough for the average canine youngster. A trained dog is a perfect home companion.

CARE OF SICK DOGS

The best advice that can be given the home pet owner, regardless of whether the pet is a dog or another animal, is do not try to be your own veterinarian. More dogs have been killed by the unintentional neglect of well-meaning owners than by almost any other single thing. It costs little to take your dog to the nearest good veterinarian, or to have him come to your house, and the chances are that prompt action will save your dog as well as the heartaches of the family.

You will know when your dog is right, and constant watching of the dog at home will tell you when something is amiss. If anything seems wrong, check him over carefully and if the condition is something out of the ordinary or of which you know little or nothing, call your veterinarian, and if you have none, find a reliable breeder and see whom he uses to keep his dogs in prime shape.

Possibly whatever is wrong with your dog is something you have done or failed to do yourself, and for the love of the dog, do not try to mask your own carelessness or mistakes through dishonesty of statement. Tell your veterinarian the exact condition of the dog, when it came on, and what might have caused it. That will give this skilled practitioner a head start in diagnosis and therein lies half the battle in the saving of the life of your dog.

Far too often the veterinarian is called in too late or the dog is taken to him hours, days, or weeks after he should have been, with the result that death is but a matter of hours.

If you have been a careful owner, you have pretty much guarded your dog against accident and bad health. You will have seen that he had clean, cool water at the right times, and foods that were nutritionally right for him. He will have had his proper exercises and have had his sleeping quarters out of dampness and drafts. Also, he will not have been allowed to roam free to joust with traffic (always a losing game), or to pick up the wrong sorts of food from the garbage pails of the district.

With this background and the fact that you have kept him well groomed, you will know that his resistance to infections will be great and the chances of riding off any disease that may be a current epidemic are very good.

Symptoms of Illness. As in the case of the human, oncoming sickness flies its banners if we but watch for them. In the dog the first signs of any trouble usually are the change from liveliness to listlessness, with the pup eating little or nothing, preferring to rest and really not resting at all. Eyes become glassy or staring and often are bloodshot. The gums lose their bright look of health and seem drained of blood—whitened— and the dog gets very hot in the nose, back of the ears, or both. Do not worry if the pup has a hot nose for a short space of time, but take some action if it hangs on steadily for more than a couple of hours.

Taking a Dog's Temperature. A rectal thermometer should be part of the equipment of every dog owner, as a check against outward signs of trouble. In the adult dog, the normal temperature is 100°; it is slightly higher in puppies. Begin to take action if the temperature is over the 102° mark and surely get busy when it passes 103°. The thermometer should be held in the dog's rectum for one minute, and the temperature taken about three times a day. Always be certain to make allowances for excitement, fairly recent feeding, and natural nervousness of the dog.

Vomiting. It is not necessary to be unduly alarmed if your dog vomits, for this is rarely an indication of a serious condition. It may come from some foreign substance in the intestines or stomach, and in the case of many dogs will come with bolting food too fast, creating a gas that literally blows the food out the way it came. Quite often, however, it comes because of worms, or from having eaten spoiled food.

Giving Your Dog Medicine or Pills. If for any reason you have to give medicine to your dog, do not put it in with the food in his dish, because the strange taste may make him shy away from the pan he has been trained to eat out of, in which case you will have to train him over again. Of course, if the medicine is a pill you can fold it in a piece of meat and hand it to your dog. But if you are giving it to him undisguised, first take him in hand gently and calm him down. If there is any danger that he might bite because of fear or nervousness, have someone help you. Placing your fingers in the wide gum-spaces between the teeth near the back of the jaws, open the mouth widely, and whether the medicine is a pill, capsule, or liquid, see that it gets down as deep in the throat as possible; the further back the better will be the chance of involuntary swallowing. Keep the head tipped and use your hands to close the mouth and keep it closed until the medicine has been swallowed. Stroking the outside of the dog's throat very gently often helps to stimulate his swallowing reflexes.

Few dogs like to take medicine, unless it is of an oily nature; in most cases oily medicines are lapped up with pleasure. But if the medicine is disagreeable, the owner must be firm and kind about it and not let the house pet get away with avoiding the medicine by working on sympathies that might cost the dog's life.

It is not too wise to build up a medicine chest for your pet, because this creates the tendency on the owner's part to be his own doctor. What things might be needed for minor treatments or emergencies while waiting for skilled help usually are found in the average house, anyway.

Constipation. Mineral oil and milk of magnesia are usually on hand and these are useful as light laxatives. It is well to observe your dog's stools, and if they are either too loose or too tight, it is likely to be a sign of trouble. As a rule, in the case of constipation, get your dog away from bones and give him some mineral oil or milk of magnesia, raise the amount of exercise, and give less food and more water. In really stubborn cases, use an enema; removing the blockage in this way generally quickly restores the dog to good health.

Diarrhea. In the case of bowels that are too loose, change the diet to something that tightens a bit, but first clean the dog out with castor oil or something of that nature, as it will usually be found that the cause is some intestinal irritation that needs to be removed. If the diarrhea has really got to the dysentery stage, which is indicated by a water, bloody, or mucous discharge and an exaggerated stiffness of gait, it may be on the road to gastritis, enteritis, or something similar, and the only safe thing to do is to call in your veterinarian.

Poisoning. If your dog gives indication of being poisoned in any way, take no chances on home remedies unless your veterinarian has advised you as to what to do while waiting for him.

First Aid for Injury. In the case of injury, obey the rules for handling a human—that is, move the victim no more than is absolutely necessary, for if a bone is broken, moving him may irritate the fractured area, tear muscle structure, or even cause the broken bone to puncture a vital organ. Keep the dog as quiet as possible and away from people until skilled help arrives. If a break is located on the leg by careful probing, you can wrap it spirally from the bottom, but not tightly.

In the case of heavy bleeding, apply a tourniquet or pressure in some way, meanwhile having had someone call for a veterinarian. If you have had first aid training for humans, that plus common sense can help you take care of the general run of injuries, such as the application of cold compresses for bruises, and the use of antiseptics for skin breaks or cuts. Iodine or a salt water or epsom salt solution work well, while baking soda can be used to stop blood flow, but never seal up a sore for the outlet is needed to let poisons out.

In the case of burns of any nature or scalds, again follow the procedure in treating humans, getting the affected area cleaned without too much pressure and applying vaseline, caron oil, or a raw oil. Soaked tea bags are also very efficient.

Exhaustion and Heat Prostration. If you come across an exhausted dog allow him a whiff or two of spirits of ammonia and then give him a little whiskey mixed with an equal part of water. In the case of heat prostration, move the dog into a cool place and apply cold water—but do not throw a bucketful at him.

Improvising a Muzzle. To muzzle a dog, which for some reason has bitten you, tape his jaws with one-inch gauze bandage, crossing it under and over the muzzle and tying it back of the ears.

Colds. One can well follow human treatments for coughs or cold in chest or throat. Keep the dog quiet, eliminating all but necessary exercise, increasing the amount of water given and allowing the dog to have the usual amount of food if he will take it; and give him a light laxative.

Distemper. If you keep up a good reserve of strength in the dog, there is little chance that he will get distemper, or if he does get it, that it will open the door to the other ills that befall a below-par dog after such an attack. The majority of dog breeders believe in one form or another of inoculation against distemper, which usually is given before the dog is four months old.

The most common symptoms of distemper are lack of spirit and appetite, watery eyes, a runny nose with pus discharge, a persistent dry, hot nose, and a steadily mounting fever. When this hits your dog, get him into a dry but ventilated place, keep the bowels open, and call your veterinarian.

Pneumonia. In the event of pneumonia, treat as in a human, with constant care and call in your veterinarian, the same as you would call the doctor for a member of your family. While your dog cannot talk and tell you he has it, you can feel it roaring away if you lay your hand on his chest.

Eye Trouble. With eye trouble that has no relation to other matters, wash the eyes out well with absorbent cotton, using a safe eye lotion advised by your veterinarian or your family doctor. If nothing else is available, milk works well.

Fits. It is very important to know something about fits, so that canine lives are not destroyed unnecessarily. For there is no question but what hundreds of innocent dogs have been slaughtered each year by unknowing police officers, called to the scene of a rather sad dog that is more scared than anything else by excited, misinformed citizens.

Running fits are a type of canine hysteria in no way related to rabies. They usually come from poor care or the lack of assimilation of proper food nutrients. Usually the dog will run recklessly but has one thing in mind—to go and hide in a dark place where he can feel safe. In the course of more or less blindly seeking a haven or some understanding, he will race unsteadily, often falling over with a slobbering or frothing at the mouth and a glassy stare.

A cleaning out of the system and a fast change of diet, mainly to raw, lean meat, usually clears up these fits in short order, and most dogs will grow out of it in a few months. Sometimes it comes as an indication of a serious need of worming, and in general its attack is on the nervous type of dog with digestive ailments, which may have been the cause in the first place. Here again, the safest thing to do, after quieting the pet and getting it where some misguided individual cannot shoot it, is to call the veterinarian.

Rabies. If there does appear to be any suspicion of rabies, put on thick gloves before handling your dog and tie him where he can reach no one. Remember that rabies comes *only* from the bite of a rabid dog and that other dog bites merely need ordinary care. Rabies is not confined purely to dogs. But dogs can and should be injected against rabies. If this and other methods of control were enforced by law in all parts of the country, there would be no epidemics of rabies.

The earliest symptoms of rabies in a dog are quietness and depression, with restlessness and a tendency to hide in dark places. At this time the dog's bark may become slightly higher in pitch. In the second phase of rabies, the bark becomes extremely high-pitched and the dog's voice may even crack. At this time the dog will run around in a wildly excited way and is likely to snap at anything he passes. Then follow paralysis of the lower jaw and discoloration of the tongue which nearly always hangs out, dripping saliva and mucous. The last stage of rabies consists of paralysis which starts in the hind quarters and spreads throughout the body. Coma and death usually follow.

Skin Diseases. Skin diseases are difficult to diagnose, are often contagious, and may persist stubbornly if not given the correct care. It is therefore best to consult your veterinarian, whether you suspect mange, eczema, ringworm, or any other abnormal skin condition, rather than try to treat your dog at home. Pecularities in the skin or coat may also be symptomatic of illnesses other than a disease of the skin itself. They may indicate worms, or something incorrect in the diet, for example. Only a veterinarian can be reasonably certain as to what the condition comes from and how to treat it.

CHAPTER IV

BREEDING DOGS

The breeding of dogs is one of the most fascinating of subjects, and it can be both an interesting and inexpensive hobby. It is indeed a matter for the most careful thought, and while one might call it almost an exact science, there are so many factors that enter into it, that even the most successful and scientific breeders run into problems they cannot answer before it is too late.

The general principles to follow are the same whether one is breeding one of the Toy breeds, such as the Pomeranians, or the larger breeds like the Great Danes. It should always be a concern of the person with the household pet that it is totally unwise to breed at all unless one has a purebred dog, because there is no market for other than purebreds, and thus the hobbyist faces a loss beyond the satisfaction of having arranged a mating that produces something.

MATING

Selecting a Mate. Assuming that the pet owner has secured a good female from a reputable breeder, he can always be certain of experienced advice from that person on the matter of what stud dog to use in the planned mating. Or the veterinarian to whom he takes his dog for periodic checkups will be happy to give him the best in advice.

If, on the other hand, the hobbyist has a good male dog (the male being known as the "dog", and the female known as the "bitch") the breeder and the veterinarian would be likely to know who might have a suitable female to which to breed the dog on whatever terms might be arranged. In any case, it is usually an improvement for either male or female to be bred.

Before any breeding is planned, it would be wise for the owner of the pet to study the pedigree of his male or female and thus be in a position to talk to others with the same breed, as it is much more than mere theory that breeding must be right "on paper" before it can be right any place else.

It would then be wise for the owner to ascertain who has dogs of that breed which might be used as mates, and to make certain that the matching of bloodlines is correct and that in physical respects the mating is right, as there is no sense of mating flaw to flaw and thus defeating the purpose of breeding, which is to produce something better than what you already have.

About as sure a gauge as the average uninitiated owner could obtain would be to visit nearby dog shows and go through the benching aisles to find the breed in which he is interested, and without really "tipping his hand", listen carefully, ask questions, and really find out what lines are producing the best new stock in that breed. Then he could safely go to owners having that stock and make the necessary arrangements. Frankly, there are few breeders who would, for the price of a stud fee, which may run from $25 to more than $100, offer to have one of their studs serve your female, unless they knew there was every reason to believe that the mating would produce something that would bring credit to them, as well as to you.

If you have a pet dog, and are not too well known in the dog-breeding world, you have more of a problem in arranging matings, unless you come along with an exceptional dog that would fit exactly into the breeding program that any breeder might have in mind to improve his stock and, of course, at least pay the costs of his hobby.

However, as the breeding of dogs is chiefly the concern of the owner of the female and it is his name that goes down on pedigrees as the breeder, this chapter will deal mainly with the problems of the owner who has a pet female that he would like to breed.

If the potential breeder does not have a female and is out to buy one, he should consider well the standard of the breed and buy a female that is structurally right by that standard of perfection, or at least has but minor flaws, and one with a good pedigree, decent disposition, and in good condition.

Whether it is a pet of some standing with the family, or a new one, the female should be put in the best of condition before the time for mating comes along, for the effects of condition start to tell on the makeup of the coming puppies right from the moment the breeding takes place. While the conditioning process is going on, the owner of the female should be studying the records—not show wins, but the record of what lies back of the studs available for that particular breeding—making sure that conformation, pedigree, condition, and temperament are right.

If you are breeding for the first time, and unless your female has had puppies for some other owner, do not take an unproved stud regardless of how attractive the bloodlines may appear or how fine a business deal can be made, but get a male that has a record of producing good puppies from the same bloodlines as are contained in the pedigree of your female.

If you have observed all these points you will be more than likely to get some fine pups that will not only reward you for their beauty, but stand you a good chance of getting your investment back a few times over. It must not be thought, however, that it is easy to make a living by breeding household pets. While there is big business involved in the whole matter of dogs, there are few persons who can make their living purely from breeding. The average "name" kennel is carried as a hobby, and the owners, as well as the rank and file of those in the competitive end of the sport, either count the breeding of dogs as a costly hobby, or they sell surplus stock to carry the load of expenses. However, it does no harm for any dog lover to invest the money, time, patience, and care and to "borrow" the skill of experts.

As has been stated previously, it is wise to breed a "maiden" to a proven stud, rather than gamble on an untried male. Another reason for this is that a first mating finds either party apt to be fractious and spoils chances of good results. The same rule applies to the use of your dog as a potential sire; it is always soundest policy to breed him to a female who has a record of success in producing puppies.

The Female's "Heat" Season. The owner of the female must exercise care during the period in which the pet might be bred, to avoid an unplanned mating with an undesirable dog. For in this receptive season the female, if permitted to run at large, will be attracted to dogs of any breed or mixture of breeds. Therefore, it is wise for the owner to keep his female pet under constant guard during her "season". This period, known as the time when the female is "in heat", varies in different females, but roughly lasts from eighteen to twenty-four days, is divided generally into two phases, with a gradual shift from one phase to the other, every six months. There are cases in which, after the first season, these periods come four, eight or even twelve months apart, and a female's first period usually comes at about the age of eight or ten months; but it is best to keep watch for signs of this season from the sixth month.

The season is generally preceded by a "waiting" period in which there is a small discharge from the external female organ, which increases and becomes darker as the first real phase of the period gets under way; this first phase lasts about ten days. The second phase, and that in which you as a breeder are most interested, comes when the external organ swells visibly, often to three and four times its normal size. That means that your female is truly in a receptive mood and you must confine her if you do not mean to breed at that season, or make your final arrangements for the breeding. During the early part of the season you will find that your female resents attention from dogs, while in the second phase she will go seeking them at any opportunity.

How To Plan a Successful Mating. It is important to plan the mating well enough in advance so that your female will not have passed her season before she is taken or sent to the male for breeding. The mating act is a natural function and as a rule it takes no skill to direct the process, but it is wisest, unless you know from experience that your female will not be too difficult, to hold her head until the breeding has been completed.

The most reliable breeding method is to take your female to the stud, breed her one day, skip a day, and then breed again on the third. In that way you are relatively certain that pups will be produced. In the case of females that have been missing, but are known to be sound physically, it is best, if possible, to let the male and female "live" together.

No responsible breeder will mate a female in her first season. As a rule, the breeding starts in the second or third season, preferably the latter, especially in the case of large, long-lived dogs, since they mature more slowly. It may be ruinous to breed too young a female, for the physical and nervous effects often spoil her for life.

After the first careful breeding, which generally leaves the female even healthier than before as well as producing a more equable disposition, there is only one general rule to follow for success in getting good puppies and not spoiling the mother, which is to skip a season— that is, breed only once a year. From a practical point of view also this is wise for the average home pet owner, whose quarters may have limited space for puppies, either in the house or in the yard.

It is usually true that females last longer if they have been bred now and then, and they seem to be less subject to the woes of older age. It is well not to breed when the female becomes really old, as that might shorten her life. And certainly if your female has reached middle age without having been bred, do not attempt it, as the passage of time might well be said to have made the passage of puppies dangerous— usually damaging both to the mother and the puppies.

Whatever the age of your female, play safe and have at least one experienced person on hand when any mating is to take place.

Spaying Females. If you get a female puppy and are certain that you will never want to breed her, and if you know that for some reason you will be unable to keep her guarded during the heat seasons, it is possible to have her "spayed", provided she is young enough. Spaying is an operation consisting of removing the reproductive organs. It is not harmful if performed between the ages of three and ten months, but you do run the risk of changing your dog's appearance and temperament, for in dogs that have been spayed there are often glandular changes resulting in the dog's tending to become too fat, somewhat misshapen, and lethargic.

Care of the Stud Dog. It is not likely that the average pet owner who has a dog will be bothered too much by calls for the dog's services as a stud, but there are some things to be observed in permitting him to be used for this purpose.

Although in competitions—shows, field trials, and obedience trials—males seem to be more popular than females, this is largely because a male can be used much more often as a father than the female can serve as a mother. While she may have five to, at the most, ten litters in her life, the stud dog conceivably could be used once a week or every ten days over a period of five to eight years.

If, as a pet owner, you want to increase the demand for your male as a stud, the best method is simply to do what you would do anyway as a matter of personal pride—keep your dog in good shape by seeing that he is properly fed and exercised so that he will develop good physical qualities. And while a pet owner must not expect, as has already been stated, to make a living from breeding his pet, it is possible for the owner of a good stud dog at least to get back the initial cost of the pet and the expense of his upkeep.

As to the best age at which to begin using a dog as a stud, there is individual variation. While records do show that a dog was used by accident at four months, and that many have come through at less than seven months, it is really unwise to use a dog until twelve months and then only sparingly until he has reached maturity for his breed. The larger breeds ought not to have their studs used at less than twenty months or two years. As for the upper age limit, again the records show us sires as old as fourteen and fifteen years, but the best mating time is usually ended at the age of seven or eight years.

In regard to how often a dog can be used, that, too, depends on the dog himself and also on how well you have kept him in condition so that he may be at his best to service females and produce the puppies that will create more of a demand for his services. It is generally accepted that while some dogs can be used twice a week for a short period and some are recorded as having gone to service that often for two to four years, once a week is enough to use any dog without shortening his useful life or even his entire life.

In most cases of "misses", the fault may be traced to the female, although gossip may say that your dog is not productive. Of course it nay not be the fault of either of the pair, but may simply have been an unproductive mating.

As for care of your dog, in general give him the same fine care you would even if not used at stud. Feed him that which you have found is best for his system; give him decent living quarters, free from dampness and drafts; do not quarter him with another male; and although you give him plenty of exercise on average days, let him have 24 hours off on the day that he is to be used to breed some female, and be sure that he has had eight hours' rest before use.

PREGNANCY AND DELIVERY

Care of Female during Pregnancy. The period of pregnancy in a normal female dog is roughly nine weeks, but it can run any time from the 58 to the 65 days, and often the female will carry her puppies over several extra days without any harm to the pups or herself.

While dogs are as different among themselves as are humans, there are few females that show any changes in the early stages of pregnancy. Gradually appetite increases and as a rule it becomes abnormal shortly before the litter is due to arrive. Size increases gradually and with it a slowly growing tendency to romp less, to sleep more, and to take more liquids. Nipples will enlarge and the breasts take shape.

The diet given the female during pregnancy will tell its story in the ease she has in delivery and in the quality of the pups. After all, you have had your female for some time before breeding and will know what agrees with her and what is upsetting to her or what she will refuse. A good diet may include meat and fish, either raw or cooked, depending on what she likes best; milk, broths, and stews; fresh vegetables except those high in starch, vegetable juices, and the water in which the vegetables have been cooked; biscuit made for dog consumption; and, at times, the dry cereals set on your own table. As you get down to the last week or ten days, cut out most of these items and concentrate on meats and fish.

Cod liver oil is excellent and might well do away with the need of giving laxatives at the later stages when there might be constipation. Make certain that fresh water is always available.

Above all, watch the activity of the kidneys and if these are not properly active, or even overactive, do not risk the backing up of poisons to such an extent as to spoil the unborn pups and perhaps forever ruin the health of your female: play safe and take your female to your veterinarian, or better yet, have him come and see her.

As in the case of the human mother-to-be, exercise is most important in keeping the muscles in good condition and fat off the frame. In fact, you might find it necessary to take the female for long walks on leash lest she get so sluggish that organs function too slowly for the good of the pups. This exercise may be toned down considerably as time goes on, and there should be little violent activity in the late phase of the pregnancy. Although a female might jump six-foot fences less than a week before bringing out an all-star litter, and the same female might lose her puppies another time because of getting too fat from lack of work, a happy medium is best if you are to have an ever-healthy mother and thus sturdy pups.

Delivery. In the majority of cases you will have little to do with the matter of delivery, known as whelping, for the female is born with the knowledge of what it is all about and will take better care of her pups if you let her and them alone. If there does seem to be trouble in delivery, unless you have a lot of experience, take no chances but call in your veterinarian, and a minute saved may mean the difference between life and death for mother and pups.

The puppies are delivered in an individual sac, which the female removes, and she also severs the navel cord that has been the individual life-line between the pup and her, doing so neatly in most cases. If at times the female has some trouble in taking care of sac and cord, she will need help from an experienced person.

The mother will lick each puppy until it is dry and nuzzle it around to make sure of life and of its getting to where it can nurse, and for no reason will she leave any pup until she knows either that it is all right and will live while she is out taking care of her needs, or that it is beyond her help or yours.

Do not handle a newborn pup unless you have to do so, for there are far more puppies killed by human handling than ever were killed by the mothers' carelessly lying on them. You have done your share as a rule, if you have provided the mother with quarters which are comfortable, warm, dry, and free of all drafts.

Of course, you will have added a bit more of comfort by making certain that the bitch has been given warm milk or broth from time to time during the whelping period. If there is much time between pups, the female will lap up a good dish of milk between "acts", but if they come fast, she will have no time for her own self and little use for seeing you or anyone else around.

The female has but one thing on her mind at that time, which is to try to bring into this world her whole litter, in good shape, and as expeditiously as possible, that she may have the further joy of nursing her brood, and woe betide the human that ventures to interfere *unless* the mother knows help is needed.

CARE OF NEW-BORN PUPPIES

General Care of Puppies. To start with, the care of the young puppies is practically the exclusive job of the mother, and the owner's share is mainly that of taking the best care of the mother, that she in turn may do the best for her pups.

Continue to make sure that the sleeping quarters are warm and dry and free of drafts, and that there is plenty of nourishing food for the mother, who will gradually switch from a main desire for milk, water, broth, and other liquids, until she is eating almost at the rate and style that she followed in the voracious days before the puppies came. Keep the meat and fish content high, with an ample supply of cod liver oil which helps act as a cold preventive as well as a laxative.

The pups' eyes are closed when they are born and remain that way until they are nine or ten days old. If, by chance, they should not be open by the fourteenth day, wash them very carefully with warm water. Up until then you will have done nothing for them except to move them as you keep the bed in the whelping box perfectly clean, and tend to the care and exercise of the mother that she may be able to do her best by them. Of course, you will have watched them to see that they are exposed to no infections of any kind; but rather than try to be

THE MOTHER DOG WILL CARE FOR HER YOUNG

doctor yourself, when something appears wrong, call in your veterinarian.

Weaning. As a rule puppies will nurse from their mother for four or five weeks, and some will try to do so as long as you will permit them. It is becoming more of an accepted practice to wean them sooner than in the old days, both to save an extra strain on the female and to get other food elements into the puppies more quickly. You can quickly tell when it's time to take more care yourself by the fact that the mother leaves them for longer periods.

It's easy to wean pups, for when they begin to get out of their crawling, hitching-along way of moving, they will wobble and stagger about investigating what they can. If by then you have not started them off by dipping their noses into warm milk, you had best do so, and if you should leave some of the mother's feeding, as long as it has no heavy meat or kibble in it, in a dish they cannot readily tip, you will find the sight and smell will attract them and they will dip in, come back out and lick their chops, and more than likely dive back in and try to get more than is quite good for them.

At six weeks or so, you can start giving them a little raw, scraped beef that is fat-free, always feeding in proportion to size. From then on, you can keep adding new things to their diet, being sure more or less to copy that diet on which you have found the mother did well, except, of course, for the heavy portions. The best system is to feed puppies sparingly but often, for this minimizes gas troubles due to overeating, and they will surely overstuff themselves if permitted to do so.

Keep their dishes very clean, scalding them after each feeding so as to lessen the peril of germs and natural infections, and be certain that cool, clean water is often available. Far better to have wet places to mop up than sick pups to pick up.

Training Very Young Puppies. There is little you can or need do in the line of training your pups when they are very tiny and just be-

The Correct Way to Lift a Puppy

The Incorrect Way
to Lift a Puppy

ginning to wobble about, especially as they are with their mother, who will gradually teach them to foul further and further away from their bed.

You should, of course, by now have divided the whelping box into two sections, divided by a board high enough to let the mother get away from the pups; the height of the board should be raised as the pups can move better. The female can thus keep her eye on them and get back to take care of them readily.

It is best along about this time to start paying attention to individual pups and, as fast as they seem about to soil or wet, usually after eating or sleeping, pick them up and put them on paper, being sure to move them in a certain route so that they will get into the habit, and before you know it they will at least keep their home clean.

The old theory that dogs should be lifted up by the scruff of the neck has long since been discredited. It is a much sounder and safer method to lift your pet by placing one hand securely under his chest, with the middle fingers between his forelegs, and the other hand under his hind quarters. Hold your dog as close to your body as possible to avoid strain on his back.

Depending on the weather and ground conditions, you can put them out of doors for their eliminations at the right time and thus build in them the knowledge that there is a right place for everything. You thus prepare them for their lives in other homes when it comes time for them to leave you and go to the homes of friends or other persons who will have bought or been given such of your litter as your quarters do not permit you to keep.

If you have taught them to eat properly and taught them house manners, at least so far as their own quarters are concerned, you will have given them a good start in life and will have built a fine reputation for yourself for raising healthy, clean puppies.

Any other information that you might need on training can be found in the section on general training of dogs, but of course remember that in this case you are dealing with an "infant" dog.

CHAPTER V

DOG SHOWS AND OTHER COMPETITIONS

The casual dog owner has begun to realize that dogs of the very breed in which he is interested meet in some form of competition very frequently. The various types of contests are designed to prove the worth of the dogs, showing that a changing civilization, while wiping out most of the work for which the breeds were developed, has not robbed the dog of his brains and working ability. The contests consist of dog shows, obedience trials, field trials, sledge dog races, and whippet and greyhound racing.

The development of these contests, which involve but a small fraction of the dog population of the United States, has resulted in giving the general public a chance to buy a far healthier, happier, smarter dog than in years gone by.

RACING

Greyhound and Whippet Races. There is but one type of dog contesting that is primarily professional and geared along the lines of horse-racing. This is the Greyhound and Whippet racing conducted at various tracks throughout the country where state laws permit the running and some form of betting. As in the case of horses, there are also amateur groups that conduct a few races a year. To see the speedsters in these competitions skimming over the ground is to see poetry in motion.

DOG RACING IS A POPULAR SPORT

Sledge Dog Races. The northern sections of the United States, in the years before World War II, had developed a fine series of sledge

SLEDGE DOGS PREPARING FOR A RACE

dog races. Thousands journeyed on ski trains each weekend to watch these powerful dogs. The development of this sport provided the American armed forces with invaluable aides that hauled needed supplies to isolated mountain and snow-bound troops.

At the present time, owners are reforming and retraining their strings and the most thrilling sledge races of all time are in the making, with an International Sledge Dog Derby being planned for the not too distant future. These races are not held entirely with purebreds, as owners are ever experimenting in the crossing of various breeds to produce speed without the sacrifice of stamina. The result will be many more units that can be used in the saving of life in the wastelands of the North where other modes of transport fail.

Basically the sledge dog teams are made up of Alaskan Malemutes, Eskimos, and Siberian Huskies, with judicious use of crossings of these breeds. Some of these sledge breeds have made notable records in show competition, proving that beauty and brawn may well be combined.

FIELD TRIALS

There is an increasing number of people and dogs taking part in the various large and small field trials of the country. These trials have been developed to fit the purposes of the breeds, and nearly every section of the country holds major or minor trials in the various breeds.

Field trials provide thrills for the galleries that come to watch them, often standing through heat or cold, fair or foul weather, entranced by seeing the dogs doing in competition an approximation of that which they would do under actual hunting conditions. And through these trials, sturdy strains that can do well in the field have brought to the buying public healthier, happier dogs that will make better pets for children or adults.

Beagle Trials. It is likely that there are more dogs and people involved in the Beagle trials than in any others, for the calendar is filled each spring and fall with a host of Beagle trials lasting from one to five days, the time being needed to run the huge entries of the various classes in the 13-inch and 15-inch varieties of the merry little hounds.

The trials are run on likely rabbit grounds, quite often leased from farmers, posted to prevent shooting and stocked under legal requirements where there are not enough rabbits to provide a good trial. Guns are not used in such a trial, nor is the Beagle expected to catch the rabbit. It is the intelligence of the run, the use of nose, and the "tongu-ing" at the right moments that wins these trials.

Dachshund and Coonhound Trials. The low-slung Dachshund, in all three coat varieties—smooth, wire-haired, and long-haired, has a type of competition similar to the Beagle. The work of this breed, per-formed with speed unbelievable in such a body, justifies the dog's name which, translated from the German, is "badger hound". Game as they come, independent and intelligent, the Dachshund through its field trial work has proved its right to be classed as more than a pet. The qualities that make this breed good in the field also make it an ideal pet for apartments and small homes.

Coonhound trials are popular to the extent that prizes are high and stiff prices are paid for winning stock or its progeny. Competition in this line is one of the oldest in the United States and came about through the boasting of farmers and sportsmen that this or that one had the best Coonhound. Much thought has gone into the breeding of the dogs used for this purpose.

Retriever Trials. There is great interest in Retriever trials, and few events for dogs attract as much attention as the National Champion-ships, which are held late in the year under conditions that well prove the stamina of these breeds. The Golden Retriever, of Russian origin and English development, in spite of small numbers, has been turning in its share of wins. The Labrador Retrievers, both black and yellow, have been dominant factors in the field for years, and like the Goldens have also done extremely well in the show end of the dog sport. The Chesapeake Bay Retriever, one of the very few breeds to have orig-inated in the United States, has also made a grand record.

The Flat-coated and the Curly-coated Retrievers have been mainly held for private hunting expeditions, while other good retrieving breeds, such as the Irish Water Spaniel, the Poodle, and the Weimaraner, seldom go into major competitions.

Pointer and Setter Trials. The big money competition in field trials comes in Pointers and Setters, with the English Setter dominating the long-haired dogs, although here and there devotees of the Irish Setter have come through with some excellent dogs. Few events are as thrill-ing as the trials where the wide ranging dogs must be followed by horse. The ability thus to range and later to find and hold game, sometimes for long periods of time, wins trials and championships and creates columns of newspaper and magazine comment.

It is of interest that a large share of the competing field is made up of doctors and other professional men, who find in these high-grade

FIELD TRIALS OF SKILL ARE EXCITING

dogs of the field a relaxation from the cares of their work. Nearly all maintain some house dogs as constant companions.

Spaniel Trials. The Brittany Spaniel, a French breed which has been known for centuries abroad, are now prominent in American field trials. Sportsmen in this breed have seen to it that their field trial dogs can also compete in the breed shows. The Brittany, although called a Spaniel, might better from his style of working in the field be termed a Setter.

From coast to coast and North to South there are a host of trials for the English Springer Spaniels and the Cocker Spaniels, the work required being perhaps the closest of all gun-dog trials to actual conditions the owner would meet if out for a day's hunting with his dog. In the location of game, the intelligence of handling and the retrieving of game after the guns have brought it down is a joy to behold, which is why galleries are ever growing and each year sees members of that gallery graduate into the competitive field.

Advantages of Field Trials. Field trials have not alone provided joy for the owners of the competing dogs and the galleries that follow each type of trial, but they have resulted in a boon to the average owner of a dog of these breeds.

The trials are in a sense a proving ground which shows the breeding that must be done to develop greater stamina and more intelligent use of natural talents. All of the dogs thus bred cannot be run in field trials and the buying public reaps the benefit by being able to buy a sounder, smarter dog.

All of the breeds used in these trials, because of generations of breeding to present a better working dog and more close association to the wishes of humans, bring up a fine line of pets. Potential obedience is bred into them, and as a rule the buyer of such a dog for a pet comes away with something of which he and his family may well be proud. This is especially true if the proper-sized breed has been selected.

Perhaps this is best illustrated by the fact that the Cocker Spaniel is by far the most popular of all breeds in the United States, being adaptable to city apartment dwelling and seemingly not harmed by the confinement that would ruin a larger dog. The breeders who led this breed from far back in the field to the number one place in registrations it has held for the last few years started out to produce a dog that would look well in the show ring and do well in the field. They wound up giving the public a very charming dog that could live anywhere.

OBEDIENCE TRIALS

The fastest growing phase of the dog sport has been the Obedience Trials, with their appeal to young and old alike, as witness the huge throngs that gather about the trial rings during dog shows. These events have had a great effect on the buying public, which desires a dog of a breed they have seen do well in these utilitarian tasks.

Placing a premium on intelligence and temperament, and at the same time preserving the classic lines of the breeds, sound breeding has made possible the purchase of dogs inherently sound in all ways.

Training for Obedience Trials. A further benefit to the potential buyer is the fact that these dogs are trained in more or less public classes, and few dog owners live so far away that they cannot, one evening a week, reach the nearest training class, where for a modest fee the owner can learn to train his own dog.

This work is usually done under the teaching of an amateur hobbyist who remembers personal problems with dogs and wishes to help others. The training has such wholesome effects on dogs that in many

MAKING A HIGHJUMP AFTER RETRIEVING A DUMBBELL

cities there have been classes started by the local humane societies. The New York City classes initiated by the American Society for the Prevention of Cruelty to Animals is a notable example of an open class for adults, as is the class for children only at Hartford, Connecticut, under the Connecticut Humane Society.

There are no tricks in the work or the competition that has developed in these lines, nor are members of the classes required to go into open competition. It is likely that less than 15 percent of trainees do take part in tests, but the whole community benefits from the training.

Representatives of more than 90 percent of the recognized breeds have taken part in training and over 75 percent have made good in trial competition. This has been proof of the fact that modern breeding has not "bred the brains" out of dogs and that therefore it is perfectly safe for any dog lover to have a purebred dog as a pet in today's complex civilization.

BROAD JUMPING SHOWS SKILL AND DEVELOPMENT

Rules of Obedience Trials. The present setup of obedience rules calls for heeling on and off leash, stand on command, coming when called, sitting when the owner stops, a minute sit and a three minute down with the owner at a distance but in sight. The work, except for the long sit and down, is done individually in the ring, while the sit and down is done with six or more dogs in the ring at the same time. Scoring 85 or better of a possible 100 three times in the Novice class leads to the Companion Dog degree.

The work in the Open classes, where 220 of a possible 250 scored three times leads to the Companion Dog Excellent degree, is more exacting. Besides heeling on and off leash, the dog must drop at owner's signal as it comes on call. In addition the dog must retrieve a dumbbell thrown first on the flat and then over an obstacle graduated to the dog's size, make a broad jump on command, and then, with the other dogs in the ring and the owners out of sight, sit for three minutes and down for five minutes.

The Utility class work calls for "speaking" (barking) on command in the sitting, down, and standing positions; picking out of a pile of objects leather, wood, and metal objects belonging to the owner; seeking

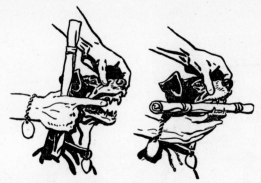

THE DOG MUST HOLD THE RETRIEVED ARTICLE GENTLY IN HIS MOUTH

back for a lost article; standing for examination similar to the show ring; and making a graduated hurdle and bar jump on command. Passing the Utility work three times at 180 or better of a possible 200

EVEN THE SMALL BREEDS ARE SPORTY

and the attaining of a passing mark in tracking, gives the dog the master degree of obedience, Utility Dog.

Tracking's practical aspects rest in the fact that a dog so trained can be a valued police adjunct for the finding of lost persons, and many a lost person has been saved from exposure through the work of these dogs. In the test classes the dog must follow a trail, made by a stranger, one-quarter of a mile long and at least 30 minutes old, and find an object left at the end of the trail.

Value of Obedience Trials. Master degrees in obedience have been secured by dogs from all six of the variety groups, including the tiny toys, which often meet the huge working dogs on even terms and beat

USING A LEASH WHEN FIRST TRAINING A DOG TO JUMP OVER A BAR

them. All of which is an answer to the repeated complaint, "I like that breed to look at, but I don't think they have much sense." Obedience trials have proved to the world that brains and beauty can go together, and that it is the individual dog that counts. Bought from a reputable breeder or dealer, bred down from healthy and intelligent stock, the dog's breed, land of origin, size, color, or coat do not count half as much as the purity of breeding.

The same principles that make for success in obedience are the ones that make for success in the relation between the household pet and his

AFTER PATIENT TRAINING A DOG WILL JUMP OVER A BAR UNASSISTED

owner. It is a matter of understanding between owner and dog, perfect teamwork, patience, kindly discipline, and health-guarding care.

DOG SHOWS

Purpose of Dog Shows. Dog shows are the window-dressing for the breeders of dogs and for the sport as a whole, and, like the cattle, horse, and poultry shows, are the proving-ground of the success of the breeding methods followed by this or that one, as well as of the buying sense of the exhibitor who is not in a position to breed his own dogs.

There is no question but that were it not for the several hundred shows approved by the American Kennel Club, there would be very few top-grade dogs in the hands of the pet owner who wishes a good dog. These shows, held indoors in major cities during the winter months and on attractive sites in parks or private estates in the milder months, attract a total of well over a million persons, who are out to see the best in dog flesh.

The shows themselves are not money-makers, except in rare instances, but they do provide the chance for exhibitors and breeders to compare notes, via the decisions of the judges licensed to do the various breeds. Exhibitors are anxious to chalk up the wins at these shows, knowing that the prestige not only is flattering but makes more valuable the breed stock on hand and possible progeny from the winners.

Through the publicity accruing from wins at these shows, the gen-

PERFORMING BEFORE THE JUDGE AT AN OUTDOOR SHOW

eral public comes out to see the dogs of all national origins and either remains to buy something good in the pet line, because the properly handled and groomed show dog is one of the most attractive animals in the world and hard to resist, or goes home, talks it over with the family, and then buys a dog. For these reasons the dog show is invaluable to buyer and breeder alike.

Kinds of Shows. Generally speaking, dog shows are of three types: sanctioned matches, specialty shows, and all-breed. Each has its place in the scheme of things. The sanctioned event may be either merely of a puppy nature, limited within one breed or open to all; or it can be limited to one breed with all ages admitted; while the most popular is the all-breed, all age match. In no case do the winners receive any points toward the much coveted championship that adds untold value to a dog and its get.

The purpose of the sanctioned event is three-fold: to maintain active interest within a club that runs a point show once a year; to give puppies and other untried stock a chance to acquire ring manners and do away with possible fears of seeing many people; and to attract more attention to dogs in the community where the show is held.

JUDGING AN OPEN CLASS

Being held in a more leisurely manner and under less strain, the match event rubs the nervousness out of beginning exhibitors and makes them ready to take their part in the major shows.

The specialty show is one that is held by a single breed club, where dogs may acquire points toward their bench show championships. As a rule, a class win taken at a specialty show means much more to the winner and people associated with or interested in the breed than a much higher win would mean in that breed, when the classes are part of an all-breed show. Here, without the confusion of other breeds being about, and interest concentrated on the one breed, the judging usually means more and the beginner can learn much more of his breed than in an all-breed show.

The all-breed member or licensed show is the key of the dog show structure. The several hundred that are held throughout the country every year run in entries of two hundred to more than 2,500, the latter being the marks hung up every year by the Westminster Kennel Club event at Madison Square Garden, New Work. The world record entry for a dog show was the 4,456 dogs drawn for the last pre-war Morris and Essex show at Madison, New Jersey.

Valuations of dogs at these shows run on a conservative figure of from $25,000 to well over a million dollars, and wins at these shows

THE WINNER OF A SPECIALTY CLASS

will hike the values of certain dogs and losses will drop the ratings of others.

In the majority of all-breed point shows, breed classification is given the majority of the breeds recognized as eligible for competition in the United States. It is from the points won at these shows that dogs may win their championship titles. Unlike other sports, the purebred dog cannot walk out of one show as a champion, even by defeating a dozen other champions.

Points. It requires fifteen points to make a bench show title, no more than five points may be taken at any one show, at least three wins of three points or better must be included in the fifteen-point total, and these "three-or-better" points must come from at least two different judges, which is a fairer valuation of a dog.

The championship points are won in competition within a dog's own breed and sex. The points in each sex are graduated in accordance with the entry that must have been defeated in taking either winners dogs, or winners bitches.

The majority of the breeds cannot bring out too high an entry in a given spot and so the American Kennel Club has assigned them the following scale: two entries in the sex, one point; three entries, two

DETERMINING THE "POINTS"

points; four entries, three points; five entries, four points; six entries, five points.

The breed demanded to have the greatest sex entries to attain points is the Boston terrier, which must have seven entries for one point, twelve entries for two points, seventeen entries for three points, thirty entries for four points, and forty-five entries for five points.

At the present time there are two ways in which a dog may acquire a larger number of points than those rated by the size of the entry in his sex in his breed. The first comes when the winners dog meets the winners bitch for the best of winners award, allowing this victor to go in against any specials for best of breed. If the dog has acquired no points and can defeat the winners bitch who has taken five points, the dog acquires five points at no loss to the bitch.

The second way to make points above breed and sex rating is to come through the classes of the breed, accomplish the rare feat of going on to take best of breed and then winning the variety group. Such a winner would automatically be given the highest number of points that there were within any of the breeds represented in that variety group.

Operating in reverse, a dog could go through to best of show many times and never attain a championship point, purely through having been entered only for specials and not in the classes.

Classes. To earn the chance at championship points through the regular channels a dog must have won one of the classes in the sex. These classes in each sex are: Puppy, Novice, American-bred Limit and Open. The puppy classes are for those youngsters of six to nine months and another class for nine months to one year, in the larger entry shows where the class can be divided; otherwise the puppy class may be entered by any purebred pup of the breed, from six months to one year old.

The winners of these classes then meet to have the judge pick the winners dogs, which gets the points allowable for the day. The arbiter also selects a reserve, which would automatically move up and take the winners points if any infraction of rules caused the winner to be disqualified. The judge then goes over the same classes for females and having picked his winner, brings them together for best of winners.

If there are any dogs entered for "specials only", and these are usually champions or star dogs kept under cover, these meet the best of winners for best of breed honors. At the same time, other judges are going over their breeds, and when completed, all of the breed or variety winners within the one variety group meet, under generally another judge, who picks the first, second, third and fourth.

Gradually working toward the apex of the pyramid, the winners of each of the six variety groups then are judged for the best of show honors. If the winner here happens to be a foreign-bred dog, the best American-bred in each of the groups meets rivals for the title of being the best American-bred in the show. In neither case is there a runnerup for these honors, for there is no second in dog show finals.

Entering a Show. Every dog entered in a purebred dog show must be registered with the American Kennel Club or "listed". By this latter term is meant that the dog is a purebred, eligible for registration, and very likely the proper papers are in the process of going through proper channels. A "listed" dog may be shown only three times before a registration certificate comes through.

Each of the shows puts out its own premium list, to which is attached a standard entry blank, with the address of the individual club given in the heading. As a rule, the blank denotes how the entry fees are to be paid and where the entry and its check is to be sent. At the present time

THE WINNER OF "THE BEST OF SHOW"

entry fees for most shows stand at $3.25, with an extra 25 cents for "listed" dogs.

At the left of the blank must be inserted the breed class to be entered and the sex. In the main body, opposite the class and sex entry, one enters the name of the dog's breed, its color, the name of the registered owner, the name of the dog, Registration Number given by the American Kennel Club, date of birth, country of birth, the name of the breeder, the name of sire, the name of dam.

At the bottom of the blank, the owner signs his name, gives his address, and names the professional or public licensed handler who may handle the dog in the event that the owner himself is not going to do it. Having gone back and checked to see that all entries are correct, enclose your blank in a properly addressed envelope to the show superintendent, and play safe on acceptance by mailing it ten days before the show; six days prior to the show the blank must be in the proper office.

If your entry is accepted, you will get an identification card with your bench number, in case the show is benched. You will also get a program of the show, which will tell you what time you are required to arrive at the show site and what time your breed goes on to be judged.

Should you have a desire to follow the shows, give your name and correct address to the show superintendent and you will get entry blanks from all the shows he runs.

The class in which you should enter your dog may change from time to time. There are people experienced in your breed who will advise you as to the correct class to enter your dog. You can keep your dog in the Puppy class up to the time that it is one year old, although, if it develops well, it might be well to move over to another class.

The Novice class is for dogs six months or over, born in the United States or Canada, who have never won a first prize in any class other than puppy classes, and includes taking winners.

The American-bred class is for dogs six months or over, barring champions, whelped in the United States of a mating consummated in the United States.

Limit classes are for all dogs, except champions, that have never won six firsts in this class prior to the closing of entries for the show in question.

The Open classes are for dogs six months or over, including champions, but in member specialty or one-breed shows that are limited to American-breds, foreign-breds may not compete.

Preparing for Shows. Preparation for a dog show actually consists of preparing the owner, especially until the owner has become a veteran of the show circuits. First there is the need of making certain that the entry blank has been made correctly and mailed in to the proper superintendent. Then one has to check connections between home and the show and in case of needing to stay overnight to make sure of reservations.

You should have a "show bag" for the things you and the dog will need at the show. Above all, make certain that into that bag or your pocket goes your show identification. You will want to take along your show lead, the type best suited for your type of dog, and a benching chain to secure your dog to his stall in shows that are benched. Don't forget your dog's brush, and if he is of the breeds that need combing, take along his comb. If he is accustomed to eating during the hours that you will be gone, take along a can or package of his food and a feeding dish, because it is not always possible to obtain dishes or food at a show.

As to preparation of your dog for the show, there are few general rules that will cover every breed, beyond the rules of common sense, which in the case of most breeds you will have followed in your day

RELAXING BETWEEN CLASSES

by day routine of taking proper care of your family pet. You will have kept him from too much exercise and given him extra feedings if he has become a little thinner or lighter than the breed standard demands. And you will have given him less food and more exercise if he has taken on too much poundage. A little too much here and there is a deterrent to the dog quite as much as to a bathing beauty.

To help your dog to stand and move right, you will have kept his nails trimmed back properly, for too long nails will destroy the balance the dog needs to "keep on his toes". By daily groomings, and any owner can find 15 minutes a day to work on a dog's coat, you will have helped the coat to look shiny and alive, and of course that same grooming will have done more to keep him clean than a series of baths, which might be ruinous. Of course, if your dog is white or partly white, you can clean up the white by a bath the day before, but generally, if there is not too much white, you can prepare the dog at the show by rubbing in and then brushing out powdered chalk.

Unless one is an expert, the coat of a dog that needs trimming, clipping, or plucking can be ruined by inexpert practice and it is far cheaper to take your dog to the nearest professional in the line and pay for a job that will have your dog in show shape as far as coat is rated. Many times dogs have been put in such coat conditions by inexpertness of handling that it has taken six months or more to put the appearance back where it belongs.

It is always best to take time to study when at a show, to find why this or that professional handler wins with his dog, or why an amateur

DAILY TRAINING PRODUCES THE WINNERS

with winning habits comes through in your breed. Not alone do you see expert ring showmanship and the getting of the most out of a dog, but you will see a dog put down in the best of condition and with the coat perfectly groomed.

You can always walk into the handlers' tent and by standing out of the way you can see how the expert works on his dogs from start to finish. From this observation you can learn how to put down your dog, but don't practice on your dog until you are sure you know what you are doing.

A dog going into the shows should be "show posed" daily, in accordance with the best traditions of its breed. Take about fifteen minutes each day to set him up, talking to him quietly to put him at ease. If this is done, by the time he makes his show appearance, it's all easy to understand and you and he will make a better impression.

Watch the winners and copy their way of doing with members of your breed, both in posing them and in moving them for the judge. Practice at home what you have seen in the ring and then both you and your dog will be more at ease in show appearances.

There is a thrill to show competition, because there is hardly anything in the world with more living beauty than the hundreds of well-groomed, beautifully posed dogs, or more flowing grace than a good dog in action of being gaited in the show ring. There is no mystery to it—merely the matter of having a good dog of fine stock and the patience for proper preparation.

Thus do the breeders and exhibitors fill the show windows of the world of the dog and through them see which are the best-looking specimens per the standard of perfection for the breed, and give the potential buyers a preview of what can be expected at the breeding kennels of the country, and what you might expect from a given mating within a breed.

The preparations means something to your dog, too, for the average dog, like the average child, likes to "show off" and knows that he is on exhibition. So much do the dogs like this exhibitionism that they mope if the owner packs the usual show bag and doesn't take them along.

CHAPTER VI

ORIGIN OF DOGS AND HISTORY OF THEIR DOMESTICATION

Among the earliest recorded evidence of the existence of dogs are rude carvings in the tombs of the Pharaohs, indicating that even in those days dogs resembling the Afghan hound or the Saluki were well known and cherished for their value in the hunt. Indeed, it has been told for thousands of years that the men of the desert would sooner give up their wives than their hounds, because they might readily acquire another wife, but a dog was a saver of life and a securer of food.

Later research and excavations in other lands may bring to light evidence of some breeds that were used at an earlier date for either hunting or guard duty, but at the present moment it is generally accepted that either the Afghan hound or the Saluki was the first breed to be domesticated and bred in the form which we know today.

There is confusion in regard to other breeds, for the rough bone scratchings found in delvings into ancient civilizations can be interpreted to mean the origins of many of the breeds which we know today. But we know, at least, that basic breeds of dogs, in their wild stage, existed when man was still far removed from recorded history.

It is generally agreed that the first picture showing dogs was found in the Tomb of Amten, in Egypt, believed to have been built between 3500 and 4000 B.C., and these were of the "gaze-hound" type. There are other ancient monuments in both Egypt and Assyria, which include dogs in depicting characteristic scenes of the age.

Some of the earliest books in the Old Testament of the Bible mention dogs, and from the more than thirty references to the dog in the Bible, it can be gathered that in those days there was a wide differentiation in type and breed, showing that the association of man and dog was well established at that time. Nothing as yet has come to light proving when man first set about domesticating the dog and turning him to practical utilitarian purposes; however, it is known that the dog was the first animal domesticated by man.

HOW THE FIRST DOGS SERVED MAN

As might be expected, the first dogs used by man were apparently trained for use in the hunting field, when hunting was not a sport but a necessity if there was to be much for the humans to eat. Undoubtedly the huntsmen for tribes, finding that these wild animals "beat" them in getting valued food, started out to trap and kill the wild dog, in order to leave a free field for man. The folk lore of many lands touches on this subject, but no authority has yet pinned the credit on the first man to reason that it would be smarter not to kill these wild dogs, but to capture and train them to work for man in the pursuit of game.

Anyone who has come in contact with wild dogs knows how crafty they can be and what a task it must have been to capture the first of them alive, and how much more of a job it was to civilize and train the dog to serve man.

History, written and otherwise, tells us of flocks of sheep and herds of cattle, and that where there was any semblance of order, the work of tribes and peoples had three main divisions: first, the rude tilling of the soil, originally done by hand and then with rude implements drawn by the ancestors of our oxen and horses; secondly, hunting for extra meat, and to that task were assigned the bravest and the smartest hunters, who already then (which was at least 5000 years ago) had the help of dogs; and thirdly, tending the flocks and the herds, and it is supposed that while centuries saw the wild dog as one of the perils of the flocks and herds and their shepherds and herdsmen, eventually some of the older "tamed" dogs that had been used by the huntsmen were allowed to stay with the live stock to ward off attacks from the wild dogs. Fierce pride of ownership made these dogs keen in repelling all animals that would do harm to their charges, and eventually all flocks and herds had their quota of dog guardians.

In the course of doing the new work, the lines of the dogs changed, and as man moved from place to place, he came across other dogs that were of different basic crosses, and by breeding the old hunting stock to these heavier dogs, the heavier shepherding breeds that we know today came into being.

It is said that man, and with him the dog, moved ever westward from Egypt, Assyria, and way stations, and with him went his flocks and his herds. Raiders would cut into these migrating tribes or bands, cut out as much of the stock as they could and take with them the guarding dogs; thus the dog stock of various sections became crossed and we get our many ancient breeds.

However, those who claim man always traveled westward have forgotten that there is a cut in from further east and north, for many thousands of years before Christ there were peoples in what we know as China and Tibet. China can well lay claim to having the most ancient breed, the Chow Chow, which served for centuries as a hunting, herding, and sledge dog, and which has had its effect on many of the other breeds which we know today. Tibet gave the world one of the basic breeds in the old Tibetan Mastiff, a big, powerful, awe-inspiring dog that is the ancestor of the majority of the larger shepherd and guardian types of dog that have been known in Europe for many centuries. In fact it is quite likely that the large majority of the nearly thirty working breeds recognized in the United States today stem back to Tibet's big mastiff.

Somewhere in the days of unwritten history, the migrators from Egypt and the Middle East crossed the trail of wandering bands from Tibet and China, and as the humans crossed, so did their dogs, and that is why we can see in many breeds structural evidences of the ponderous mastiff and the speedy dogs of the desert.

In time, man moved on to the midlands of the present Europe, bringing with him some dogs which were adapted to the needs of the country, and others which developed themselves to fit into the environment. The difference in coat density to cope with weather conditions was nature's own way of aiding these animals which were so necessary to the existence of those days. Man did the rest in breeding only the strongest, the fastest, and the most sagacious specimens.

Man also trained his "best friend" to handle the herding and guarding duties of the particular country, and each one had its own problems that had to be met in a different way. Several centuries ago, man used his head well enough to know that the handling of herds and flocks needed two types of dogs, and to this day in many countries it will be found that the large, slow moving direct descendants of the Tibetan mastiff are used for the actual guardianship duties, while a smaller, faster dog was used in the herding detail, able to cut back and bring up stragglers and to sound the alarm of danger from a distance.

It is evident that even in the Middle Ages, they knew something of breeding, and that they handled the two-way job in different ways. Sometimes they bred down from the big dogs, either using the smaller specimens of the breed and creating a still smaller dog of the same type; or else they crossed the standard herding dog of the country with a smaller local breed or, going outside and picking up likely stock with which to create the size of dog desired for the fast work.

There are other examples that show no relationship whatever between the guard dog and the herding dog, and it can be assumed that wandering bands brought in these dogs from the outer world, very likely having stolen them.

The ancient breeders knew what they wanted for utilitarian purposes and bred until they arrived at their goal. Man went on in this fashion, and then with type established, he stopped, and we have those breeds today. Such breeding for practical purposes has gone on steadily, and each of the known breeds today was created for some specific reason, with the youngest of the present-day utility dogs going back more than sixty years, while others are re-creations of old breeds.

DEVELOPMENT OF PRESENT-DAY BREEDS

The development of breeds was not always along the lines of dogs to meet the working needs in guardianship and herding, for the huntsmen of various tribes were busy, too, making new breeds to cope with the wild game situations as they changed from one area to another. And so from the speedy dogs of the desert, the Afghan hound, the Saluki, and the Greyhound came the many sporting and hound breeds that we know today, the vast majority of which are able to trace their ancestry back 100 years to untold centuries.

In some cases these hunting dogs show traces of the Chow Chow; others, of variations of crosses down from the dogs of the desert, often crossed back to the smaller breeds that had come from the dog of Tibet. It is believed that these varied hunting breeds were more developed by man's watching the dogs hunt in their own way and breeding to take advantage of native abilities.

Dogs living along salt or fresh water were basically what we know as retrievers, while others were accustomed to getting their food by catching game on the ground. Man then went to work to slow down these dogs and trained them to get the game and bring it to the owner, rather than devour it themselves. The dogs that were adept at game location and flushing were taught to point and hold game until the master could come up for the kill.

All dogs were originally hunters, and many breeds that have been turned to other purposes or bred down in size—often from more than fifty pounds to a mere five today—frequently revert to type and do a grand bit of work in the field, or else can be trained so to do. Game sense and nose has not been bred out of all breeds with the passage of time.

The retention of nose is proved today by the variety of breeds which take part in and pass the tracking tests which are a "must" if a dog is to acquire the coveted U.D.—Utility Dog—degree. It is understandable that sporting and hound breeds might be expected to pass such a test and that the working breeds should come through on the basis of their ancestry.

The records show that representatives of all six variety groups have earned their U.D. and wound up in a blaze of glory on the basis of creditable tracking. The classic example is that of a five and one-half pound Pomeranian turning in one of the most perfect bits of tracking seen in recent years. This feat was partly training and partly a reversion to ancient type, for the Pomeranian came down from the work dogs of Pomerania, which in turn descended from the sledge dogs of the North which, to exist, had to be trail-blazers and finders.

The history of the domestication of dogs shows an immense mutual gain for both man and dog. The latter has found himself with a home, safe from prey. Man's advantage, thanks to his ingenuity and sense of breeding for specific purposes, gained a great working aide that guarded home, family, and livestock. Man got a grand hunting companion that in early days often spelled the difference between living and starving. He got a faithful friend that always has been regarded as one of the greatest of all morale-boosters.

In addition it can be said that progress went with the dog, for as man settled new lands, he took along his dog and his cat, and without them there could have been no permanent settling of new lands, no continual raising of food. Rats and other vermin would overrun the farming belts of the nations were it not for the presence of dogs and cats, and in that blessing alone, it has been worth man's while to capture the wild dog, domesticate him, and train him in practical fields. It has paid many-fold for the development of the breeds of dogs which exist in the world today, some in all countries, nearly all lands being the point of origin of at least one breed.

Not only are dogs still doing their original work as guards, hunters, and sledge dogs, but thousands of them are leading the sightless and making it possible for them to be equal members in society. In ancient days, dogs were used well in warfare and very often the tide of battle in tribal warfare went to the side with the most and the best war dogs. The old Romans developed the system of variety groups almost as we have them in our dog shows today, and one of their classifications was "War Dogs". In World War II, dogs did their work well as patrol, sentry, scout, sledge, and messenger dogs, and none ever turned traitor or sold out his side.

Dr. Edwin H. Colbert, Assistant Curator at the American Museum of Natural History, traces the dog back to the Miacis, a small civet-like creature, which existed about 55 million years ago, and is claimed as the common ancestor of the dog and bear families.

Coming on up the trail that led to the development of the dog as we know him today, Dr. Colbert notes that about 55 million years ago the apparently not too bright Miacis gave rise to two lines, one of which was the ancient ancestor of the bear, and the other of which was the Cynodictis, which can be termed the forefather of the whole dog family. Then, about 20 million years ago, the Cynodictis split its descendants two ways, winding up about a million years ago with the Lycaon or African wild hunting dog and the Cynodesmus. From the Cynodesmus came the present-day members of the animal group known as the Canids, including the wolf, the fox, and the dog (Canis). In the course of the dog's development, changes in leg length in proportion to body size have brought about the increased ability to move quickly.

The Colbert report gives strong backing to the many authorities who claim that the dog is largely descended from the Eurasiatic wolf. Yet against that, we have scientific study showing that while a wolf and a dog may mate, the resultant progeny will be sterile. However, it is known that during the long centuries that man has been working on the domestication of dogs, often dog has slipped out of the human environment and gone back to the wild and mated with his untamed kin.

The resemblance between dogs and certain other animals is strong: wolves, foxes, coyotes, and jackals are especially similar in appearance to the longer-muzzled dogs.

Oddly enough, while Dr. Colbert feels that the first "canids" evolved in North America some 15 to 35 million years ago, this continent has evolved very few of the recognized breeds. The United States can lay claim to but six, shares one with England, Canada has five excellent hunting or working breeds to its credit, and Mexico has two breeds.

Such indications as we have as to what the prehistoric ancestors of the dog probably looked like suggest that if man has much to thank the dog for, surely the dog must thank man for scientific breeding for practical purposes that has materially aided nature in making the dog so easy to look at, so graceful, and in some cases so aristocratic. The mutual attraction of man and dog has indeed paid rich dividends on both sides.

Part Two

CATS

CHAPTER VII

CHOOSING A CAT

A cat is a beautiful and intelligent animal, with an admirable dignity of manner, independence, and individualism, as well as the capacity for warm affection and devotion which are so desirable in a family pet. The cat-owner is often fascinated by his pet's interesting habits and behavior, takes pride in its graceful appearance, and enjoys the love and loyal companionship which his cat provides in its response to human understanding. In addition, cats are easy to train, adapt themselves readily to nearly any surroundings, and are naturally clean in their habits.

IMPORTANT CONSIDERATIONS WHEN SELECTING A CAT

Choosing the Cat Best Suited to the Whole Family. If you have decided that you want a cat for yourself or for your family, you will, of course, want to know how you can be sure to select one that will have all the characteristics you are looking for in your pet—what breed to choose, and how to judge the temperament and quality of the individual cat or kitten. If the pet is for your family, the first thing, obviously, is for the members of the family to agree on what type of cat they want—whether they want a kitten or a full-grown cat, whether they want a playful, active disposition or prefer a quiet, reserved temperament, and what breed, color, and type of coat they prefer. In other respects choosing a cat is not as complicated as choosing a dog, for cats do not vary so much in size as dogs do, and on the whole the various breeds of cats adapt themselves equally well to city or country

CHOOSING THE KITTEN FOR YOU

homes, to adults or children, and to the temperaments of their new owners; nor are there so many cat breeds to chose from as there are dog breeds.

Deciding Between a Cat and a Kitten. If you buy a mature cat, you will know exactly what you are getting in regard to appearance and temperament, rather than having to trust, as in the case of a kitten, that your pet will develop into the fine specimen you had in mind. Also, your mature cat will undoubtedly be already house-trained,

A CAT AND HER KITTENS

and is likely in general to be more settled in its behavior. Kittens, however, are not very hard to train, and offer the advantage of more active, playful behavior which to many people, especially young children, is worth the mischievous phase the kitten may go through. Even kittens vary in temperament, however; you may prefer one with plenty of spirit, or you may pick one that is more timid and gentle. If you are selecting a kitten, be sure its eyes are bright and its gums pink, for these are signs of good health. If possible, look at the kitten's mother and father as well as at the kitten itself to be sure you are getting a good specimen of the breed. The breeder will also be able to furnish you with the kitten's pedigree, so you can predict to some extent what your pet will be like at maturity. Since cats are the most individualistic of pets, do not expect any exact pattern of behavior based on some other cat you have known of the same breed, but if you are buying from a reliable breeder, you can reasonably expect to get the fine cat you wanted as well as one that is clean and free of disease or infection.

CLASSIFICATION OF CAT BREEDS AND THEIR COLOR QUALIFICATIONS

The Six Recognized Breeds. There are six pure breeds of cats which are recognized by the Cat Fanciers' Association, and there are definite standards for each breed which we will take up individually in the next chapter.

In the Long Hair group and the Domestic Short Hair group, there is a great range of color and markings within each breed, and also special class standards for each individual color within these breeds. In the Manx breed there is also a rather large range of color and markings. In the Siamese, Abyssinian, and Peke breeds, however, only one or two colors are recognized as standard within each breed. In choosing a cat you will therefore want to consider not only which breed you prefer, but also which standard color within that breed.

In preparation for the discussion of breeds in the next chapter, we shall first list here the Standard Color Divisions (which apply to the Long Hair, Short Hair, and Manx) as recognized by the Cat Fanciers' Association; and then we shall discuss the individual colors, describing fully the standard requirements for each recognized color.

As the colors for the Siamese, Abyssinian, and Peke breeds are so limited, they are reserved for the next chapter under the discussions of those particular breeds.

The Standard Color Divisions. The best authorities agree upon the following Color Divisions:

Solid Color Division	Silver Division	Tabby Division
White, Blue-Eyed	Chinchilla	Brown Tabby
White, Orange-Eyed	Shaded Silver	Red Tabby
Black	Silver Tabby	Tortoise-shell
Blue	Smoke	Blue-Cream
Red		(also Silver Tabby)
Cream		

Additional Colors
Mackerel (or Ticked) Tabby
Manx
Parti-colored Manx (any color
 with white—or any mixed
 colors)

Additional Classes
Siamese Blue-Point
Siamese Seal-Point

Detailed Descriptions of the Standard Colors. The following chart gives a detailed description of each of the Standard Colors which are mentioned in the preceding divisions:

WHITE: Pure white, no colored hairs. Eyes, deep blue or deep orange.

BLACK: Dense coal black, sound from roots to tip of fur; absolutely free from any tinge of rust on tips or smoke in undercoat. Eyes, copper or deep orange.

BLUE: Color blue not drab, lighter shade preferred, one level tone, without shading or marking from nose to tip of tail, and sound to the roots. Eyes, brilliant copper or deep orange.

RED: Deep, rich clear, brilliant red, without shadings or markings; lips and chin same color as coat. Eyes, copper or deep orange.

CREAM: One level shade of cream, sound to the roots. Eyes, brilliant copper or deep orange.

CHINCHILLA: The undercoat should be pure white, the coat on back, flanks, head, and tail being sufficiently tipped with black to give the characteristic sparkling silver appearance; the legs may be very slightly shaded with the tipping, but chin, ear tufts, stomach, and chest must be pure white; any barring or brown or cream tinge is a fault. Eyes to be green. Rims of eyes, lips, and nose to be outlined with black. Center of nose to be brick red.

SHADED SILVER: Shaded Silver should be pure unmarked silver, shading gradually down the sides, face, and tail, from dark on the ridge, to white on chin, chest, and belly and under the tail; the legs to be the same tone as the face. The general effect to be much darker than a chinchilla. Any barring or brown or cream tinge to be considered a fault. Eyes to be green. Rims of eyes, lips, and nose to be outlined with black. Center of nose to be brick red.

SMOKE: A smoke cat must be black, shading to smoke, with white undercoat and black points and mask, light silver frill and ear tufts. Eyes to be brilliant copper or deep orange.

SILVER TABBY: The color of a silver tabby should be a pale clear silver with broad dense markings; to conform in pattern to those described for brown tabby; any brown or cream tinge to be considered a drawback; eye color to be green or hazel.

BROWN TABBY: Ground color, including lips and chin, rich and tawny. Markings dense black, clearly defined and broad (not narrow pencilings). Legs, evenly barred, the "bracelets" coming high up to meet the body markings. Tail barred. Barring on neck and chest, or "necklaces" distinct, like so many chains. Head barred. Cheek swirls and swirls on sides of body, each continuing in an unbroken ring. The marks upon the face and between the ears and down the neck to meet the "butterfly" on the shoulders, which divides the head lines from the spine line. Back markings, to consist of a distinct black stripe down the middle of the back with stripes of the ground color on either side of it, and black lines on either side of them. No ticking. Eyes, copper or deep orange; copper preferred.

RED TABBY: Ground color, red, markings (as described for brown tabby) to be a deep rich red. No ticking. Eyes, copper or deep orange.

TORTOISE-SHELL: Black, orange and cream, bright, clearly defined and well broken, that is patched and not brindled. Half of nose black, half orange, known as the "blaze". No tabby markings. Eyes, copper or deep orange. (Objections: Colors brindled rather than broken, solid color on face, legs or tail.)

BLUE CREAM: The two colors, blue and cream, to be well broken into patches, bright and well defined. Eyes, brilliant copper or deep orange. (Objections: Colors brindled rather than broken, solid color on face, legs, or tail.)

Making Your Choice. When deciding what breed of cat, and what color coat you prefer, the preceding charts should be of help, as well as the discussion of the individual breeds in the next chapter. Then, if possible, go to a few local cat shows. There you will see fine examples of the different kinds of cats, with their various coats, markings, and colors, and you can decide which type most appeals to you.

Where and How to Buy a Cat. Then find a reputable breeder who raises that type of cat. If the cat is to be a pet for the whole family, it is advisable to take the family along and let them help select the particular cat that seems to have the disposition and appearance that they prefer. This also will present an opportunity to know in advance if the cat you are considering will take to the different members of the family.

If you already have a dog, it may be wise to take the dog along, too, and introduce it to the cat. This is often not as difficult as one might suppose. Not all dogs regard cats as their enemies, and vice versa. If introduced gently and gradually, the chances are the animals will get used to each other and will become as friendly as if they were two dogs or two cats. Cats and dogs living in the same home often grow extremely fond of each other, play together, and in general live in peace and harmony. They have even been known to act protectively toward one another in the presence of strangers or other animals.

introduced gently and gradually, the chances are the animals will get used to each other and will become as friendly as if they were two dogs or two cats. Cats and dogs living in the same house often grow extremely fond of each other, play together, and in general live in peace and harmony. They have even been known to act protectively toward one another in the presence of strangers or other animals.

CHAPTER VIII

BREEDS OF CATS

We will now describe individually the cat breeds recognized as pure-breds by most cat fanciers' clubs. These include the Domestic Short-haired cats, which are often called merely house cats or alley cats even when they are purebred; the Persians and Angoras, now generally considered as one breed and known in cat-show language as Long-hairs; the Siamese, which comes in two types—the blue-point and the seal-point; the Manx, which has no tail; the Abyssinian; and the Peke-faced cat. Although the Burmese is often thought of as a separate breed, most cat clubs do not recognize it as such because there are virtually no pure-bred Burmese cats, for all of them have some Siamese or other strain in their make-up. At the end of this chapter we discuss briefly a number of other kinds of cats. Most of these are quite rare, and are not officially recognized by most cat fanciers as purebreds. Each kind, however, has very definite individual characteristics and, therefore, we feel they should be mentioned in this book.

At the end of each of the individual discussions on Domestic Short-haired Cats, Long-haired Cats, and Manx Cats, you will note a reference made to *The Standard Color Divisions,* which appears in the previous chapter. As there are so many recognized color combinations for all these kinds of cats, for the convenience of our readers we have included the table, with detailed descriptions of each of the colors, in the preceding chapter, rather than repeat the list after each cat breed.

PURE-BRED CATS

Domestic Short-haired Cats.
The Domestic Short-hair is the breed
most commonly seen in the United
States, although relatively few of
them are seen at cat shows for the
simple reason that their breeders
and owners seem rather reluctant to
compete against the glamor of the
imported breeds and their descendants. Yet, in addition to the popularity of the Domestic Short-hair as
a house pet, this breed has been

DOMESTIC SHORT-HAIRED BLOTCHY

known to take high honors in the
ratings of outstanding judges at cat
shows. There is an accepted standard
for the breed in both the United
States and England, and a classification is given its members for show
ratings. When there is an entry of
them at any of the various fanciers'
shows, the best can compete for
best cat in show, and since, as in
dog shows, the best-of-show judge
must rate them on their own standards, the so-called alley or house cat

is eligible for walking off with the
major honors of that particular
show.

There is not the perfection or
evenness in breeding attached to the
Domestic Short-hair that exists in
the other breeds, for we find among
them the tabbies of silver, brown,
orange, blacks, whites, blues, various grey shadings, and the tortoise-
shell that is often called calico. Then
there are creams, greens, and various shadings including those called
"tiger cats" because of their stripes.
The "tabby" markings also refer to
the stripes. However, they are
wavy, which makes them differ
from the tiger markings.

Where the other breeds of cats
obtain their shadings from selective
breedings, which also produce the
eye colors, there is not so much attention paid to these features by the
breeders of the Domestic Short-hair.
This seems a pity, because the competitive rules of cat shows demand
that color of coat and eye must conform to standards laid down for the
long-hairs. Colors must be well defined in all cases, and the eyes are
required to conform to the standard
set for long-hairs. For instance, the
whites must have a heavy blue or
orange eye; the blacks must have a
copper or orange eye; and the same

is true of blues, reds, and creams. In the case of the chinchillas and silvers, the eyes must be green. The masked

SHORT-HAIRED SILVER TABBY

silvers and silver tabbies have green eyes, while the brown and red tabbies and the tortoise-shells have copper or orange eyes.

In body build, the Domestic Short-hairs are more slender than other breeds and likely to be faster and possessed of more vigor, with longer noses, higher perched ears, and heads slightly less rounded. The chest

DOMESTIC SHORT-HAIRED TABBY-STRIPED

must be deep, the body well-knit, and the tail thick at the base, tapering toward the tip and carried fairly level. (See *The Standard Color Divisions* in the previous chapter.)

Long-haired Cats. Persians and Angoras, formerly considered two separate breeds, have, through inter-

breeding, become one, and in show nomenclature they are designated as Long-hairs. The various color combinations of the Long-hairs are much the same as those of the Do-

BLACK PERSIAN

mestic Short-hairs described above. The standard for the body conformation calls for a deep chest, low on the legs, and a massiveness of shoulder and rump. The neck should be fairly short to support a rather massive head that is a setting for a broad skull, wide-set ears that are rounded, a broad and snub nose, powerful jaws, and full cheeks. The eyes, regardless of color, must be

BLUE PERSIAN

wide set, very bright and expressive, round, large and full, with a serene gaze.

The back is level, with a tail that

is fairly short and set lower than the back but not so much that it dusts the floor as the cat moves. The legs are strong and rather thick, with the foreleg straight as a ram-rod and all paws compact and large. The hair is long and fine over all

SILVER PERSIAN

the body, and combed out to be full of life, very fluffy, with an immense ruff, plenty of feather on the ear, toe tufts, and a very full brush. No "buttons" under the chin are allow-able: this is an outright disqualifica-tion.

The solid colors must be truly solid, pure from the roots to the tips of the hairs, and, as stated in the standards for the Domestic Short-hairs, the eyes must be those called for with the particular coat color. As noted before, orange or copper are the eye colors called for more than anything else, although there are a number of the breed col-ors that demand a green eye. Ac-cepted coat colors are white, black, blue, red, cream, chinchilla shaded silver, smoke, silver tabby, brown

tabby, red tabby, tortoise-shell, and blue cream.

LONG-HAIRED SILVER TABBY PERSIAN

There is no accurate record as to when the Long-hairs were first brought to the United States from

TORTOISE-SHELL

various Oriental and Turkish ports by seafarers. The Persians possessed silky and abundant coats as well as

ANGORA

broad skulls. The Angoras, which came from the Turkish province of the same name, had narrower heads and their hair was longer on the stomach and pendant, as in the case of the Angora goat.

It is evident that the first of these cats were brought to Maine by traders, and it appears that they throve best there because the cold climate was best for their heavy coats. Even today in the coastal towns of Maine there are proportionately as many long-hairs as there are short-hairs in most other sections of the United States; they are sometimes called "Maine Coon Cats" and have no show classifications.

Many persons seem to think that the Chinchilla is also a separate variety of cat, but actually it is not, and comes in show classifications as competing in the Long-haired division, the same as the aforementioned thirteen coat and eye colors of the Persians. The good Chinchilla possesses green eyes, which offset the pure cream coat that must be free of any and all markings. Some mistake the masked silver for a Chinchilla, because some of them have a body that is Chinchilla with the same green eyes and a black or dark silver face. The coat of a pure Chinchilla is much to be envied by Milady, who yearns for a Chinchilla coat made from the famous rabbit that has become a big money industry. The Chinchilla cats make a fine, distinctive house pet.

The Long-hairs that are shown on the circuits today come mainly from stock imported from the cat fanciers of England, and in some cases got their start from fanciers who emigrated with their stock from England and are responsible for most of the cat societies of this country as well as for our competitive shows. (See *The Standard Color Divisions* in the previous chapter.)

Manx Cats. The Manx cat, native to the Isle of Man, is the strange-looking breed which has no tail.

MANX

The breed has an almost impish look about it, especially when one of its members spots a cat with a tail, almost as if it desired to say that the tail was of no use in catching a mouse, which is the cat's traditional function.

It is believed by some authorities that the Manx cat actually is a product of selective breeding and that the tailless cat came into existence through a series of breedings of cats with short tails, and that eventually the result was no tails at all. It is known that in present breedings of Manx cats there are apt to be kittens with stumps or short tails.

There are other distinctive features of the Manx cat, the chief one being a very short back with very high hindquarters which produces the rabbit-like gait. The flanks are very deep and the rump well rounded. The head is large and round, but not as snubby as the Persian, and the nose is half-way between that of the Long-hair and the Domestic Short-hair. The coat color has many variations and does not count for much in the standard. It is generally accepted that the color combinations of coat and eyes must be the same as for the Long-hair cats.

Manx cats are very individualistic, brave, and loyal, and have been known to recognize their breeders or former owners many years after parting with them. The first Manx cats appear to have come to America in about 1820. (See *The Standard Color Divisions* in the previous chapter.)

Siamese Cats. The ancestry of the Siamese cat is lost in legend and the haze of mystery that surrounds many of our animals. It is known that these cats have dwelt in the palaces and temples of Siam and Burma for well over 200 years, and that probably their history goes back far beyond that time. They are now very popular among American buyers of pets.

The Siamese cat is medium in size, with a well-muscled body that bears no trace of fat, so that it is fast in action and very graceful. The head is wedge-shaped, long and narrow, with well-defined ears that are broad at the base and very pointed. The tail is thin and tapering and not very long. The legs are thin, and the hind legs are somewhat longer than the forelegs.

There are two color-types, the blue point and the seal point. While there are show classifications for the blue point, these are rather rare and are more or less rated as a sport. The real royal Siamese cat is the seal point and is colored a clear fawn, shading to a deep chocolate brown over most of the face, with fawn between the ears. Tail, ears, legs, and feet are brown. When born these cats are white and it is most interesting to watch them slowly get

SIAMESE, SEAL POINT

the fawn to chocolate shadings as they grow older. The eyes are blue, with a slight oriental cast toward the nose. The darker the eye, the better the cat. They are rated as very smart and are known to be good hunters. Often they can be trained to fetch, heel, and carry out other commands more usually associated with dogs.

It seems reasonable to assume that the exotic Siamese came about through breeding the royal cat of Burma with the Annamite cats when the Siamese and the Annamese conquered the Burmese some 300 years ago. These almost holy cats had bushy tails and long hair. The Burmese cat that we know today is generally considered to be a variation of the Siamese and not a purebred. Its coat is chocolate or sable brown, with seal brown points, and the eyes are orange, golden, or yellow. It very much resembles the purebred Siamese in disposition.

The first two Siamese cats to leave their native country went to England as a gift from the uncle of the king, Prajadhipok, and these two founded the line that started the Siamese Cat Club of England. Once well established, the line soon came to the United States, and here a flourishing club exists, although the number of Siamese is very small in comparison with the Long-hairs.

Abyssinian Cats. It is generally agreed that the famous sacred cats of Egypt came down from the wild Caffre cats, a species that was native to Asia and parts of Africa, and there seems to be no logical reason to doubt but that the Abyssinian is a direct descendant of the Caffres of ancient times, which evidently came into the tame stage through Egyptian efforts back in the days when they were mummified when dead and laid to rest in ornate caskets. These Caffre cats resembled the Egyptians, and were not unlike our present day Domestic Short-hairs. For geographical reasons, if for no other, it would seem logical that the Caffre was the old-time ancestor of the Abyssinian.

Quiet and dignified, with an unusually soft voice, the Abyssinian cat

ABYSSINIAN

is an excellent pet for those who are willing to treat it with the kindness and gentleness that its particularly sensitive nature requires. It is an extremely graceful cat of medium size, with a long, tapering tail, small paws, and very large, bright eyes that are remarkably expressive. The eyes may be hazel, yellow, or green. The head is long and rather pointed, with sharp ears that are relatively broad at the base. Its short, fine coat may be ruddy brown or silver, with black or dark brown ticking.

Abyssinian cats are somewhat rare in the United States, but for many years they have been quite common in England.

Peke-faced Cats. As its name implies, the Peke-faced cat, which is an addition to the Persian breed, resembles the Pekingese dog in the contours of its head and face, and the closer the resemblance, the better the cat is considered. This breed has only begun to be recognized recently, and is the result of carefully selective breeding which has accentuated the Pekingese characteristics.

As in the Pekingese dog, the nose is very short and flattened, and the muzzle is wrinkled. The large, full eyes are very round, prominent, and brilliant, set wide apart, and may be copper or deep orange. The coat colors are solid red or red tabby.

Japanese Kimono Cats. Not very well known and without any known standard for the breed, the Japanese Kimono cat nevertheless warrants being mentioned here because of its interesting black markings, on a lighter body-color, which resemble a woman wearing a kimono. These cats first made their way to England on sailing vessels, having previously been stolen from their owners. In England they were bred and from there the breed went to other sections of the world.

Other Cat Groups. There are a number of other kinds of cats, which, though not officially recognized as purebreds, have quite definite characteristics. Among these are: the Burmese cat, Tibetan Temple cat, Bush-tailed Burmese cat, and French Burmese, all of which are related to the Siamese; the Bobtail cat, so-called because of its short tail and hopping gait (related to the Manx); the Himalayan White Persian, whose nose is split to aid him in breathing when going over high mountains; the Mexican Hairless, which, as its name implies, is hairless; the Kink-tailed cat, whose tail is kinked; the Pendulous-eared cat, who has drooping, pendulous ears; and many others which are even more rare than the ones just mentioned above.

CHAPTER IX

CARE OF CATS

KEEPING YOUR CAT HEALTHY

Basic Rules for Care of Cats. There are few four-legged pets which cause less work or bother than the cat. The basic rules to follow in the care of the cat are the same as for all other living pets: make certain that the cat has a decent place to sleep, one that is always clean, draft-proof, and dry; make sure there is fresh clean water for the cat whenever it needs it; keep the cat clean always; and feed it properly.

Feeding Your Cat. Feeding the proper amounts and the right foods is an important factor in the life of your cat, and various authori-

Two Healthy Kittens

ties all have proven rules in the matter of feeding. The best guide to the diet of your cat is to follow the rules set forth by the breeder from whom you buy your new pet. Naturally you will have bought from a person who has had success with the breed of cat that you buy, and if you have gotten a healthy kitten or grown cat, you can rely on the fact that whatever system produced it is the one for you to follow. All cats do not thrive on the same diet, and it is wise to follow whatever has brought the cat along to the good state in which you get him, although you will at times have to change when you note that your pet has gone "off his feed". It is always well to see that there is variety in the feeding. Animals, like humans, get tired of one monotonous diet for a length of time, or, on the other hand, your cat might get so used to the one type of food that he will not eat a new food on a day when you cannot find what you usually give him.

Meat is a basic food for cats and lean beef seems to work out the best for them. Some cats will eat it raw and others like it cooked. That much you will need to find out for yourself. If your cat is one that has the country space in which to roam, he will stay in good health on almost anything that you feed him. But in most cases your cat is pretty well confined for safety's sake, and you must think of mixing vegetables and cereals with his food for bulk and roughage. This makes up for the grasses and other items picked up by the roaming cat.

Now and then give your cat raw or cooked liver, heart, and the like. Bread and milk are much appreciated, and a supply of milk should always be kept on hand. Fish is so much a part of the cat's diet that cats have even been known to go out and catch their own fish. Canned salmon or mackerel are excellent for your cat.

There are prepared cat and dog foods on the market on which cats thrive, but they should not be used all the time. However, to play safe against the day when you may travel with your cat or when the refrigerator may be low, keep a few cans of the best foods on hand and your pet will never go hungry.

It is well to remember that your cat likes his food warm and appetizing, so add a dash of salt to bring out the flavor, and now and then put in a bit of garlic salt. Do not let food stay in the dish all day. What your cat does not eat almost at once, pick up and either throw away or put in a cool place. To allow foods to remain about not only is unclean but will cause either mold or fermentation and then your cat will get a gassy condition that often leads to serious complications.

Olive or peanut oils are good for the cat in limited amounts but do not agree with all cats. Whether or not these agree with your cat you must learn by your own observation. If you feed him canned fish you will be likely to get enough oils into his system.

Dried bread, bran, or other cereals can be mixed with the cat's food each day, and often the home pet will like dog biscuit that has been soaked in broth or the juices that come with canned fish.

Some authorities state that a cat should have about half an ounce of food twice a day for every pound of body weight, but here again you must use your own judgment and see how well your cat is doing on the amount and kind of food you are giving him. Much depends on

PROPER FEEDING IS IMPORTANT FOR THE DEVELOPMENT OF KITTENS

the amount of exercise he gets. In general, after three months of age feed him twice a day, with a dish of milk at noon in addition.

Your cat should have his own special dishes for food and water.

Cats are very fond of the herb known as catnip and are usually benefited by a teaspoonful of liquid catnip given about once a week.

Keeping Your Cat Clean. A cat is always licking itself to be clean, for it is a most fastidious animal. However, it must be remembered that a good brushing for any animal is necessary each day, and constant grooming keeps the coat more alive and therefore lessens the chances of skin ailments that so often can lead to other troubles that might well cost the life of your cat.

GROOMING AND BATHING

Grooming Your Cat. One cannot help taking pride in the handsome looks of the family cat, and nothing improves a cat's appearance so much as daily grooming with a stiff-bristled brush. It is a pity to see a cat with a coat that would be gorgeous if it were not unkempt, matted, or full of burrs and other items picked up in roaming. It takes but about fifteen minutes a day to brush the coat of even the longest-haired cat you can get. Neglect of this grooming often makes it necessary to take the cat to a veterinarian to have the mats removed. Sometimes these must be cut out, with the result that the coat looks

DAILY GROOMING WILL KEEP YOUR CAT HEALTHY AND CLEAN

mangy or at least unkempt, and this can lead to other troubles. Also, a cat which has had brushing every day will have its skin oils stimulated and this means a far healthier skin condition, which in turn means that you will have a far healthier animal all around.

Put the cat on your lap in a crouching position to brush the back and then turn it over for the underparts of the body. Slow and easy strokes of the brush will do the trick. While some contend that combs cannot be used, this is not always true and it is possible to have good results from the use of a steel comb that has a rounded edge on each tooth.

It is well now and then to rub in fuller's earth and then brush it out, for you will find that mere brushing does not remove all dirt, nor does it eliminate "catty" odors.

Now and then it is well to wipe out your cat's eyes with cotton that has been dipped in a warm solution of boric acid, and you can save much of the chance of ear cankers through a weekly swabbing of the ears with dry boric acid or now and then with olive oil or other oils.

Not all cats take to grooming. Some will show objections by nastily clawing the owner. Therefore it is wise to wear stout canvas gloves when grooming your cat.

Bathing Your Cat. On the subject of bathing a cat, authorities often times disagree, with the majority stating that dry cleaning is far the safer for many reasons. One objection to the bath is the elimination

AN OCCASIONAL BATH MAY BE NECESSARY

of skin oils that are so needed for good coat and health, and another is the great risk of pneumonia. A good daily brushing usually suffices to keep a cat clean under ordinary circumstances, but if your cat gets into some messy or bad smelling things and you must give a bath, be very careful about how you do it. Do not have the water above blood temperature, and rather than dip the cat in a tub, have someone help you and stand the cat in a tub or sink and pour the water over it. As in grooming, wear gloves. Use a liquid soap, preferably of the eucalyptus oil variety, as others are apt to hurt the sensitive skin of the cat. Dry the cat as well as you can, and then wrap it in a turkish towel and keep it away from all drafts.

Removing Fleas. Proper brushing and combing will do much toward keeping your cat free from fleas. In spite of this care, however, your pet may catch these insects from other animals. If this happens, you can buy a flea powder and follow the directions given on the container, but be sure you buy a brand which is especially intended for cats, as some of the flea powders which are sold for dogs may do your cat a great deal of harm. It is also possible to purchase a comb made especially for removing fleas, as we have already mentioned in our discussion of removing fleas from dogs. As with dogs, too, bathing may help reduce the number of fleas but does not entirely get rid of them.

TRAINING

Training and Discipline. As with dogs, the most important points in training cats to obey are to use a friendly but firm tone in giving commands, to praise and pet the cat when it responds correctly, to be

With Gentle Handling a Cat May Learn Many Tricks

consistent in your demands, and to persevere patiently until the cat learns what you want him to do. Punishment for mistakes may consist of a disapproving attitude and tone of voice or, if necessary, a smart but harmless rap on the hind quarters. Never, under any circumstances, strike your cat on the head. These principles apply to any sort of training, from housebreaking, which is discussed below, to teaching tricks such as jumping through hoops or over a stick.

Gentle handling, a kind attitude, and avoidance of teasing, mauling, or any other treatment that is likely to make a cat nervous, frightened, or hurt, are the best prevention against being scratched or bitten. Cats who have always been treated gently tend naturally to sheath their claws whenever they are picked up, petted, or handled in any way. Children should be taught to lift cats carefully and not too often.

If you want to train your cat to walk on a leash, first let it get used to the leash and collar by allowing the cat to smell these new items. Then, using gentleness at all times, put the collar on your cat for a little while every day; later attach the leash for short periods of time. Thus, having gradually grown accustomed to these items and not afraid of them, your cat will let you lead it outdoors. A harness may be used instead of a collar, especially if the cat pulls very hard. It is most important to remember that if your cat is on a leash you must pick up the cat the moment you see a dog, for a cat on a leash cannot protect itself against enemies.

Housebreaking Your Cat. Housebreaking a cat is, in most cases, easier than housebreaking a dog. The best method of breaking a

A WELL-TRAINED CAT SHOULD HAVE HIS OWN SLEEPING QUARTERS

kitten is to give it a box of sand and make it know that that box is its own property. If the box is in a convenient place, the kitten will instinctively use it. Crumpled pieces of newspaper in the box may be substituted for sand if the latter is not readily available. Older cats will also use a sand box, if it is not possible for them to get outdoors often enough. Kittens may begin their sand-box training when they are as young as three weeks.

CARE WHEN SICK

Treatment for Various Conditions. If your cat is constipated, a teaspoonful of mineral oil added to its food once or twice a week will probably help. This is also advisable if your cat has swallowed puff-balls of its own fur, as cats often do. Swallowing fur usually causes vomiting. If the vomiting persists, however, take your cat to a veterinarian. Diarrhea may be an indication that some dietary adjustment is necessary, but since it may also be a symptom of more serious conditions, a cat with diarrhea should be taken to the veterinarian. It is very important for cat owners not to try to treat cats without a veterinarian's advice when there are signs of illness, even if it seems to be only a cold or an upset stomach. If the veterinarian prescribes medicine or pills, ask him to show you how to give them to your cat.

Toys and Scratching-Posts. Although most people believe that cats are able to entertain themselves quite adequately by playing with their tails and similar activities, a cat with special toys of its own is more

A Scratching Post Will Help Save the Upholstery

likely to leave your things alone and get into less mischief. Some will like catnip mice and rats, or bags stuffed with catnip. Others like balls, or rubber mice, and some are very content when given spools to roll around.

Another way to protect your personal belongings from the hazards of your cat's activities is to provide a scratching-post on which the cat can exercise its instinctive desire to sharpen and strengthen its claws. You can get one at a pet shop. It should stand high enough so that your cat, in reaching up, can stretch itself to his full length against the post. Scratching-posts save unnecessary damage to furniture legs, upholstery, and the bottoms of drapes.

CHAPTER X

BREEDING CATS

In breeding cats, it is not wise for the novice to try to handle the
matter himself. It is best to seek the guidance of a breeder experienced
in raising the breed of cat that you possess. For the owner who has
bought a cat purely as a house pet and does not wish to be bothered
with the care of a litter of kittens, there are catteries which, for a fee,
take care of the cat when it comes in season, and either protect it
against breeding or have it mated and rear the young, sometimes on
a cash basis and sometimes for a split of the litter. If, however, you
are interested in mating your cat, it will be worth your while to
make arrangements with the owner of a fine specimen of your cat's
breed.

Mating. While females reach maturity between the ages of five and
eight months, they should not be bred until they are at least a year old.
It is generally thought that males should not be used for stud until
they are at least three years old, although they are mature at nine to
twelve months. They are considered suitable for use as studs until they
are about fourteen years old.

The female's season, which lasts for three to fifteen days, occurs three
times a year. This, of course, is the time for mating. If you do not want
to breed your female during that particular season, you must keep her
away from the many males that will gather around your home until the
season is over. These stray males will then cry and howl, perhaps for
a whole day and night, before they go away. If you want to breed your

cat, it is permissible to mate her as often as three times during the same season, but no more than that in a single season.

Pregnancy. The average period of pregnancy for cats is about sixty-three days, although this may vary by a few days either way. During pregnancy the cat should be handled only when it is absolutely necessary and then with the greatest of care and gentleness. If you must lift her, give her support under her hind feet so there will be no strain in the abdominal region.

Feed her plenty of raw beef, adding raw liver once or twice a week, and between meals give her broth and extra milk. Half a teaspoonful of brewer's yeast added to her food several times a week will be good for her own milk when she eventually nurses her kittens.

She will become less and less active as the time for delivery approaches, and will sleep a lot. Just before the kittens are born she will become restless but will remain near her box.

It is advisable to prepare a bed for the kittens ahead of time, in a warm, dark, quiet place that is well ventilated but not drafty. Thus the expectant mother will have a chance to get used to her young ones' sleeping-quarters.

Delivery and Nursing. Cats have little trouble in bringing forth their young and caring for them. Your mother cat will bite the cord, break the sac in which each kitten is born, clean off the kittens as well as herself, place the kittens in their bed, and then get in the bed with them to allow them to nurse. You will not ordinarily need to do anything to help in the delivery, but if anything unusual occurs, you will have to call a veterinarian.

Care of New-born Kittens. If there are more than four or five kittens in the litter, you may have to feed some of them by hand. Or, if the mother refuses to feed any of them, as sometimes happens, you will have to feed them all. Your veterinarian will tell you exactly how much warm milk to give them, and how often, and he will instruct you in the care of the mother's nipples in the event that they cake. New-born kittens whose mothers cannot feed them may be fed with a medicine-dropper or a doll's bottle with a nipple.

Do not handle the kittens except when it is necessary, as when you want to clean their bed. Since their eyes are closed for the first five days after they are born and do not open fully until they are about ten days old, the kittens should be kept in a dark place at first and only gradually be exposed to light. If their eyelids stick together after their eyes have opened fully, bathe the eyelids with a boric acid solution or apply a bit of white vaseline or a drop of cod liver oil.

Weaning Kittens. When the kittens are three or four weeks old, they may be gradually weaned. The process should not be hurried, but for the sake of the mother cat it should be completed by the time the kittens are two months old. To wean a kitten, dip your finger in warm milk and moisten the kitten's mouth with it while holding its head directly over the bowl of milk. The kitten will soon learn to lap the milk from the bowl. Then add a teaspoonful of scraped beef to the diet, increasing the amount gradually. Feedings should be at least every three hours at first. Later on, the intervals between feedings may be lengthened until the kitten is satisfied with three feedings a day and milk at night. Kittens that seem reluctant to be weaned should be kept away from the mother for a few hours at a time and gradually for longer periods, so that they will be hungry enough to want to eat from a bowl.

Altering and Spaying. Male cats that live in surroundings where they cannot roam about and have natural contact with other cats may, if their owners do not plan to mate them, be altered before they reach maturity. The operation should take place between the ages of three and six months. Not only does this prevent night prowling and fighting, but it results in a more contented pet. Neutered male cats are often, in maturity, larger than cats that have not been altered.

If the owner of a female does not want to breed her and cannot provide adequate supervision and restriction during the mating or "heat" season, the female can be spayed. This is a complicated operation. It should be performed at the age of about four months.

A veterinarian must, of course, be consulted if a cat owner is considering having the pet altered, whether it is a male or female.

CHAPTER XI

CAT SHOWS

Purpose of Shows. Many cat shows are held throughout the country, and they serve to keep up the interest of breeders, who compete for the cash, ribbons, and trophies that denote who is breeding the best in their respective line. As in the cases of dogs, horses, cattle, and poultry, there are standards for each of the breeds, and the judges rate the specimens before them on the basis of how closely they conform to the written standard of excellence. Often, as in the case of other animals, the best-of-show will go to the cat that has the most personality and superior showmanship. Long-hairs predominate in taking down show awards, mainly because there are more clubs devoted to pushing their merits, and possibly this creates a better breeding program.

Qualifications for Entering a Show. To show your cat, you must have it registered with some show association or club, and then you obtain the show rules and classifications. Following that you make certain that you have your cat in the best of health and carefully groomed. Make certain that the coat is in top condition. No judge will take a second look at a cat that is not in excellent condition.

Preparations for the Show. Make sure that you have a sturdy carrier in which to transport your cat to the show. Do not feed your pet just before leaving home, but at the show you may either feed it your own pet formula, or obtain chopped beef from the show's feeding committee.

Don't leave your cat alone in its exhibition cage, because it can easily be upset with many strangers around if it loses sight of its own family. A cat can thus get so badly upset that it may claw the judge and thus lose all chance of winning the awards its condition might entitle it to take home. Also it is wise to be about because one never knows what a poorly-advised stranger might do.

If you can't take the cat to a show yourself, do not try to send it, for there are too many things that can happen to it on a long journey, such as neglect of feeding and exercise. Oddly enough, it is far easier to ship a dog than a cat, possibly because public handlers are more used to taking care of the needs of a dog than a cat and dog crates are sturdier and therefore more protective of the animal.

Under no conditions should you enter your cat in a show unless you know fully the rules of that show and the complete standards of your breed. It is not a difficult game for the novice, if that novice is willing to study well all conditions of showing cats, and it is a lot of fun to know that your cat has been good enough to take home at least a blue ribbon. Then too, if you have done any winning, you can more readily sell any surplus stock you may breed.

CHAPTER XII

ORIGIN AND HISTORY OF DOMESTICATED CATS

It is impossible to do more than guess at the origin of cats as we know them today, although we can trace the development of certain new breeds. We know the make-up of the entire cat family, including those of the wild, such as leopards and tigers. Their habits are similar in most respects, and we find the house cat reacting in much the same way when cut loose to forage for itself.

Early History of Cats. We know that the cat goes back many, many centuries and that it was held in worship in ancient Egypt and other ancient countries. It is supposed that all cats were wild in the days before the founding of the Egyptian, Assyrian, and other early civilizations, and that the smaller ones came to the campfires of roving tribesmen, just as the wild dog did, and that these early cats soon got over their wild ways, and became interdependent with man.

Cats must soon have found out that by being with humans they were assured of food scraps to augment their wild diet. Even so, the cats kept their independent demeanor, which is so much a part of their charm today, for the cat is the most independent domestic animal in the world. This aloofness is the very thing that made it respected and worshipped in the ancient days, and the very expression on the cat's face led the ancients to believe that within the cat was the soul of some deceased ancestor. It is because of the myths that were allowed to grow up around cats that we really know too little of their actual beginning and the real start of their domestication.

Man's First Uses of the Cat. The tribesmen that first kept cats did so because they noted how fast rodents and other vermin disappeared when there were cats about, and realized, especially when the tribes began farming and raising grain crops that needed storage, that they had fewer shortages and less disease when there were cats on hand. Thus cats served a role in the history of civilization.

It was not until recent years that both cats and dogs became mainly pets, but even today there are thousands of cats maintained because of the work they do in eliminating various rodents which destroy valuable foods and records that are not replaceable.

Prehistoric Origin of Cats. Dr. E. H. Colbert, of the American Museum of Natural History, prepared a short article on the origin of the domestic cat to correspond to his discussion of the origin of dogs which we have mentioned in Part One of this book. He states that if we go back far enough that cats are descended from the small, civet-like creature Miacis, the very same creature who was a very early ancestor of the dog. Colbert indicates that at some point the more cat-like descendants of Miacis branched off from the more dog-like animals. And the cat-like group later divided into two main branches. Of these the gigantic Smilodon or saber-toothed cat became extinct a few thousand years ago, and the other branch developed all the modern cat-like animals, which belong to the group known as Felis, of which our modern cats are the modern representatives.

Part Three

RABBITS, SQUIRRELS, AND OTHER SMALL DOMESTIC ANIMALS

CHAPTER XIII

RABBITS

SELECTING RABBITS AS PETS

Of the smaller animals that can be raised as pets, either indoors or outdoors, rabbits are among the most popular and interesting. These docile members of the rodent family respond affectionately to kindness and become extremely devoted to those who care for them. If you choose rabbits as your pets, you will be surprised at how readily they will learn the sound of your footsteps and turn to watch your approach, whether you are bringing them food or not, and you will be touched by the expressive way their eyes keep following you as long as you are in sight. For while a rabbit's intelligence is not so highly developed as that of a dog or a cat, he is nevertheless a smart little animal, as his ability to preserve his life in the wild has proved.

How to Handle Rabbits. The gentle ways and soft furry coats of pet rabbits appeal greatly to children as well as to adults. Children should be taught, however, that rabbits must *not* be picked up by the ears. The traditional notion that this is the correct way of handling them is a greatly mistaken one. It is permissible to grasp a rabbit by the ears only if the other hand is used at the same time to support the weight of the rabbit's body. Children, however, may not remember to do this and so should not handle rabbits by the ears at all. It is generally advisable, in fact, not to choose a rabbit as a pet for a child who is too young to understand how to take care of it. Unlike some very tolerant and hardy dogs, rabbits will not survive rough handling on the part of youngsters. But for children old enough to recognize the needs of these mild little creatures, rabbits are delightful pets.

If your sole purpose in keeping rabbits is to have pleasant pets for yourself or your family, it is better not to acquire more than one or two. A larger number is suitable only if you want to raise rabbits as a full-time and rather costly hobby or as a financial venture. To try to combine fun and business in raising rabbits is a mistake, for it is not likely to be profitable and very probably will develop into a more time-consuming job than you expected.

Advantages of Domestic Rabbits. It is highly inadvisable, too, to try to take in a wild rabbit and make a pet of it. In the first place, wild rabbits are not likely to live long in captivity. Secondly, wild rabbits often carry rabies, and you would be running the risk of starting an epidemic of this disease among your neighbors' dogs, to say nothing of the risk involved in your own or your children's handling of a potential rabies carrier.

Just as with acquiring other kinds of animals, the safest method is to get a rabbit from a reputable breeder. For the established rabbit breeders have been extremely careful to see that the animals they raise are free from disease. And before you buy a rabbit, it is wise to find out where you can get the advice of a qualified veterinarian on the care of your new pet. Medical attention, in case your rabbit should need it, should be available on short notice.

BREEDS OF RABBITS

As for choosing among the breeds of rabbits, your selection can be based only on your personal preference among the various types, colors, markings, and sizes. The methods of feeding, breeding, and caring for rabbits are the same for all breeds.

Your choice will, of course, be influenced also by how much you want to spend. The breeds which commercially are valued the most highly because of the richness of their coats—the Angora and Chinchilla, for example—will not necessarily be more lovable as pets than other breeds.

The various breeds of rabbits differ from one another mainly in coat color, coat textures, and size.

In thinking of pet rabbits, perhaps the first to come to mind is the favorite white rabbit with pink eyes, and next undoubtedly would come the reddish-tan coated rabbits, which look very much like the wild bunnies seen in the woods and fields. There are excellent breeds of these two popular colors, and there are also fine breeds with black and white coats, as well as black and tan, tortoise-shell, grey, blue, and silver varieties.

We will now take up the individual breeds of rabbits, giving brief descriptions which will be of help to you when making a choice of a pet rabbit for your family.

Angora. The white Angora rabbit, particularly the albino variety with pink eyes, is the standard white rabbit, and very popular as a pet. However, his long and wooly coat needs constant attention in order to appear well groomed. This may be bothersome to the average pet owner, and should be considered. If you choose an Angora be sure not to put hay in the hutch, as this mats

ANGORA

his coat even more. If well cared for the Angoras are handsome pets.

Belgian Hare. The Belgian Hare's coat is reddish-tan, with black ticking. His ears are tipped with black, and his tail is white. This breed is one of the most popular, among children especially. This

BELGIAN HARE

is probably due to the fact that he is so like the very familiar American wood rabbit, which we commonly call "Cotton-tail".

Broken-colored. The coat colors of the Broken-colored rabbit are as the name implies, very definitely divided. The combinations of contrasting colors may be blue, black, grey, fawn, or tortoise-shell.

One popular variety of the

Broken-colored rabbit is the *Dutch-marked*. His back may be half dark, and half white; usually with white feet, tail, and face. The Dutch-marked rabbit is very small, and extremely gentle, which makes him an excellent pet for little children.

BROKEN-COLORED (DUTCH-MARKED)

Lop-eared. The Lop-eared rabbit's coat may be any color. He is one of the oldest known breeds, and one of the largest. His appearance is rather comical, as his ears are very large and pendant. Because of this peculiarity, he makes an unusual and interesting pet.

LOP-EARED

Himalayan. The Himalayan rabbit's appearance is very distinctive. The main areas of the coat, including the back of the head, being white, but with black nose, ears, feet, and tail. Although these black

markings are so characteristic, the Himalayan is partially albino, for he

HIMALAYAN

has pink eyes. The Himalayan is a comparatively small rabbit.

English. The English rabbit's coat is white, with a black, blue, or fawn stripe down his back. He is often referred to as the "English Butterfly" because of the markings

ENGLISH

around his eyes, ears, and tail. He is one of the larger breeds of rabbits, weighing around eight pounds.

Polish. The Polish rabbit's coat is usually white. He is the smallest of all the rabbit breeds; having a very short body and small ears. His eyes, however, are very large and striking.

Flemish Giant. The Flemish Giant's coat is dark gray, with white ticking, and his stomach is pure white. Other colors have been bred, such as light grey, black, and white, but the usually dark greys and some blacks are the only ones that have been popular. The Flemish Giant is the largest of all the rabbit breeds, and weighs around eleven or twelve pounds. His body is stocky, and his legs are very strong.

Silver. The Silver rabbits come in three varieties: Silver Fawn,

SILVER

which is orange with white hairs; Silver Gray, which is blue-black, with white ticking; and Silver Brown, which is chestnut with a

bluish undercolor. They are all quite small, and weigh only five or six pounds.

Blue and Tan, Black and Tan. The coat colors of the Blue and Tan rabbit, and the Black and Tan rabbit, are very similar to that of the silver rabbits. The main difference between the two varieties being their size. The Blue and Tans and Black and Tans are quite a bit smaller, and weigh only about three or four pounds.

Other Rabbit Breeds. Among the other rabbit breeds which you may choose from are the many types of New Zealand rabbit, the White Satin, Silver Fox, Silver Marten, Blue Vienna, and the many Champagne d'Argent types.

FEEDING RABBITS

Best Food for Rabbits. Be certain that your pets are fed at regular intervals, lest they waste away on you. Clover, hay, alfalfa, vegetable tops are most welcome, and to keep their teeth in condition as well as the rest of the system, make sure they have plenty of root vegetables, such as carrots and turnips. You will find, too, that like their wild brethren they appreciate live twigs and bark on which to gnaw. Try to see also that they get newly picked green foods, such as lettuce, celery, and other leafy vegetables such as you perhaps raise at home. If you raise nothing, dip the green stuffs in cold, fresh water before presenting it to your pets, for the rabbit actually gets most of his water from the moisture content of food.

Importance of Drinking Water. Your captive bunny, however, needs plenty of fresh water besides what he gets in his food, so it is

wise to anchor down a non-tippable dish and see that it is refilled with
water at least twice a day.

If you feed them well, give them lots of fresh water, and see that the
hutch is always clean, your pets will have a long life.

RABBIT HUTCHES

Kinds of Hutches. One or two rabbits may be kept in a hutch within
your home and, if raised with the greatest of care, will live healthily to

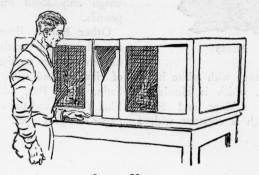

INDOOR HUTCH

a normal age. A good-sized outdoor hutch, however, and an ample en-
closed yard are preferable if your ground-space permits such an arrangement.

In some country localities it may be safe to let pet rabbits roam at
large provided they have a suitable hutch to return to in case of danger.
But since rabbits are a natural prey to a number of other animals, it is
wisest to keep your pets confined in some space large enough to allow
them plenty of exercise and adequately protected against their enemies.
In a sense, these animals are better off in protected captivity. They have
no feelings of enmity for other animals and never start fights, but are
often attacked and have no fighting equipment but their alertness and
their speedy legs. Indoors or outdoors, therefore, they should be protected by wire mesh.

Building a Hutch. For a pair of rabbits, a hutch should be at least 48 inches long, 30 inches wide, and 30 inches high. If the pair are of opposite sexes, however, it is well to prepare for six or eight tenants; this means providing a hutch 5 feet long, 3 feet wide, and at least 3 feet high.

Build the hutch so that it is readily cleaned, and make certain that it is raised from the ground and set in such a way as to be dry, free from drafts, and exposed to as much sunshine as possible. Make sure that the hutch is not easily tipped over or opened, and then build an ample run out from the hutch.

OUTDOOR HUTCH

Outdoors, it is safest to run medium-heavy wire yard-fence up to a height of six feet, and use what is known as a "turn-in", only in this case you should make both a "turn-in" and "turn-out", which is really a wired "V" at the top of the fence, about one foot high and set at a 45-degree angle. Set your wire in the ground to a depth of at least 18 inches and tamp the dirt over it solidly. This will prevent your rabbits from digging down and tunnelling out of their enclosure, and at the same time prevent dogs and other digging animals from tunnelling in.

BREEDING RABBITS

Nest Boxes. The hutch should contain a nest box or two, built into one of the corners furthest from the light. These should be 12 inches wide, 12 inches high, and about 16 inches long. This is where the mother rabbit will go to have her young, and while you will provide bedding here, as in the rest of the hutch, of dry hay, excelsior, or straw, do not be surprised if as delivery time comes near the mother rabbit throws out your bedding and makes up her own, even pulling fur from her own body to make a downy couch for her young.

When to Breed Rabbits. Rabbits can be bred safely when they are seven months old or when they weigh about seven pounds. About a month later there will be young rabbits, which should be left alone for forty-eight hours with mother as the only caretaker. Then you will want to weed out the less perfect of the young ones and leave the mother with no more than six or eight to care for, which you will check from time to time. Wean them at eight weeks, and then separate them by sexes and place them in their own compartments.

Care of Doe and New-born Rabbits. It is best to allow your doe (female rabbit) at least a month's rest after the first litter is weaned before breeding her again, but from the second litter on you can re-breed her almost immediately each time, as three to five litters a year are safe for a doe that has been fed and cared for properly. Keep your buck (male) rabbit in his own hutch at all times, and bring the does to him to be bred.

While the young are not completely weaned until they are eight weeks old, they will start at the age of three weeks to get part of their feeding from their mother's feeding dish or hay rack, and by watching closely you will learn when to set down individual feeding stations for them and thus promote proper growth.

Feeding Doe and New-born Rabbits. During the nursing period the doe needs at least half a pound of food a day. Growing rabbits, after weaning, need about four ounces of feeding a day, and this increases as they grow larger. These amounts in both cases refer to prepared foods and do not include green stocks or hay that you would use as a basic diet. The amount of the latter will be determined by your own judgment as you watch the progress of your rabbits. A feeding rack of bright, clean hay is essential to their health.

CHAPTER XIV

SQUIRRELS AND CHIPMUNKS

MAKING FRIENDS OF SQUIRRELS AND CHIPMUNKS

The squirrel and the chipmunk are not usually looked upon as pets for the household, and while many of us know of people who have kept them confined in cages, this is generally frowned upon, for it is cruel to attempt to cage these cute and beautiful little animals. However, we can feed them and make friends with the furry little creatures, and it is not at all uncommon in sections where there are trees for the squirrels to come down onto the family porch first to pick up nuts that you have left for them, and eventually to come into your home through an open window, take a nut from your hand and scamper off with the prize.

How to Handle Squirrels and Chipmunks. It is common sense to permit these tiny animals to have full freedom and not to try to over-domesticate them. In the first place, their freedom of action is what produces their main beauty. Secondly, being creatures of the wild, they cannot last too long in captivity, and this imprisonment can in time make them sour of nature and thus ready to take out their resentment on the first thing they can bite with their two sharp front teeth. If that happens to be your finger, the chances are that if you do not take immediate care of it, you will get blood-poisoning.

Do not take that to mean that squirrels and chipmunks are really unfriendly to man, for there is hardly a wild animal anywhere that is more generally friendly. He merely wants to come and call on you, and, as he gets to trust you, accept your hospitality and scamper off, free as the wind and able to call on someone else. Rest assured that if you treat him right, he will be back to look for you, and if he happens to meet you in a city park or in the woods, he will get to know you quite well.

Quite naturally, his favorite abode is in the hollow of a tree, but in the city you can quite often find him making his home in the eaves of houses or other places where he can find comforting warmth.

SQUIRRELS

Where to Find Squirrels. In the public parks of cities the squirrels are encouraged to become at home in the trees, and children have the chance to become acquainted with them and to help them out through the winter months when their food is generally covered by snow and frozen ground. Of course, where nuts are plentiful, the squirrel becomes a hoarder and stows away enough to carry him fairly well through the winter. However, it is well to remember that often the storehouse gets frozen up and then we humans must see to it that enough food is put out for them. Nuts, seeds, berries, certain barks, and young shoots form the main part of their diet.

Red squirrels prefer the seeds of coniferous trees somewhat more than do the grey squirrels, and both are known to take mushrooms up into a tree fork and eat them leisurely.

Characteristics of the Squirrel. The squirrel has but two hard front teeth and nature is kind enough to replace them should they be broken. He sits on his hind legs while eating, holding the food in his fore paws, with the bushy tail erect as a plume. This tail also is useful in helping him jump from tree to tree, and as a boa to wrap about him and keep him warm when he rests or sleeps in the winter.

There are many different varieties of squirrels in wild life, but we of the built-up community are most familiar with the red and the grey varieties. The American Indian more or less revered these little animals, and it was part of the folk-lore or legends of the tribes that knew them that they were protected by a god for their work in planting trees throughout the forests. It is true that many forest trees that bear nuts had their origin in the over-supply of nuts the squirrels planted to ward off winter hungers, and the Indian, being truly grateful for anything that led to more food, held the squirrel in high esteem. One legend is that the Indian God of Creation called all animals into a session and asked for help in continuing existing forests and even extending them on lands where no trees grew. In turn each animal found an excuse for getting out of work, except the squirrel. As a reward he was given the nuts to eat and a bushy tail to preserve his balance in the trees.

A Squirrel Is a Friendly Pet

Squirrels are rather long-lived, some having been checked as attaining as much as fifteen years in active, outdoor life, living either in a hollow tree, or as is often the case after the young are born, in a twigged nest in a tree.

Breeding Habits of Squirrels. When squirrels mate, usually there are four young ones, which take about thirty-five days to get over being blind, and after they have had another month, the parents move them outside, carrying them by the loose skin on the belly so that the young one can hold on by wrapping body and paws around the mother's neck.

CHIPMUNKS

Where to Find Chipmunks. The chipmunk is attractively marked, with its striped back, and is often called the stripe-backed squirrel or ground squirrel. The latter name comes from their scurrying about the ground and building their nests in the ground very cleverly. In captivity, they would have little chance to do this, and thus, they too, are best as casual pets, met on the ground.

Oddly, there is never loose dirt to indicate the entrance to the home of the chipmunk, for it digs into one side, and as it goes back and throws the dirt, it finally has that side plugged up. Then it gets down

A CHIPMUNK WITH ATTRACTIVE MARKINGS

about two feet, makes a commodious home, and digs out the other way, leaving just enough entrance to squeeze through, and this entrance generally is covered with a leaf of some sort.

Breeding Habits of Chipmunks. The young chipmunks arrive in the spring and Papa Chipmunk has to have another tunnel home while Mama rears her young, which appear in public first when a bit over a month old, but it takes a little while longer before they have their full coat of fur. The chipmunk's storehouse is its home, and for much of the winter season it hibernates in a sort of coma.

CHAPTER XV

GUINEA PIGS, WHITE MICE, WHITE RATS, AND HAMSTERS

GUINEA PIGS AS PETS

To the average person, the guinea pig is associated with experimentation for the benefit of mankind. But these little creatures can serve also as interesting and appealing household pets. They require little care, and are rather hardy, easy to feed, and so friendly that they make pleasant companions for young or old. They may be kept in city or country places with only reasonable precautions for their safety. Although they have the word "pig" as part of their name, they are not related to the pig, but come from the same basic rodent family as the rabbit, squirrel, beaver, porcupine, mouse, and rat, and, like them, are of chewing, gnawing habits. Their other name is the *Cavy* and they are native to South America and the West Indies.

Breeds of Guinea Pigs. There are many types or breeds, the most popular being the sleek-skinned Bolivian and the short-haired Abyssinian. There are also some long-haired species that naturally need more care to keep them healthy through cleanliness.

Unless there are strangers around for whom he might have an aversion, the guinea pig makes an enjoyable pet, always a busybody running in and out of his house and around whatever enclosure you can give him. If you are really a kindly soul, you will buy him a mate, and you will be amused by his chattering to her, for guinea pigs love company and are somewhat tragic-looking if always alone and not in a family where there is human companionship.

Characteristics of the Guinea Pig. Although many persons have the impression that these are stupid little fellows, they actually are alert and keen, and it is not long before they learn your footstep and the sound of your voice, and will set up an excited squealing while racing madly about the pen, waiting for you to appear.

GUINEA PIGS ARE POPULAR AS PETS

Housing Guinea Pigs. They take up little space, and you can build a house, big enough for four, that need be but two feet long, one foot wide, and a foot high. Build it strong and raise it so that the occupants are not subject to ground or floor drafts and dampness. If you have the place to do it, and can have them outdoors part of the time, slope the roof to carry off rain and carry the pitch beyond the walls for further protection. Hinge the top for ready cleaning and make sure you can hook this roof so that marauders may not pry in and remove your pet. Sawdust, over which a thin layer of straw is thrown, provides the ideal resting place, although they much prefer to have you pick them up so they may snuggle against you.

Your pet will last longer and be happier if you build an exercise enclosure, as large or larger than the house, raised off the floor or ground and with fairly heavy wire surrounding three sides and across the top. The floor here should have sawdust on it, and it takes little time to add more to their enjoyment and your pleasure by building in a few inclines.

It is important that you keep both the house and play enclosure clean, removing the old sawdust and straw every other day, as a dirty hutch causes illnesses.

Feeding Guinea Pigs. Feeding is rather simple, and you can put in an ample supply and your pet will take care of his needs as he feels hungry, which will be much of the time. Under no conditions feed table scraps. Carrots, beets, parsnips go well, as do oats, bran, tender hay, grass, clover, dandelion greens—in fact, any sort of green, leafy dish.

Be certain that your guinea pig has plenty of clean water, which should be placed in a container that is anchored down against tipping. The water should be changed at least twice a day. If you have a pair and they mate, be sure the female has milk daily, along with her other feedings. The babies will be out nibbling along for themselves after very few days, and until they are about a month old they should be given milk, dried-out bread that is soaked in milk, some little green stuff that is dried, and a helping of bran mash.

If your pet happens to get sick, be sure the temperature of the quarters is between 60 and 70 degrees, feed him warm milk, wrap him in a woolen cloth, and perhaps give him two drops of castor oil.

How to Handle Guinea Pigs. While your guinea pig loves to be cuddled and enjoys being stroked generously, be certain in handling him that he is not allowed to fall or jump from your hands, as his fat little body with the tiny feet at the ends of short legs cannot stand the shock. Both hands should be used to pick him up, one to grasp him gently and the other to give him solid support underneath.

Treated properly, the guinea pig is about as inexpensive and enjoyable a pet as a family whose living quarters are not too commodious could have. This lovable little animal will return all the affection you lavish on it.

WHITE MICE AND WHITE RATS

White Mice. There are few small pets more amusing to watch than white mice that have been given playthings and a properly equipped cage. Their antics with a piece of hard wood about the size of a large spool, for example, and the way they make use of the stairways or inclines to the upper quarters of their cages, are fascinating. The white mouse requires little care and attention, and is highly recommended as a pet for those with small homes.

Housing White Mice. The housing problem is settled with a strongly-built cage of which three walls, the roof, and the flooring are of smooth, hard wood, while the front of the cage is covered with strong wire mesh. The cage should be about 2 feet long, 1 foot deep, and 18 inches to 2 feet high. The reason for the height is that mice like to climb, and therefore a second story, set back from the mesh, should be built with an incline leading up to what would appear like a mezzanine. The roof should be hinged for easy cleaning, at which time the

WHITE MICE ARE COMICAL

mice should be shooed into a small compartment about 6 inches square. This tiny compartment will be used by the mice when they want to hide away for sleep. A light covering of hay makes the best bedding for them, although sawdust may be used.

Feeding White Mice. Fresh water should be given at least twice a day and placed in a container that cannot be tipped. Now and then they appreciate some condensed or evaporated milk, thinned down. Oddly, perhaps, cheese, meat, and sweets should not be given to the captive mouse. Cracked corn, plain or rolled oats, canary seed, scratch feed, wheat, carrots, and lettuce all are good for your pet.

There always should be feed in the mouse home, for it has been found that even slight fasts can be fatal, but at the same time, one should avoid foods that tend to make mice fat and lazy. A bit of apple now and then is good, as is watermelon with seeds left in.

Keeping White Mice Healthy. The white mouse is naturally a very clean animal if given any chance, and it is highly entertaining to watch them clean themselves often. To keep them healthy and thus better able to entertain you, it is necessary that their quarters be spotlessly clean always, and draught-proof.

Breeding Habits of White Mice. If your mouse is bred, you will find she is an excellent mother and all you need to do for her is to give her fresh milk that is not cold, and a rather good supply of bread soaked in milk.

White Rats. In general, the care of the pet white rat is the same as for the white mouse, except that living quarters should be made almost twice the size, with all details in proportion. The white rat will be found to be a highly intelligent, amusing pet, especially if bought young and brought up by you. However, it is not generally advised that white rats be kept as pets where there are very small children, as rats are rather nervous, and lack of understanding on the part of the little children is apt to lead to trouble. Adults and older children who have been taught how to get along with them will find white rats pleasant as pets. One word of caution: if you have a pair, put the buck out by himself during the pregnancy of the mother and while she is rearing her young.

HAMSTERS

The hamster, well known to scientists for its definite service to mankind in the laboratory, is an affable creature with much value as a home pet, especially for those with small living quarters. The little rodent is

HAMSTERS MAKE INTERESTING PETS

attractive in its golden coat of rather short hair, is little more than five inches long over all at full growth, and often weighs no more than four to six ounces. It has a short tail and looks not unlike a miniature bear, especially when it puffs out its muzzle pouches.

Feeding and Housing Hamsters. Hamsters are easy to feed, and it has been said that they are not unlike the "grey ghost" of the dog world, the Weimaraner, in that they will try eating anything. The best foods for them are carrots, peanuts, cabbage, dog food, calf meal, and similar food materials. Do *not* give them water, as they take all the moisture their systems require through their food when there is a reasonable proportion of leafy things.

Housing is simple. The type of hutch used for guinea pigs is suitable for hamsters. Be certain to use mesh wire over the open spots in such a way that cats, dogs, and other potential enemies do not get at your pets.

Hamsters came to the laboratories of England, and thence to the United States, from Syria. The first were found in an eight-foot burrow in the country near Aleppo and all the laboratory hamsters are descendants of the female and twelve young that were found at that time.

Breeding Habits of Hamsters. Hamsters multiply rapidly, and the young are easy to rear. They will have litters that run from two to fifteen, and will keep on having them up to a year of age, when normally they are through. They can mate at forty-three days.

If you start to raise them, be certain to separate the females from the males and all the young, and do not disturb the females because they are easily upset and are likely to eat their offspring.

Part Four

BIRDS

CHAPTER XVI

CANARIES

The canary is one of the most popular pets in America. Beautiful in color as well as in song, it is also one of the hardiest of caged birds. It is naturally clean in its habits and requires very little care.

VARIETIES OR TYPES OF CANARIES

It would be impossible to list accurately all the various types of canaries known today, for every now and then some group of fanciers

THE EVER POPULAR CANARY

comes up with what proves to be a permanent new type. But it is well for the potential buyer to know most of the following varieties: Buff Norwich; White Roller; Yellow Warbler; Color Fed Yorkshire; Yellow Yorkshire; Mottled White Dutch Frill; White Canary; Norwich Canary; White, Green, Mottled, and Blue Yorkshires; Color Fed Norwich; Buff Dutch Frill; Green Roller; Crested Warbler; Cinnamon Warbler; Warbler Canary; Roller Canary; American Roller, a low-singing bird with a particularly lovely song; Crested Norwich; Border Fancy, so-called because it belongs on the Scotch-English border; Scottish Fancy; Lancashire, reputedly the largest of them all; and the Lizard Canary, rich and silky in plumage texture, with gold and silver varieties.

If possible, go to a large pet or bird shop that carries a number of these and make your selection.

CARE OF CANARIES

Feeding Canaries. The canary is, of course, a descendant of the seed-eaters that roamed wild and were able to pick up exactly the right balance of seeds and grasses. Even though he is now domesticated, however, the problem of feeding him is made easy by the fact that so many companies put together the ideal seed packages for him, and you can buy them not only at your pet shop but also at most grocery stores.

What is known as canary seed and sweet rape are really their staple diet and should be kept in a well-anchored seed cup at all times, for the average bird is not apt to gorge itself and become sick. For Rollers the proportion seems to be quite a bit more rape than canary seed. Wild grasses are all right, in fact their use ought to be encouraged, provided that you are certain they are mature, as the unripe grasses are very apt to start diarrhea. A very few hulled oats are good at times, but never give the cracked oats unless you have a bird that is underweight and needs a quick pick-up. Take them off the cracked oats as soon as possible, or they will get much too fat to sing.

A bit of really green food each day should be in the diet, such as the outside leaves of lettuce, cabbage, spinach, water cress, and the tops of celery. Do not give your bird any candy, cake, or other sweets. Never forget to keep a piece of cuttlebone attached to the side of the cage.

Kinds of Cages. The prospective canary-owner should not attempt to make his own cage for the first canary, but should buy a good metal one that has an easily removable bottom and equipment. The size and price should be determined by your purse and the spot in your house where you will place the cage. It is always well to get a cage large enough for two birds, with a stand that has a good base so that the cage will not easily be tipped to the floor or through a window. The cage should, of course, be kept out of drafts at all times.

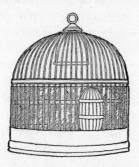

CANARY CAGE

Where to Place the Cage. It is customary to place the canary's cage by the window that lets in the most light, and this is correct, for they are birds of the day. However, when you go to bed at night, cover the cage with a cloth made for the purpose, or a towel, arranged to keep out the cold and extra light, without shutting out the air entirely. In the hot months, be sure to arrange a cloth over one part of the cage so that the bird may be able to get out of the glare of the sun now and then.

General Care of the Cage. Perhaps the only work you will ever really do for your new household pet is to clean his cage. This should be done at least once a day, for there is nothing that will do harm to your canary faster than a filthy cage. It takes but a few minutes to take down the cage, wash the bottom pan with hot water and dry it thoroughly, put in some clean white sand, and then wipe down the sides of the cage. At the same time take out the perches one by one and scrub them in hot water, being sure to rinse off any soap you may have used. It is best, too, always to empty and wash the seed and water dishes every day and put in fresh food and fresh water. You thus eliminate chances of any filth, of the creation of a hiding place for vermin.

Bathing Canaries. A shallow dish containing water should be placed on the bottom of the cage every day for the bird's bath. Most birds bathe without any coaxing soon after the little tub is put in place.

Illnesses. There are a number of common canary ailments which require simple treatment that can be administered at home.

For *constipation,* give your canary a drop of mineral oil and as much soaked-up milk and toast as he will eat at once, and take it away before it sours. Also give him more greens.

For *diarrhea,* remove the feathers from the vent and wash the section in warm water, drying it with a soft rag; apply a soothing ointment. Give buttermilk in place of water and have seeds only for feed.

For *anemia,* that is, when your bird looks color-drained, add to his regular seed some hard-boiled egg food every day, sprinkled over with poppy seed; a bit of cracked oats each day; and put fresh green water cress and a piece of orange in his cage twice a day, removing them when the bird has had his fill.

For *colds,* put a bit of mentholatum at his nostrils with a toothpick or matchstick, then for twenty-four hours replace his drinking water with a solution of one teaspoonful of epsom salts in a pint of water. Keep him warm and make arrangements outside the cage for fumes of eucalyptus oil in boiling water to reach the bird. Keep the cage partly covered. Feed him about the same as for anemia. This care is good also in case of *asthma,* but for asthma also use two drops iodine in one ounce of drinking water for three days.

Baldness comes from one bird's picking another's feathers, from mites, or from a skin trouble caused by lack of nourishment.

If your bird has a *broken leg,* split a quill the length of the leg, spring it open and encase the leg, then tape it up and put the bird in a cage without perches. Put food and water on the floor of the cage and cover it so that the sight of action outside will not make the bird move too much. The leg will heal inside of a week.

Sore eyes may come from many causes, but it is best to regard them as an infection and keep your canary away from other birds. Use a solution of boric acid as used for humans. Put drop of castor oil or a 10 percent Argyrol solution on each eyeball.

Scaly legs and sore feet usually come from a dirty cage. Sometimes they come from insect bites. Soak scaly legs for about five minutes in warm water and apply vaseline. Do this every day and do not pick off the scales. On the sore feet put a drop of iodine.

Rickets is a disease caused by improper diet, and lack of sunshine. If the bird is badly affected, you will have to destroy him. If the disease is not too bad, however, give him all the sunlight you can.

Skin tumors are caused by a blockade of a pore. Wait for the tumor to get taut, then cut it lightly with sterilized blade and remove the substance. Wash it out with a sterile solution and leave it alone until it has healed.

Moulting Season. Late in the summer your canary will lose a great many of his feathers and will stop singing. This is the moulting season. At this time you should give him extra nourishment. The prepared mixtures known as "song-restorers" are a good addition to his diet during the moulting season, although the bird will naturally get his voice back, as well as getting new feathers, when the season is over.

BREEDING CANARIES

Choosing a Mate. The best results in breeding are usually brought about by mating birds of opposite colors—a pale bird with one of bright plumage, for example—as well as of different song qualities. February or March is the best time. The pair should be put in a separate cage.

Caring for the Eggs. After three days, put a nest in the cage so that the birds can line it. In another three days the first egg will be laid. Since the male birds often eat the eggs, it is advisable to remove them with a spoon, substituting false eggs, until the last one has been laid. Then put back all the eggs. The hen will sit on them until all are hatched, which takes about thirteen days.

Caring for the Young Chicks. The male bird usually feeds the female who stays in the nest and feeds her chicks by regurgitation. However, if the male is at all troublesome, he may be taken out of the cage. The chicks leave the nest at about the age of three weeks. If at this time the mother is about to breed again, it may be necessary to remove the young ones from her cage to prevent her from plucking their feathers in order to line the nest again. Chicks who pluck at each other's feathers should be separated, too.

The sex of the birds can be determined by the fact that the vent of the male extends outward and downward while that of the female is swollen and rounded.

ORIGIN AND HISTORY OF THE CAGED CANARY

We know, from records going back perhaps 400 years, that the original wild canary was a small greyish-green bird bearing yellow patches on its body, and that although the wild males had fair voices, they did not compare in range and tonal quality with the canary as we know it today.

Early Migration of the Canary. As the name suggests, canaries were first discovered on the Canary and Madeira Islands. They were, therefore, originally a semi-tropical bird. The first record of the domesticated canary was late in the sixteenth century. It appears that a trading ship bound for Italy took on, as part of its cargo, quite a number of the wild birds. Storms came up and the little ship was wrecked off the Isle of Elba, west of Italy. The little birds made their way to the island and became thoroughly at home. Not long after this, as occasional historical references show, they were confined in cages in Italy, where they were held in high regard as singers.

Origin of the Present-day Varieties. Traders and travelers soon carried some of the birds into other European countries, where they rapidly became popular, especially in England and Germany. As far back as the early days of the seventeenth century we find they were being successfully crossed with native British song birds. By about a hundred years later these crossings had produced at least twenty-five different varieties of canaries in England, among them some of the more popular types known today.

In Germany they were raised in cages and crossed with the native

Siskins and Linnets to such an extent that little trace was left of the little birds that were originally found on the Canary Islands. Out of these breedings came beautifully mottled songsters. The climate of both England and Germany is so different from that of the land of the canary's origin that the birds developed more stamina, a longer life-span, and bigger chest expansion which made for more song.

The Canary's Popularity in America. Until about fifty years ago there was no breeding program in the United States, but shiploads of the birds were brought over from Europe. Gradually the hobby of keeping pet canaries grew here, and today the United States breeders can more than hold their own with the rest of the world. Many cities and towns in America have a canary society, the members of which gather to discuss progress in breeding and what else can be done to breed the perfect canary. There are many annual shows at which prizes are awarded. Some of these clubs are for members who breed all va-rieties of the canary, while in other communities there are individual clubs sponsored by the followers of the different varieties, such as the Norwich and the Yorkshire.

CHAPTER XVII

PARROTS, PARAKEETS, AND LOVE BIRDS

Few pets suitable to the average household can be more colorful or provide more entertainment than the sturdy members of the parrot family, which is a large one indeed and includes shell parakeets, love birds, macaws, cockatoos, lories, and lorikeets, besides the true parrot which we shall discuss below. At the present time, we are dependent on the young of birds already in the United States, as there is a ban on the importation and shipment of birds of the parrot family because they transmit psittacosis, a very serious infectious disease. Because of the popularity of parrots as pets, and with the hope that psittacosis will one day be eradicated, we include parrots among the household pets discussed in this book.

PARROTS

Training Parrots to Talk. The outstanding feature of the parrot, besides his glorious and varied coloring, is, of course, his ability to talk. To teach a parrot to talk, it is best to start when he is young. Begin by repeating a single word, over and over. When the parrot has learned to repeat that word after you, teach him a few more. Then begin teaching him short sentences.

Cages for Parrots. Make certain that your parrot has a cage large enough to permit him to move around comfortably, and observe the same rules for keeping the cage and the bird clean as we have already mentioned in connection with canaries. Have plenty of clean sand on hand to put in the bottom of the cage and be sure to scrub it out at least once a day. Always keep the water dish well filled with cool, clean water.

Feeding. Parrots do well on many types of diets. Sunflower seeds seem to be the most generally acceptable to the majority of members of

GREEN PARROT

the parrot family and usually is the basic diet for them. The "Polly want a cracker" saying is not mere talk, for we find that the majority of parrots do like crackers of nearly all types, particularly soda crackers.

Fruits, mainly apples, are good for parrots of all types, and like all birds, they should be supplied with fresh green vegetables, such as the outside leaves of lettuce and cabbage, making sure to wash them clean first. It is best to dry them, too, as the moisture from wet vegetables in the bottom of the cage makes it messy and does your parrot's feet no good.

General Care of Parrots. It is a good idea to give your parrot a name, preferably of one syllable. You can be sure that the bird will soon respond to it.

Another good practice is now and then to give the bird a bit of freedom by letting him out of his cage. When you first do this, make certain that you are in a room that is closed off from the rest of the house and that no member of your family is apt to open one of the doors and let him go too far. Also make sure that there are no open windows, for your bird may go adventuring and be lost.

If your parrot shows any signs of illness, be sure to consult a veterinarian. Good diet and proper care of the cage are, of course, the best preventives. If given adequate care, parrots live for a very long time.

LESSER SULPHUR-CRESTED COCKATOO

Varieties of Parrots. There are many varieties of parrots, differing from one another in size and color and in their ability to learn to talk.

Among the most popular varieties are: the Mexican Double Yellow Head, African Gray Parrot, Panama Parrot, Cuban Parrot, Mexican Redhead Parrot, Cartagena Parrot, Amazon Parrot, and Macaws (which we discuss more fully in the following paragraphs). There are also several varieties of Dwarf Parrots.

MACAWS

Macaws, the largest members of the Parrot family, also are among the most magnificent in coloring. They come in many color combinations and seem to sense their own beauty. While for the most part they are kept in aviaries, they do very well in single cages, providing they have ample room.

Cages for Macaws. For all these members of the Parrot family, as in the case of canaries and other caged birds, we strongly advise getting

GREEN WINGED MACAW

a cage that is more than adequate for their size, and make sure that it is set on a solid pedestal that is not easily tipped over. Place it by a window that will give the birds the most light in your house. However, again it is urged that in the really hot months some sort of covering be placed over part of the top of the cage, so that the birds can have a shady place to perch part of the time.

Feeding Macaws. You may feed macaws a mixture of sunflower seed and hemp, oats, wheat, canary seed, and dari. Also some greens, boiled corn, and peanuts may be added to your macaw's diet.

Varieties of Macaws. There are eight varieties of macaws, some of which are very popular in America. A few of them are: the Military Macaw, the Blue and Gold Macaw, Green Winged Macaw, and the Scarlet Macaw. The colors of all macaws, as with most other members of the Parrot family, are extremely vivid and very beautiful. Macaws are not generally known for their ability to talk.

SHELL PARAKEETS

Shell Parakeets are the diminutives of the general tribe of parrots. They are among the most gorgeously colored of all birds. Shell parakeets are often called "Love Birds", but true Love Birds are not as thin and graceful or as brilliantly colored as shell parakeets.

GRASS GREEN SHELL PARAKEETS

In buying shell parakeets, one generally buys a pair of them, male and female, whether intent on mating them or not. They do much better for you as companions when there are more than one of them, although there is little reason to believe the old saying that if one of a pair of love birds dies, the other soon will die too.

If possible, it is very interesting to keep more than one pair of different varieties in the same cage. In this way you can have many beautiful colors adorning your cage, as well as learn the varied and characteristic habits of the different pairs.

Housing Shell Parakeets. You may house your shell parakeets either in a cage or an aviary, depending on where you plan to keep them, and whether or not you plan to breed them. However, always try to have room for at least two birds.

The cage or aviary should be equipped with water, seed, and health grit troughs, perches, and nests (if you plan to breed your birds). Your parakeets should have light and fresh air, but should be away from drafts at all times.

Feeding Shell Parakeets. Ordinary bird seed is not good for parakeets. A healthy mixture to feed your birds is two parts canary seed,

ALEXANDRINE RING-NECKED PARAKEET

two parts large yellow millet, and one part large red millet. Parakeets may be given most greens, but sparingly, with the exception of lettuce.

Breeding Shell Parakeets. If you plan to breed your parakeets, be sure to keep some cuttlefish bones and egg shells in the cage or aviary. These will help prevent the female from becoming egg bound (difficulty in laying eggs), and from producing soft-shelled eggs.

Parakeets will mate during almost any season of the year. They will usually produce four or five broods a year; each brood having five or more little ones.

Nests. It is very important to have a nest ready at all times in your cage or aviary, if you plan to breed your birds. The nesting box should be about 5″ × 5″ × 8″, and should have a concave bottom so the eggs won't get cold from rolling around. No lining is necessary for these nesting boxes, as the hen will lay the eggs on the floor and then sit on them until they hatch (usually about eighteen days after they are laid).

Colors of Shell Parakeets. Shell parakeets come in many, very lovely colors, the body and tail feathers usually being more vivid than the head, neck, and wing feathers which, however, are often interestingly marked. Some of the more popular colorings are: bright green with yellow; violet, cobalt, or azure blue with grey; and canary yellow with white.

LOVE BIRDS

As we have said before, many people who refer to love birds are really speaking about shell parakeets. The true love birds have chubby bodies and their tails are short and wide. A familiar wing coloring for

NYASSALAND LOVE BIRDS

love birds is green body feathers, with reddish, brick, or yellowish feathers at top of head.

Care of Love Birds. For the most part, the care of love birds is the same as it is for shell parakeets, which we have just mentioned above.

The cages or aviaries can be the same. The nesting boxes, however, should be about one-third larger, and lined with raffia, coarse straw, or the like.

Feeding Love Birds. Love birds may be fed the same vegetable greens as parakeets, but their main food mixture differs slightly. It should consist of one part large millet, two parts canary seed, and two parts sunflower seed.

Breeds of Love Birds. There are seven breeds of love birds which are popular as household pets. These are: Masked, Peach Faced, Nyassaland, Black Cheeked, Fischer's, Madagascar, and Abyssinian.

CHAPTER XVIII

FINCHES AND OTHER CAGED BIRDS

FINCHES

Among the varieties of caged birds that are a pleasure and adornment for any home are the members of the Finch family. These lovely little birds are hardy and therefore not too much trouble for the average family. They offer a wide range of attractive colors, some have delightful voices, and all are amusing in their antics.

With finches, as with parakeets and love birds, it is preferable to buy a pair rather than a single bird, for birds thrive much better with company than by themselves. You may want to have several pairs, each of a different variety, which will always make your cage or aviary a gay, colorful, and cheerful spot in your home.

Housing Finches. Those who wish to have only one or two pairs will probably want to have their pets in a cage somewhere in the house. Always remember to keep your birds away from drafts.

As with the other birds we have mentioned, the cages should be fully equipped with water at all times, seed cups, and perches. For cleanliness purposes, it is wise to keep newspaper folded on the floor of the cage. As birds like to bathe frequently, it is important to place a shallow bowl of water on the floor of the cage so that your pets may go in and out at their leisure.

Those who wish to raise finches in quantity will probably find that an outdoor aviary is the most satisfactory form of housing. Finches are subject to the same types of diseases as we have already listed for canaries, and the treatment of birds with these illnesses is the same too, as for canaries.

CAGES SHOULD HAVE AMPLE ROOM FOR ONE OR TWO PAIRS

Feeding Finches. The most basic and healthful food for finches is the regular Finch Mixture. They may also be given greens, health grit, cuttlebone, spray millet and sometimes a little Peptone.

Some people feed their finches live insect food while they are feeding their young. Others, however, prefer to feed them commercial Insect Food. Nestling food mixed with hard boiled egg is also very good when they are feeding the youngsters.

Breeds of Finches. We will briefly describe here the main characteristics of a number of the more popular and common breeds of finches.

The *Society Finch* has always been bred in captivity, so knows nothing but cage and aviary life. For this reason, the Society Finch is a very good choice for those who are raising these birds for the first time.

Both the male and female sing a little, but the male's song is much more jubilant, and is often accompanied by a little dance.

The three main color combinations of the Society Finch are: fawn and white mottled; brown and white mottled; and pure white.

The *Strawberry Finch,* a native of Malaya and India, is about one-third the size of our canary. It is sweet of note, possesses gorgeous coloring, is very docile, and costs relatively little. It is especially important for this and most high-colored birds to make sure that they have a place in their cage where they can get some shade, lest their color fade and moulting start too early and too often.

The *Cordon Bleu Finch* is one of the loveliest in color of all the finch breeds. His head, throat, breast, and sides are, as his name implies, Cordon Bleu (French blue). His beak is crimson with a black tip. His back and upper wings are brownish green. As in most breeds, the colors of the female are essentially the same but not quite as vivid as the male.

SOCIETY FINCH

STRAWBERRY FINCH

ZEBRA FINCH

The *Lady Gould Finch* is outstanding among finches in brilliance of coloring. There are two color varieties. One is red headed, and the other is black headed. The body and flight wings colors are the same for both varieties, and are extremely vivid, particularly in the male. The back is solid green, the flight feathers being darker, shading to almost black. The chest is a rich purple, and the lower breast and abdomen is a golden yellow. The back of the neck and shoulders is a turquoise blue which shades into a bronze green on the shoulders. The many interesting tones and shades of color make the Lady Gould Finch the most striking of all.

The *Zebra Finch* is one of the gayest and liveliest of all the breeds. They are hardy little birds, and therefore easy to raise.

The beak of the Zebra Finch is coral red. The cheeks are orange. The head and back are grey, which extends into the dark grey rump. The tail feathers are black and white horizontal stripes. The throat has black and white diagonal stripes. The sides of the body, just below the wings, are orange with white spots, and the legs are bright red.

Other Finches. There are numerous other breeds of finches whose colors are very interesting and beautiful. These include the Shaft Tail, Bluish, Bicheno's, Butterfly, Cherry, Crimson, Cuban Olive, African Fire, Firetailed, European Goldfinch, Lavender, Masked Grass, Melba, Parson, Red Crested, Saffron, Spice, Star, Sharp Tailed, Indian Silver Bill, White Eared Grass, and others.

Breeding Finches. If provided with the proper nesting boxes and nestling food, you will find that breeding finches, as with other birds, is not a difficult task; in fact, one that you will not have much to do with, as the birds themselves are very aware of the needs of their young.

You will find that the male and female will take turns sitting on the eggs. The brood may be from five to ten eggs, and will take about sixteen days to hatch.

Where to Buy Finches. The foregoing discussions of some of the more colorful and popular breeds of finches should help you when making your selection of a pet bird. Also, in every large city there are dealers, or large general stores that maintain fine bird departments, where you may look over these birds before you make your first purchase. If they do not have the particular type of bird that suits your fancy, you may be sure that they know where there are such birds on the market and will either obtain them for you on order or refer you to breeders or importers of the variety.

OTHER CAGED BIRDS

Troupial. At the other end of the scale of size from the finches we find a bird that is about three times the size of the canary: this is the Troupial or Bugle Bird. It is a native of South America, about ten inches long, with a rich, sweet song. It is readily tamed and very hardy, living mainly on fruits. It thrives on bananas, likes a bit of grated carrot thrown in, and appreciates it if you give it grasshoppers and other insects. Remarkable whistlers, Troupials are easily taught to imitate bugle calls, hence the alternative name of Bugle Bird. A Troupial's cage should be at least 24 inches long, 18 inches wide, and 15 inches high.

Shama Thrush. Another very interesting bird is the Shama Thrush, a truly handsome dark fellow who has a voice much like the Mocking Bird, but considerably sweeter. He will virtually talk to you from early morning until his bedtime. He likes what are known as meal worms, as well as the commercial insect foods, fresh greens, and plenty of fruit. He comes originally from India.

Various Other Birds. There are many other small caged birds which make very interesting household pets. We will list here some of the different families, and the varieties within each family.

Among the Waxbills we have the Black Cheeked, Orange Cheeked, Red Faced, St. Helena, Rosy Rumped, Sydney, Common (African), and Crimson Winged.

The Weaver family includes the Blood Bill, Cinnamon Crowned, Grenadier, Napoleon, Orange, Red Headed, and the Taha, as well as the Paradise and Pintail Whydahs.

Among the Tanagers there are the Scarlet, Superb, Violet and Yellow, Ariel, Sulphur Breasted Toucans, the Spotted Bill Toucanet and Donaldson's Touraco, as well as the Pekin Nightingale and the Pin Tailed Nonpareil.

The Doves provide us with the Bleeding Heart, Indian Green Winged, Diamond, Harlequin, Plumed Ground, Crested Bronze Winged and the Triangular Spotted.

The Nicobar Pigeon and the Java Rice Bird have their adherents, as do the Bullfinch, the Black Hooded Nun, the Great Barbet, Embroidered Barbet and the Blue Throated Barbet.

The Buntings are the Indigo, Lazuli, Nonpareil, Rainbow, and Varied, while the Cardinals are Green, Mexican, Brazilian Pope and Brazilian Crested.

SUMMARY OF THE CARE OF SMALL CAGED BIRDS

Housing. Cages should be too large for your new pets, rather than too small. Buy a cage that is practical and not all "gingerbread", for the squared-off cage with no frills is much easier to keep clean and hence less likely to breed mites and other pests.

Be sure that you can place it by a window where the pet will get plenty of sunlight. Be certain, too, that it is placed on some sort of pedestal that is sturdy and will not be knocked over by the least breeze. The cage should also be placed in a spot where all the family agree it is to remain, for your bird will not like being moved about too much. Then set up your food pans in places where they cannot be tipped over at all, and also where the newcomer readily can find them. Be sure that they are filled with the best type of food recommended by experts on your bird.

Next take care that the water cups should also be properly anchored, easy to find, and easy for you to remove and keep clean. They should be filled with fresh water at all times. It is best that you start out by filling these with distilled water, rather than risk diarrhea and such diseases that can result from impure water. Presently you can change to boiled water for a few days, and then gradually have the local tap water added until your birds are adjusted to it.

Cover the bottom of your cage with newspaper or brown paper and be sure that you have the so-called Health Grit handy in an open dish. This is most important, as the grit actually enables the bird to masticate its food. Grit also must be kept on the floor of the cage that your pet may keep its feet clean. This eliminates many ills. Do not, for any type of bird, forget to fasten a piece of cuttlebone to the side of the cage, well up from the floor and near a perch where the bird may easily reach it. This not only serves to sharpen the beak, but is also a valuable food source.

It is a good idea to paint the cage with a durable enamel, so that it is more readily cleaned and germ-proof.

Be sure that you and the rest of the family stay away from the new birds for a bit, so that they may adjust themselves without excitement.

Caution the family that there must not be an *en masse* descent on them at any time, for that will make them nervous and they will be always fluttering away from the sight of a human being.

As with canaries, cover your bird's cage with a light cloth at night in the summer weather, and with a heavier one when cold weather comes.

You know from experience that all birds like to bathe, so be sure that you have a bathing dish ready before you bring your bird home. A shallow dish on the floor of the cage will serve the purpose.

Feeding. Besides following the advice we have given you in this book, and further advice of your dealer in feeding your pet birds, it is well to have some understanding of the basic elements of their diet. Health grit means a sharp grit that helps cut foods and in turn is a part of the diet of the bird, containing salt, charcoal, sulphur and iron sulphate, bone and shell. Green food means any newly-picked edible green that grows in your locality and includes lettuce, cabbage, celery tops, alfalfa, spinach, dandelion, turnip tops, water cress and certain grasses. Birds will eat many different types of fruits, but not all are good for all birds. It is best not to experiment. As a rule, apples and now and then a bit of orange are all that are safe. One-fifth of the prepared food called Finch Mixture is the usual canary-seed; the remainder is one of the millets of which one-half is the tiny yellow or white, another good share is the large yellow and a very small part is the large red. You can buy at most bird shops the tiny Indian millet in the head, which has been picked by hand just ahead of maturity and tied in bunches. Your bird will love this food.

Most ardent bird lovers make sure that they buy one of the prepared insect foods that are readily available. In varying proportions it has suet, hemp meal, ant eggs, dried insects and other items. Balanced seed mixtures generally include charcoal, poppy, flax, lettuce, red pepper, thistle, and other seeds the birds normally would eat were they in the wild. Now and then you may feed your bird hard-boiled egg (but not too much at a time) mixed finely with unsalted cracker meal, or even bread that has been thoroughly toasted or dried out and then ground very finely. This last is known as a nestling food and is fed to the very young. It is also good to combine this with seed when your bird seems a bit run down.

Part Five

FISHES

CHAPTER XIX

PLANNING A WELL-BALANCED AQUARIUM

Several hundred years ago the Chinese began to breed the Golden Carp in captivity and to develop the brilliant hues we see today in our Goldfish, the first of the marine life to be used as a home decoration and hobby. From China the hobby of caring for and breeding small fish spread to Japan and, about 300 years ago, to Europe and eventually to America. Little wonder that this pastime has remained widely popular. Lively, colorful fish in a glass container are pleasingly decorative and interesting, a source of delight and fascination to children, and a relatively inexpensive hobby if not carried to elaborate extremes.

CARE OF THE AQUARIUM

Well-balanced Aquariums Need Little Attention. If you are planning an aquarium, it is wise to consider the fact that there should be a proper balance between plant and animal life, and that these must be planned in proportion to the size of the tank and the amount of water it contains. For the balanced aquarium is virtually self-sustaining —that is, it will probably require no more than about fifteen minutes of your attention each day under ordinary circumstances. Fish are, indeed, one of the least troublesome of living hobbies, and the well-planned aquarium will remain a clean one with little effort on your part. If the right materials are selected at the start, you will not even need to change the water in the tank. It will be necessary only to replace the amount of water that evaporates each day, although in extremely hot weather or in an overheated apartment or house it is often advisable to siphon out about half the water and replace it with fresh water that has been aerated.

The Kind of Aquarium to Choose. Of course you will want a container of a size in keeping with the available space in your home. It is important, too, to choose one with a large enough opening at the

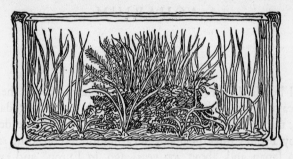

A WELL-BALANCED AQUARIUM

top to permit adequate air-surface for the water. The old-fashioned fish bowl with a narrow neck is therefore inadvisable. It is far better to have a rectangular tank, with the depth of the water at least equal to the width of the tank, and the length of the tank about twice the width. Always be sure that your water level is within two inches of the top of the tank. And, of course, keep your air-surface and your amount of water more or less in proportion to the number of fish and their size.

The best tank for the average home, and one that will give the most pleasure in proportion to its cost, is one which holds about 18 gallons of water and which is 24 inches long, 12 inches wide, and 15 inches deep. Such a tank can easily take care of eight 2-inch fish, or 16 inches of fish, to allow some leeway in regard to the one-inch-per-gallon rule. To these fish you may add two tadpoles and ten snails. Use two inches of sand in which the plant life may root and, as in the smaller tank, see that no more than one-fourth of the flooring is covered with plant life.

Where to Place the Aquarium. Location of your aquarium has much to do with its condition, the amount of work you will have to do, and the pleasure you, your family, and your friends will have from the fish. If you keep the tank or aquarium where there is a southern exposure, you are going to have so much sunlight that plants will grow out of proportion, algae will accumulate too rapidly, and the water will rise to such a temperature that the tank will often become deficient in oxygen. Your fish will then come to the top often for air, and if this goes on too long they will die.

PLANTS AND OTHER MATERIALS FOR THE AQUARIUM

Vegetation and Sand for the Aquarium. Your tank should have 1½ to 2 inches of sand or gravel, and the former should be washed, rough sand that will not pack down like cement. Do not have more than one-fourth of your tank-bottom devoted to vegetation, the proper stock of which can be obtained from any dealer in pet fish and supplies. Anacharis and Fanwort are among the easiest to obtain and best serve the purpose, which is the absorption of carbon dioxide for which they trade oxygen, so vital to all types of fish. Watch your vegetation carefully and remove any parts that die, for these will decompose and in so doing will absorb the precious oxygen and foul up your tank, with resulting loss of fish life.

The Amount and Kind of Water to Use. The best water to use in your tank is that from a nearby pond or river, or even a cistern, for this water is more natural to fish life. Where the water in your tap is soft, not mineralized, and does not contain much chlorine, you may safely use it, but experts say that this water should be permitted to stand for five to ten days before it is poured into the fish tank. It is true that a fish does need minerals, but it is much better for it to get them in its diet rather than from the water in which it lives.

The temperature of the water for the average pet fish may be 50 to 80 degrees in the winter and 65 to 80 in the summer. Goldfish can stand it colder, but other types of fish should have water nearer to 80 degrees. By all means make certain that your tank is placed so that the fish are guarded against any rapid rises or drops in temperature.

Oddly enough, it is better if most of the light that reaches the fish and the tank vegetation comes from artificial sources. Lights for this purpose are easily rigged up and at the same time provide a bit of warmth for the water in which your pets live.

Advantages of Scavengers. The smallest aquarium that is practical is one of five-gallon capacity. This size is capable of sustaining two goldfish of 2-inch length (not counting the tail), one tadpole, and four snails. In selecting the latter, get those which do not feed on the vegetation. If you have fish other than goldfish, consider their size in "fish inches" in relation to water capacity. Regardless of the size of the tank, you can figure roughly that each gallon of water is good for one inch of fish.

The reason for including a tadpole is that it acts as a scavenger and consumes all waste matter in the tank. The snails are considerable help in keeping down the amount of algae, thus saving you too many forced scrapings or cleanings of the sides of the tank. Even so, you may have to clean the tank sides now and then for a clearer view of your pets. In that case, use a flat sponge and then remove the sediment by means of a rubber siphon or a glass dip tube.

When your tadpole becomes a small frog, put a resting place in the tank that rises above the surface of the water so the frog can come up for air; otherwise it will drown.

Kinds of Fish for the New Pet Owner. If you are new to raising fish as a hobby, it is advised that you start with goldfish, which are hardy, then graduate first to the toughest of the tropicals, and then move on to the more delicate.

In the following chapters we will first discuss goldfish as pets; then tropical fish; and ending with brief discussions of turtles and tadpoles.

CHAPTER XX

GOLDFISH

As an aquarium fish the Goldfish is, of course, extremely attractive, and as was mentioned previously, for the beginner it is very easily taken care of. In addition, it has long been known that goldfish can stand more rigors of weather than other fish kept as pets, and like all members of the carp family, can even stand being frozen into blocks of ice

COMMON GOLDFISH

and be alive and healthy when thawed out. They can be bred out-of-doors in mild weather, and if successive pools are established and the pets move from one to another where not too much force of water drops into the pools, they will do even better than in the house.

From these facts, it is easy to see that the common goldfish is the hardiest fish ever placed in a private or public aquarium. He is also the common ancestor of all the more colorful newer varieties that have been developed by selective breeding through the centuries.

Varieties of Goldfish. As the majority of these types would be unavailable to the average person who would want goldfish for the amusement of his family, we will touch only upon the more readily available.

First let us say that there are two distinct color classes, one being brilliant and metallic and the other softly delicate. The first is the scaled variety that starts out a drab, mousy color and changes to red at about six months. The others are called "scaleless" because of the transparency of the scales. These start out white and later have a wide color range; they are not too easy to obtain.

Next to the Common Goldfish, the *Comet* is hardiest, with flowing lines of grace. The Comet is so much of a jumper, especially in the spring, that it is wise to keep a netting over the top of the tank. Incidentally, this is a good practice with all pet fish, for the netting keeps out fish-hunting cats.

The *Fantail* is probably the most popular of the strange varieties, with double tails as their most striking feature. Some do not have these tails entirely divided and are then known as Webtails. Both types are of rare grace and beauty. Being inbred, the Fantails are not as hardy as the Common Goldfish, but still can live many years with the proper treatment.

The so-called *Lionhead* is the strangest Goldfish of them all, with a head-covering like a raspberry and a thick body. This variety needs plenty of room.

The *Veiltail* is a higher development of the Fantail, with lower fins and tails broad, long, and gracefully flowing. It takes about two years or more for these to attain full development, and it is said that after the fins are fully developed, the feedings must be light lest the fins split from congestion.

It is said that the *Telescope Goldfish* is most characteristic of the grotesque beauty of much of oriental art. These curious fish were developed by the Chinese and the Koreans, and get their name from their protruding eyes. They have more variety of color than all the rest combined, and this is the only type that sometimes comes in black. The black ones are called Moors, and are often rated as a distinct variety.

Besides coming in every conceivable goldfish color, the Telescope sometimes shows mottled effects, with small points of brown, yellow, white, red, and lavender, liberally sprinkled with black. These are called Calicos and are especially sought if the colors are many, finely mixed, and have lavender or blue predominating.

The *Shubunkin* is of Japanese origin and has many good qualities, among them hardiness, activity, and the fact that they are excellent breeders. They are much like the Calico Telescopes, with a more greenish-yellow hue.

Feeding Goldfish. Regular commercial prepared foods, in dried form, can be purchased at any reliable pet shop. You may also want to add other foods to your fishes' diet for variety. Suitable for such variation are small amounts of: chopped fish, beef, shrimp, oyster, liver, canned salmon, boiled spinach, crumbs of crackers, and bits of yolk of boiled egg. It must be remembered that these foods should always be given in very small quantities, from the end of a knife perhaps, several times a day. Be sure not to over feed your fish. After a few feedings you will be able to judge exactly how much to give your fish; just enough to be consumed in a very few minutes.

Other Advantages of Goldfish. Besides their advantages as pets, goldfish are valuable as destroyers of mosquitoes. If you put them in a stagnant pool near your home, a rain barrel, or near other breeding places of mosquitoes, your trouble from these sources will stop. The larvae of mosquitoes is an excellent food for the younger goldfish, and if given nothing else to eat, these young ones will keep your place more free from mosquitoes than the larger fish will.

CHAPTER XXI

TROPICAL FISH

Anyone who chooses tropical fish as pets need never lack for variety, for there are well over 300 different kinds of these beautiful little fish which have been brought into the United States, and many more than 100 of these varieties are fairly readily procurable. So fascinating are they, with their bright colors and quick, graceful ways, that often one who starts with a small tank and is at first content with the simpler and hardier varieties soon is tempted to expand his hobby and winds up with a dozen or more tanks of various sizes and shapes, in spite of the increased work and expense and possible crowding in the space available in the home.

Without attempting even to list all the tropicals that have been brought to this country, we will concern ourselves with the more popular types, and their care.

As is the case with all types of pets, it is better not to go in for tropicals at all unless you are willing to take the little time that is necessary to feed them at the right intervals and to buy them the correct food, which is very easily obtained at the pet stores in your community. Food and other supplies for your finny pets are available also through most of the mail order houses.

It is possible to accommodate a few more inches of tropicals in a given tank than of goldfish. The water must be kept clean and at the correct temperature, which usually ranges from 55 to 80 degrees, although at times tropicals might stand 85; 65 to 75 is more nearly what they should have.

POPULAR VARIETIES OF TROPICAL FISH
AND THEIR CARE

It is best that one start with the hardiest of these little fish and learn from them, and then if time and money permit and the urge is there, go on to more and better equipment and stock up on a number of rarer fish. In this connection it is well to note that new varieties are turning up all the time and that there are explorers roaming the world in search of new and more colorful fish as well as better specimens of known varieties. Most people, however, start their collections with Guppies, Swordtails, Angel Fish, Zebras, and Platys.

Paradise. It is believed that the first of the tropicals to be imported was the Paradise, which remains

PARADISE

one of the most attractive of them all. Its colors vary some with changes in temperature, which for this type may range from 60 to 95 degrees Fahrenheit; they breed at 80 degrees. More change in color is noted when there is excitement for the fish, possibly in the chase for mating. The males' color is generally dark with vertical bars of deep red against blue-green, tail fin of deep red, and a metallic blue to streamer ends of

fins. The female is more subdued in color.

The Paradise is a type that puts its eggs in bubbles provided by the male, who picks the eggs up in his mouth and when all breeding is done, cavalierly discharges the female. It is one of the toughest of all the pet fish and also almost the cheapest to buy. Dried granular food goes well with them, but they like a variety of boiled fish, chopped oysters, flies, and small worms.

There are other popular fish in the same group as the Paradise, such as the many Bettas and the Gouramis, one of the latter being the odd Croaking, so called because of its guttural sounds at mating time. Temperatures, feedings and breeding habits are about the same as for the Paradise. These bubble-nesters can be bred in lily ponds where the temperatures do not drop under 65, and under such conditions they need little care.

Swordtail. The Swordtail gets its name from the male, which is the one that develops this appendage, and then only at first breeding time. The general color is a deep green, with a dark contrasting line of red down the body. Here is a case where the mother produces her young alive—anywhere from twelve to one hundred at a time. The female shows she is set to produce when she gets fattish and then dark near the vent. This type of fish is called viviparous (produces living young, instead of eggs), and fertilization by the male takes place

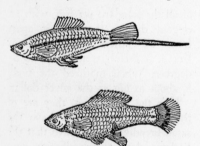

SWORDTAIL (MALE WITH SWORD, AND FEMALE)

in the egg duct of the female and lasts for four broods. This is the easiest kind to raise, because they can be given powdered fishfood almost at once. It is best to get the parents out of the tank unless you have ample plant life in your tank in which the young can hide and thus avoid being eaten by their parents.

Guppy. The Guppy, best known of all tropical pets for the amateur, is also known as the Rainbow Fish.

GUPPIES

The male is ever so much smaller than the female, but carries all the color of the family. The Guppy is another of the live bearers, and the same precautions must be followed with them all. There are never any two of the male Guppies that are exactly alike, and if there are enough of other going broods on hand, they are less likely to eat their young. However, it is well not to take chances. Very rapid multipliers, they start breeding at six months. Their cost and upkeep is low.

Chanchito. The Chanchito is one of the biggest of tropical fish, often 4 to 5 inches long, and although they belong to the scrappy Cichlid family, they are reasonably peaceful, save when mating and protecting their young. While their courting may be a battle royal, when the young come, they work devotedly for them. They tear out all plants or objects in the aquarium that might hide enemies. Eggs are laid in even rows with room for water circulation, which is taken care of by the parents, who take turns at fanning the water with their tails. When the young arrive they are hustled into a hole in the sand at the bottom of the tank. Production is so heavy that often it seems as if a cloud has come up from the sand.

Jewel. The Jewel fish is of the same family as the Chanchito. It is smaller but with the most brilliant of all coloring known in pet fish. In the mating period both sexes take on a bright red color on the under part of the body. The body and fins are evenly dotted with tiny metallic blue spots. Breeding habits are similar to other breeds of the family, save that these appear to be more trusting and do not tear out plants.

Zebra. The Zebra is as striking as might be assumed from the name. It is ever moving and always pleasant to other fishes, and its metallic blue stripes against a yellowish

ZEBRA

background are very fascinating especially with the fast action of these fish. These are egg droppers with no adhesive quality in the eggs, so that marbles ought to be piled up on the bottom of the tank, and the

eggs allowed to drift down for protection. To be safe, the parents should be taken out of the tank and eggs left alone.

Angel Fish. The Angel Fish, or Scalare, is one of the most attractive

ANGEL FISH

of all the standard pet fish, with an elegant dignity that sets it apart from all others. Coming from Brazil, it prefers water at 70 to 85 degrees. When matured the body is about as big as the silver dollar.

Like the Chanchitos, they are of the Cichlid family, and have the same breeding habits, save that the Scalares drop their adhesive eggs on the leaves of the Giant Sagittaria, and move them from place to place on the leaves. In color they are mainly a bright silver with vivid black markings that seem to have a special elegance as they move gracefully through their tank.

Mollienisia. The black Mollienisia are very popular as pets because of their color, which is a rich velvety black. That is where they have gotten the more familiar name of "Black Mollies". Their offspring,

BLACK MOLLIE

however, are sometimes only splotched with black; these are not preferred.

Another form of Mollienisia are the Blue Mollies, which vary in color from jet black to light blue, or blue bodies with black spots.

The popular Sailfin, another form, are interesting because of the male's large dorsal fin, which he unfurls and carries erect when courting.

It is important to remember that more than one variety of Mollies should not be kept in the same tank when breeding.

Platy. The Platy, which is also known as Moon Fish because of a

beautiful colors as pure red, pure black, all shades of gold, metallic blue, and varying shades of yellow to orange, have been produced. The probability of producing so many interesting colors through such selective breeding has made the Platy a joy to those who wish to breed pet fish.

Pearl Danio. The Pearl Danio is a very attractive choice for any collection of tropical fish. They are

PEARL DANIO

among the egg-layers. Their colors are very soft and beautiful; being blue, violet and pink, with a stripe of red running along their bodies. There is a touch of green on their fins.

Tetra. A valuable addition to the fish fancier's aquarium is the neon

PLATY

TETRA

crescent-shaped spot of black at the base of the tail, is very popular.

Through careful breeding such

Tetra. Many consider it the most magnificent of all the tropical fish. This is because of the two vivid red and blue vertical stripes that go from the ventral fin to the tail. The stripes look almost fluorescent, and for that reason these fish have been named "neon" Tetra.

Mouthbreeder Family. Mouthbreeders are quite a remarkable family, and worth having for study alone. After the eggs are deposited and fertilized the mother takes them into her mouth—often there may be 100 of them—and cares for them this way until they hatch, and for some time after that. Like those of the Chanchitos, the eggs must have water circulation, which the mother provides within the mouth. No one ever has discovered just when the eggs are hatched, but when the mother sees there is no danger she lets them all out to swim around, and at the slightest sign of danger, they go back to mother. This keeps up until the mass of the brood are too big for the nursery. The mother Mouthbreeder cannot be tempted to take one morsel of food during all the time she has the responsibility for her brood.

Barbus Family. Two members of the family known as the Barbus have many good points in their favor for your choice as pets. They get along with other fish, adapt themselves to wide ranges of temperature, live for a long time, breed easily, and will reward you with their beauty and grace; at breeding time the male takes on a diffused rosy glow. All members of the family drop adhesive eggs and breed very much like Goldfish.

African Killifish. The African Killifish, or Blue Gularis, is a cousin of our Bullhead Minnow. It is a striking individual, having a dark patch of reddish-orange on the tail fin and lower part of the body that contrasts with the general bluish cast, with a tinge of purple, of the remainder of the body. This is overlaid with deep black and brown markings between which we find light, reflecting scales. Since this fish is a great leaper, one must keep a glass cover over the tank. After the eggs come, remove the fish for the safety of the eggs.

POPULAR SMALL DOMESTIC FISHES

Minnow. The Minnows are one of the small domestic fishes which are always popular as pets, and are an interesting addition to your aquarium.

MINNOWS

The *Shiner* is probably the favorite Minnow, though there are approximately 225 known species.

Other Small Domestic Fishes. There are many other domestic fish that add color and interest to the aquarium. Among the more widely known of these are: Horned Dace, Suckers, Chubs, Golden Orfe, Tench, Catfish, Eels, Darters, and Sunfish.

CHAPTER XXII

TURTLES, TADPOLES, AND SALAMANDERS

We have taken up all the favorite aquarium fishes, and in this final chapter we shall consider turtles and tadpoles which though not fish at all are entertaining and very interesting aquarium pets. At the end of the chapter we shall make a brief mention of salamanders, which thrive in a terrarium or dry glass-enclosure.

Turtles. There are few communities in which one cannot find a pet supply shop which carries little turtles for pets, and these same shops also have the very little equipment that is needed for such pets, as well as the proper foods for them. If you go to one of these shops, you will usually find that these little turtles have gaily-painted shells, which will help brighten any room. The equipment for a tiny turtle, which costs very little, consists mainly of a small aquarium, or you can use any ordinary round or oval glass bowl. A metal container deep enough to keep your turtle from climbing out can also be used, but it is much more fun to have an all-glass container so you can more easily observe the actions of your pet.

Place in your container some brightly-colored pebbles, and a flat stone or two, and be sure that the stones stand high enough out of the water to create an "island" on which the turtle can get out of the water and at least imagine he is sunning himself. Be certain to keep the water clean and at about room temperature, varying from 60 to 80 degrees. It is a simple process to clean out the "home" of your little pet two or three times a week. Put the turtle into some other safe container while you clean off the island and the pebbles.

Put the bowl or aquarium in a light place, but be certain that it does not remain too long in the direct rays of the sun. Keep this in mind when you leave the house for the day and know that no one will be around to change the position of the turtle's bowl, for the direct sun coming through your window and then through the glass of the bowl will make your small pet very uncomfortable.

TURTLES

Turtle food, which most often is dried ant-eggs, can be bought in any pet store, or you can send away for it to a dealer. Observe your pet for a few days, and remember the advice the dealer gives you, so that you do not dump in too much food and thus dirty up the water and create an unsanitary condition. While the turtle food will be the main item of diet, turtles as well as humans like a change or addition now and then. A small amount of lean, raw beef, finely scraped, will do your pet a great deal of good if not used too often. He will also appreciate finely cut-up green lettuce, other leafy salad greens, chopped tiny beet leaves, and rainworms.

It is well known that variations in food and shifts to control the amount of sunshine for your pet will go far to prevent blindness. Many experts suggest that at the appearance of a white film over the eye, help should be given by means of a few drops of cod liver oil put into the turtle's mouth with a small medicine-dropper. Or you might swab over the eyes with a solution of boric acid.

As the type of turtle which you keep as a pet will not feed on land, remember always to place whatever food you are giving him in the water. You will be able generally to tell how much health your pet has by watching him suddenly move about his aquarium and try to climb the sides to get out onto what he thinks he sees outside his own immediate world.

Tadpoles. Many persons adopt tadpoles as home pets, and others have snails and other types of small shellfish. There are shops which

EARLY AND FINAL STAGES OF THE DEVELOPMENT OF A TADPOLE TO A FROG

deal in these pets and the proper equipment for them, and in these shops you can also receive information on how to take care of such pets. The advantages of keeping tadpoles and snails in the home fish aquarium, and the kinds of snails that are suitable for a fish-tank, have been discussed in the section on planning a well-balanced aquarium. If you get a tadpole for a pet, you must remember that before very long he will develop into a little frog. At that time you must provide him, as we also pointed out in discussing the aquarium, with an island on which he can come up for air.

Salamander. An interesting pet for a terrarium is the salamander. A terrarium is a bowl or rectangular glass-enclosed box, similar to an aquarium but kept dry. Salamanders do not live in water, but want a damp and moist atmosphere. Therefore, the terrarium should be equipped with plants, ferns, small stones, and pieces of wood or bark, with water in a dish for the salamander to drink.

Since insects are important as food for salamanders, a glass lid should be placed over the terrarium after providing insects to be eaten.

SALAMANDER

Salamanders also eat small worms, spiders, small snails, and practically any small insects are suitable. As they have no teeth, salamanders are perfectly harmless. They grow to be two or three inches long.

During the day the salamanders will be found under one of the objects in the terrarium, as they are active only at night. This is because the night air is cool and moist, and as they breathe through their skin, it is easier for them at that time.

The salamander looks much like a lizard, having a long body and tail, small head, and protruding eyes. There are several varieties of salamanders, of which the most popular color for pet owners is the Red-backed Salamander.

Index

INDEX

Abyssinian Cats, 201
Affenpinscher, 92
Afghan Hound, 43, 44
African Killifish, 282
Airedale Terrier, 70, 71
Alaskan Malemute, 61
Alexandrine Ring-Necked Parakeet, 256
All-breed member dog show, 167
Altering and spaying male cats, 215
American-bred class, 172
American Foxhound, 35, 36
American Kennel Club, 5, 11, 13, 165, 169, 170
American Museum of Natural History, 220
American Roller Canary, 244
American Society for the Prevention of Cruelty to Animals, 161
American Water Spaniel, 25, 26
Anemia in canaries, 246
Angel Fish, 280
Angora Cats, 198
Angora Rabbits, 225
Aquarium, advantages of scavengers for, 272
care of, 269, 270
planning well-balanced, 269–272
plants and other materials for, 271, 272
where to place, 271
Asthma in canaries, 246

Baldness in canaries, 247
Barbets, 263
Barbus Family, 282
Basenji, 39
Basset Hound, 35
Bathing canaries, 246
cats, 207
dogs, 105–106
Beagle, 34, 35
trials, 157
Bedlington Terrier, 81, 82
Belgian Hare, 225
Belgian Sheepdog, 54
Benching chain, 172
Bernese Mountain Dog, 66
Best foods for rabbits, 227
Birds, 243–265
Birds, dogs and cats in same household, vii
Black and Tan Coonhound, 37

Black and Tan Rabbit, 227
Black Mollie, 281
Black Persian, 197
Bloodhound, 38
Blue and Tan Rabbit, 227
Blue Gularis, 282
Blue Persian, 197
Blue Vienna Rabbit, 227
Bobtail Cat, 202
Border Terrier, 73, 74
Borzoi, 43
Boston Terrier, 97, 98
Bouvier De Flandres, 64, 65
Boxer, 55, 56
Breeding canaries, 247–248
    cats, 213–215
    dogs, 143–154
    finches, 262
    habits of chipmunks, 234
    habits of hamsters, 240
    habits of squirrels, 233
    habits of white mice, 238–239
    rabbits, 230
    shell parakeets, 256
Breeds of cats, 195–202
Breeds of dogs, 15–105
Breeds of rabbits, 224–227
Breed standards, usefulness of, 10
Briard, 51
Bringing new and old pets together,
    vi–vii
Britanny Spaniel, 26, 159
Broken-colored (Dutch-marked)
    Rabbit, 225, 226
Broken leg of canary, treatment of,
    246
Brushing the dog, 106
Brussels Griffon, 91, 92
Bugle Bird, 262

Bulldog, 99, 100
Bull Mastiff, 58, 59
Buntings, 263
Burmese Cat, 195, 202
Bush-tailed Burmese Cat, 202

Caged canary, origin and history of,
    248
Cages, care of canary, 244–246
    placing of, vii
Cairn Terrier, 77, 78
Canaries, bathing, 246
    breeding, 247, 248
    early migration of, 248
    feeding, 244
    illnesses of, 246
    kinds of cages for, 244, 245
    moulting season of, 247
    origin of present-day varieties,
        248, 249
    popularity in America, 249
    varieties of, 243, 244
Canary cage, general care of, 245,
    246
Cardigan Welsh Corgi, 59, 60
Cardinals, 263
Care of aquarium, 269–272
    canaries, 244–247
    cats, 203–211
    doe and new-born rabbits, 230
    dogs, 105–142
    female dog during pregnancy,
        149–150
    finches, 259–260
    goldfish, 275
    guinea pigs, 236–237
    hamsters, 239–240
    love birds, 257
    macaws, 254–255

new-born kittens, 214–215
new-born puppies, 151–154
parrots, 251–253
rabbits, 227–230
salamanders, 287–288
shell parakeets, 255–256
sick dogs, 136–142
small caged birds, 264–265
stud dog, 148
turtles, 285–287
white mice, 238
young chicks, 247–248
Cat breeds, classification of, 189
Catfish, 283
Cat shows, 217, 218
Cats, Abyssinian, 201
altering and spaying of, 215
Angora, 198
bathing, 206
Black Persian, 197
Blue Persian, 197
breeding of, 213–215
breeds of, 195–202
care of, 203–211
Chinchilla, 199
choosing, 187–193
delivery and nursing of, 214
Domestic Short-haired, 196, 197
Domestic Short-haired Tabby
Striped, 197
early history of domesticated,
219, 220
feeding of, 203–205
grooming, 205, 206
housebreaking, 209
Japanese kimono, 202
long-haired, 197–199
Long-haired Silver Tabby Persian, 198

man's first uses of, 220
Manx, 199, 200
mating of, 213
origin of, 220
Peke-faced, 202
pregnancy in, 214
pure-bred, 196–202
removing fleas from, 208
scratching post for, 210
Short-haired Silver Tabby, 197
Siamese, 200, 201
Silver Persian, 198
standard color chart of, 190–192
standard color divisions of, 190
Tortoise Shell, 198
toys for, 210
where and how to buy, 192, 193
Cats and dogs in same household,
vii
Cats and kittens, deciding between,
188
Cavy (Guinea Pig), 235
Champagne d'Argent rabbits, 227
Chanchito, 279
Chesapeake Bay Retriever, 30
Chihuahua, 95, 96
Children and individual pets viii
Children and rabbits, 223
Chinchilla cats, 199
Chipmunks, 231–233
breeding habits of, 234
how to handle, 231
where to find, 233, 234
Choosing healthy dogs, 18
Chow Chow, 101, 102
Chubs, 283
Classes in dog shows, 170
Clumber Spaniel, 26, 27

Coat, trimming, clipping, and plucking of, 124–127

Coats for dogs, 113

Cocker Spaniel, 19–21
English, 21

Cod liver oil, 117

Colbert, Dr. E. H., 220

Colds in canaries, 246
in dogs, 140

Collar, training dog to, 133–134

Collie, rough, 48, 49
smooth, 49

Colored Bull Terrier, 83

Comet Goldfish, 274

Common Goldfish, 273

Connecticut Humane Society, 161

Constipation in canaries, 246
in dogs, 139

Cordon Bleu Finch, 261

Curing dogs of jumping on people, 131

Curly-coated Retriever, 32, 33

Dachshund, 39–41

Dachshund and Coonhound trials, 158

Dalmatian, 100

Dandie Dinmont Terrier, 81

Darters, 283

Delivery of dogs, 150, 151

Development of dog breeds, 181–182

Diarrhea in canaries, 246
in dogs, 139

Discipline and punishment of dogs, 129–131

Distemper, 140

Doberman Pinscher, 54, 55

Dog biscuit, 118

Dog feedings, amount and frequency of, 119–121

Dog shows, 155–175

Dog's mate, selecting, 143–146

Dog's nails, care of, 123

Dog's sleeping quarters, 108

Dog's teeth, care of, 123

Dogs, 3–184
bathing, 105, 106
breeding, 143–154
breeds of, 15–105
brushing, 106, 107
care of, 105–142
care of sick, 136–142
clipping coat of, 124–127
coats for, 113
colds in, 140
constipation in, 139
curing of jumping on people, 131
delivery of, 150, 151
diarrhea in, 139
discipline and punishment of, 129–131
distemper in, 140
exercising of, 108–110
exhaustion in, 140
eye trouble in, 140
feeding of, 114–121
first aid for injury of, 139
fits of, 140, 141
giving medicine or pills to, 138
grooming of, 122–127
heat prostration in, 140
history of domestication of, 177–184
housebreaking of, 127
improvising a muzzle for, 140
mating of, 143–149

origin of, 177–184
plucking coat of, 124–127
pneumonia in, 140
poisoning in, 139
prehistoric origin of, 183, 184
rabies in, 141
selection of, 3–13
skin diseases of, 142
sleeping quarters for, 108
spaying female, 147
sweaters for, 113
symptoms of illness in, 137
taking temperature of, 137
training of, 127–136
training to "Sit" and "Down",
  131
trimming of, 124–127
variety groups of, 9, 10
vomiting in, 138
where to buy, 12, 13
worming of, 110, 111
Dogs and cats in same household,
  vii
Dog shows, 165–175
  entering, 170, 171
  kinds of, 166–168
  preparation for, 172–175
  purpose of, 165
Domestic rabbits, advantages of, 224
Domestic short-haired cats, 196, 197
Domestic   Short-haired   Tabby-
  striped, 197
Doves, 263
"Down", training dog to, 131–133
Dutch-marked (Broken-colored)
  Rabbit, 226

Early history of the cat, 220
Eels, 283

Eggs as dog food, 116
English Rabbit, 226
English Cocker Spaniel, 21
English Foxhound, 36
English Setter, 17, 18
English Springer Spaniel, 21, 22
English Toy Spaniel, 89
Entry-point scale, 169
Eskimo Dog, 60, 61
Exercising your dog, 108–110
Exhaustion in dogs, 140
Eye trouble in dogs, 140

Fantail Goldfish, 274
Feeding canaries, 244
  cats, 203–205
  doe and new-born rabbits, 230
  dogs, 114–121
  finches, 260
  goldfish, 275
  guinea pigs, 236–237
  love birds, 257
  macaws, 254
  rabbits, 227
  shell parakeets, 256
  sick dogs, 121
  white mice, 238
Felis, 220
Female dogs, care of during pregnancy, 149
  heat season in, 146
  relative merits of, 7
Field Spaniel, 22, 23
Field trials, advantages of, 160
Finches, 259–262
  breeding, 262
  breeds of, 260, 262
  feeding, 260

Finches—*Cont'd*
  housing, 259
  where to buy, 262
Finch mixture, 265
First aid for injury to dog, 139
Fish as dog food, 117
Fish, dogs, and cats in same household, vi–vii
  kinds for new pet owners, 272
  placing of, vii–viii
Fishes, 269–288
  Goldfish, 273–275
  popular small domestic, 283
  tropical, 277–282
Fits, in dogs, 140, 141
Flat-coated Retriever, 32
Fleas, removing, from dogs, 112, 113
Flemish Giant Rabbit, 226, 227
Foods for grown dogs, 116–118
  for puppies, 116
Foxhound, American, 35, 36
  English, 36
French Bulldog, 98, 99
French Burmese Cat, 202

German Shepherd, 53
German Short-haired Pointer, 28
Giant Schnauzer, 63
Golden Orfe, 283
Golden Retriever, 31, 32
Goldfish, 273–275
  feeding, 275
  varieties of, 273, 274
Gordon Setter, 18, 19
Great Dane, 56, 57
Great Pyrenees, 67, 68
Green food, 265
Greyhound, 41
  races, 155

Grooming, advantages of, 122
  cats, 205–207
  dogs, 122–127
  utensils for, 126
Grown dogs, choosing, 5
  foods for, 116–118
Guinea Pigs, 235–237
  breeds of, 235
  characteristics of, 236
  feeding, 236–237
  housing, 236
  how to handle, 237
Guppy, 279

Hamsters, breeding habits of, 240
  feeding and housing, 239
Harrier, 37
Health grit, 265
Heat prostration in dogs, 140
Himalayan Rabbit, 226
Himalayan White Persian Cat, 202
Hook worms in dogs, 111
Horned Dace, 283
Hound, Afghan, 43, 44
  Basset, 35
Hound Group, 9, 33–47
Housebreaking dogs, 127–129
Hutches, rabbit, 228, 229

Insects as food for pets, 288
Irish Setter, 17
Irish Terrier, 71, 72
Irish Water Spaniel, 23
Irish Wolfhound, 44, 45
Italian Greyhound, 94

Japanese Kimono Cats, 202
Japanese Spaniel, 88, 89
Java Rice Bird, 263
Jealousy among pets, vii

Jewel Fish, 280
Judging at dog shows, 167, 170

Keeshond, 102, 103
Kerry Blue Terrier, 76
Kink-tailed Cat, 202
Kittens, care of new-born, 214
    weaning, 215
Komondor, 51, 52
Kortahls, E. K., 29
Kuvasz, 68

Labrador Retriever, 30, 31
Lady Gould Finch, 261
Lakeland Terrier, 72, 73
Lancashire Canary, 244
Leash, training dog to, 133–134
Lhasa Apsos Terrier, 79, 80
Licensed dog show, 167
Limit classes for dogs, 172
Lion Dogs, 86
Lionhead Goldfish, 274
Lizard Canary, 244
Long-haired Cats, 197–199
Long-haired Silver Tabby Persian, 198
Lop-eared Rabbit, 226
Love Birds, 257

Macaws, 253–255
    cages for, 254
    feeding, 254
    varieties, 254, 255
Making friends of squirrels and chipmunks, 231, 232
Male dogs, relative merits of, 7
Maltese, 89, 90
Manchester (Black-and-Tan) Terrier, 84
Man's first uses of the cat, 220

Manx, 199, 200
Mastiff, 57, 58
Mating of dogs, 143–149
Meat as dog food, 118
Mexican Hairless Cat, 202
Mexican Hairless Dog, 96
Miacis, 220
Milk as dog food, 116
Miniature Pinscher, 94, 95
Miniature Schnauzer, 84, 85
Minnows, 283
Mollienisia, 280
Mongrels, disadvantages of, 11, 12
Monkey Dog, 92
Moon Fish, 281
Moors (Goldfish), 274
Morris and Essex show, 168
Moulting season of canaries, 247
Mouthbreeders, 282
Muzzle, improvisation of, 140

Nest boxes, 229, 230
Newfoundland, 66, 67
New and old pets brought together, vi–vii
New pet owner, kinds of fish for, 272
New Zealand Rabbit, 227
Nicobar Pigeon, 263
Non-sporting Group, 10, 96–103
Norwegian Elkhound, 46, 47
Norwich Terrier, 74
Novice class, 172
Nyassaland Love Birds, 257

Obedience training classes, 136
Obedience trials, rules of, 162
    training for, 160, 161
    value of, 164

Old English Sheepdog, 50, 51
Open classes, 172
Origin of caged canary, 248–249
　　cats, 219–220
　　dogs, 177–184
Otterhound, 46

Papers, pedigree, 11
Papillon, 87, 88
Paradise, 278
Parrots, cages for, 251, 252
　　feeding, 252
　　general care of, 252
　　training to talk, 251
　　varieties of, 253
Pearl Danio, 281
Pedigree, certificate of, 11
Peke-faced Cats, 202
Pekingese, 86, 87
Pembroke Welsh Corgi, 59
Pendulous-eared Cat, 202
Performing before judge, at dog
　　show, 166
Planning a mating of dogs, 146
Platy, 281
Pneumonia in dogs, 140
Pointer and Setter trials, 158, 159
Pointer, German Short-haired, 28
Pointers, 27–29
Points, 168
Poisoning, 139
Polish Rabbit, 226
Pomeranian, 87
Poodle, 100, 101
Prehistoric origin of cats, 220
　　of dogs, 183, 184
Protecting your belongings against
　　dogs, 131
Pug, 93

Pulik, 52
Puppies, choosing, 5
　　foods for, 116
　　general care of, 151, 152
　　points in selecting, 5–7
　　training of very young, 153, 154
　　weaning of, 152
　　whining in, 129
Purebred cats, 196–202
　　dogs, 8, 11, 12

Rabbit hutches, 228, 229
Rabbits, 223–230
　　advantages of domestic, 224
　　Angora, 225
　　Belgian Hare, 225
　　best foods for, 227
　　Black and Tan, 227
　　Blue and Tan, 227
　　Blue Vienna, 227
　　breeding, 229, 230
　　breeds of, 224–227
　　Broken-colored, 225, 226
　　care of doe and new-born, 230
　　Champagne d'Argent, 227
　　children and, 223
　　danger of wild, 224
　　Dutch-marked, 226
　　English, 226
　　feeding, 227
　　Flemish Giant, 226, 227
　　Himalayan, 226
　　how to handle, 223
　　importance of drinking water
　　　for, 227, 228
　　Lop-eared, 226
　　nest boxes for, 229, 230
　　New Zealand, 227
　　Polish, 226

selecting as pets, 223, 224
Silver, 227
Silver Fox, 227
Silver Marten, 227
when to breed, 230
White Satin, 227
Rabies, in dogs, 141
Racing, dog, 155–157
Rainbow Fish, 279
Raising variety of pets, vi–viii
Red-backed Salamander, 288
Registration number, for dog show, 171
Retrievers, 30–33
Retriever, Chesapeake Bay, 30
Curly-coated, 32, 33
Flat-coated, 32
Golden, 31, 32
Labrador, 30, 31
Retriever trials, 158
Rickets, in canaries, 247
Rottweiler, 56
Round worms, 111
Russian Trackers, 31

St. Bernard, 65
Salamander, 287
Saluki, 42
Samoyede, 62, 63
Scaly legs in canaries, 247
Scavengers, advantages of in aquarium, 272
Schipperke, 103
Schnauzer, Giant, 63
Miniature, 84, 85
Standard, 64
Scottish Deerhound, 45
Scottish Terrier, 77
Scratching posts, 210

Sealyham Terrier, 78
"Seeing Eye", 12
Selecting dog's mate, 143–146
Selection of cats, 187–193
of dogs, 3–13
Setter, English, 17, 18
Gordon, 18, 19
Irish, 17
Several pets in household, vi–viii
Shama Thrush, 263
Shell Parakeets, 255–257
breeding, 256
colors of, 257
feeding, 256
housing, 255
nests for, 256
Shetland Sheepdog, 49, 50
Sheepdog, Belgian, 54
Old English, 50, 51
Shetland, 49, 50
Shiner, 283
Short-haired Silver Tabby, 197
Show bag, 172
Show posing, 174
Shows, dog, 155–175
Shubunkin Goldfish, 275
Siamese Cats, 200, 201
Siberian Husky, 62
Sick dogs, care of, 136–142
Silver Fox Rabbit, 227
Silver Marten Rabbit, 227
Silver Persian, 198
Silver Rabbits, 227
"Sit", training dogs to, 131–133
Skin diseases of dogs, 142
Skin tumors in canaries, 247
Skye Terrier, 80, 81
Sledge Dog races, 156
Sleeping quarters for dogs, 107–108

Small caged birds, care of, 264, 265
  feeding, 265
  housing, 264
Small domestic fishes, 283
Small household pets, viii
Smooth Fox Terrier, 74, 75
Society Finch, 260
Sore eyes in canaries, 246
Sore feet in canaries, 247
Spaniel, American Water, 25, 26
  Brittany, 26, 159
  Clumber, 26, 27
  Cocker, 19–21
  English Cocker, 21
  English Springer, 21, 22
  English Toy, 89
  Field, 22, 23
  Irish Water, 23
  Japanese, 88, 89
  Sussex, 24
  Welsh Springer, 24, 25
Spaniels, 19–27, 159
Spaniel trials, 159
Spaying female dogs, 147
Specialty show, 167
Sporting Group, 9, 16–33
Squirrels, 231–233
  breeding habits of, 233
  characteristics of, 232, 233
  how to handle, 231
  where to find, 232
Staffordshire Terrier, 83
Standard color divisions of cats, 190–192
Standard entry blank for dog shows, 171
Standard Schnauzer, 64
Strawberry Finch, 260
Stud dog, care of, 148, 149

Suckers, 283
Sunfish, 283
Sussex Spaniel, 24
Sweaters for dogs, 113
Swordtail, 279
Symptoms of illness in dogs, 137

Tadpoles, 287
  as scavengers, 272
Tanagers, 263
Tapeworms, 112
Telescope Goldfish, 274
Temperature, taking, in dogs, 137
Tench, 283
Terrarium, 287
Terrier, Airedale, 70, 71
  Bedlington, 81, 82
  Border, 73, 74
  Boston, 97, 98
  Cairn, 77, 78
  Colored Bull, 83
  Dandie Dinmont, 81
  Irish, 71, 72
  Kerry Blue, 76
  Lakeland, 72, 73
  Lhasa Apsos, 79, 80
  Manchester (Black-and-Tan), 84
  Norwich, 74
  Scottish, 77
  Sealyham, 78
  Skye, 80, 81
  Smooth Fox, 74, 75
  Staffordshire, 83
  Toy Manchester, 93, 94
  Welsh, 72
  West Highland White, 79
  White Bull, 82, 83

Wire-haired Fox, 75, 76
Yorkshire, 90, 91
Terrier Group, 9, 69–85
Tetra, 281
Tibetan Temple Cat, 202
Ticks, removing, 113
Tortoise Shell, 198
Toy Group, 9, 85–96
Toy Manchester Terrier, 93, 94
Toy Poodle, 91
Toys for cats, 210
Tracking, 163
Training dogs, 127–136
    equipment for, 134
    to collar and leash, 133–135
    to come when called, 135
    to "down", 133
    to "sit", 132
Trials, Beagle, 157
    Dachshund and Coonhound, 158
    Pointer and Setter, 158, 159
    Retriever, 158
    Spaniel, 159
Tropical Fish, 277–282
    African Killifish, 282
    Angel Fish, 280
    Barbus Family, 282
    Black Mollie, 281
    Blue Gularis, 282
    Chanchito, 279
    Guppy, 279
    Jewel Fish, 280
    Mollienisia, 280
    Moon Fish, 281
    Mouthbreeders, 282
    Paradise, 278
    Pearl Danio, 281
    Platy, 281

Rainbow Fish, 279
Swordtail, 279
Tetra, 281
Zebra, 280
Troupial, 262, 263
Turtles, 285–287

Utility class work, 163
Utility Dog, 163

Varieties of pets in same household, vi–viii
Vegetables, preparation of, 117
Veiltail Goldfish, 274
Vomiting in dogs, 138

Waxbills, 263
Weaning kittens, 215
    puppies, 152
Weavers, 263
Webtail Goldfish, 274
Weimaraner, 29
Welsh Springer Spaniel, 24, 25
Welsh Terrier, 72
West Highland White Terrier, 79
Westminster Kennel Club, 168
When to breed rabbits, 230
Whining, of puppies, 129
Whippet, 41, 42
    races, 155
Whip worms, 112
White Bull Terrier, 82, 83
White Mice, 237–239
    breeding habits of, 239
    feeding, 238
    housing, 238
    keeping healthy, 238
White Rats, 239
White Satin Rabbit, 227
Wild rabbits, danger of, 224

Wire-haired Fox Terrier, 75, 76
Wire-haired Pointing Griffon, 28, 29
Working Group, 9, 47–69
Worming your dog, 110, 111
Worms, types of, 111, 112

Yorkshire Terrier, 90, 91
Young canary chicks, caring for, 247

Zebra Fish, 280
Zebra Finch, 262